Forgotten Features of the Founding

The American Republic: The First One Hundred Years

Series Editors: George Anastaplo, Loyola University of Chicago School of Law and John Murley, The Rochester Institute of Technology

No other period of American history offers the theoretical challenges of the century that began with the calling of the First Continental Congress and ended with the ratification of the Fifteenth Amendment.

Authors are encouraged to submit studies of statesman, documents and events of the period.

Forgotten Features of the Founding: The Recovery of Religious Themes in the Early American Republic, by James Hutson

Forgotten Features
of the Founding

The Recovery of Religious Themes
in the Early American Republic

James Hutson

LEXINGTON BOOKS
Lanham • Boulder • New York • Oxford

LEXINGTON BOOKS

Published in the United States of America
by Lexington Books
A Member of the Rowman & Littlefield Publishing Group
4501 Forbes Boulevard, Suite 200, Lanham, Maryland 20706

PO Box 317
Oxford
OX2 9RU, UK

British Library Cataloguing in Publication Information Available

Library of Congress Cataloging-in-Publication Data

Hutson, James H.
  Forgotten features of the founding : the recovery of the role of religion in the new
American republic / James Hutson.
    p. cm.
  Includes bibliographical references (p.) and index.
  ISBN 0-7391-0570-1 (cloth : alk. paper) — ISBN 0-7391-0571-X (pbk. : alk. paper)
    1. Church and state—United States—History—18th century. 2. United States—
Politics and government—18th century. 3. United States—Church history—18th
century. I. Title.

BR516.H783 2003
322'.1'097309033—dc21

2003040095

  Printed in the United States of America
∞™ The paper used in this publication meets the minimum requirements of American
National Standard for Information Sciences—Permanence of Paper for Printed Library
Materials, ANSI/NISO Z39.48–1992.

For WTW Jr.

Contents

Preface

The first three chapters in this volume identify and explicate religious themes which prevailed during the Founding Period but which are of scant interest to today's scholars. These themes are: the conviction that the doctrine of a "future state of rewards and punishments" provided religion with the means of producing social and political benefits; the assumption that the civil magistrate should play the role of "nursing father" to religious institutions; and the belief that rights were moral powers, grounded in religion.

These themes are related, in one way or another, to the widespread conviction during the Founding Period that, since religion produced public policy benefits, government should enlist it as a partner and support it vigorously, even with tax revenues if possible. Since state-supported religion is perceived in twentieth-century academic circles to be regressive, themes affiliated with it are not appealing topics for scholars, who, as Herbert Butterfield famously observed, prefer to study "progress" and its antecedents, which by today's academic standards means the separationist views of Jefferson, Madison and their allies.

The forgotten themes were very old, one dating from pre-Christian times and others from the fourteenth and sixteenth centuries. That they flourished in the United States during the Founding Period demonstrates how traditional and conventional the religious mentality of the country was, not surprising in a solidly Christian nation, as the new republic indisputably was. This fact may be on the way to joining the list of forgotten features of the Founding, if recent claims that the new American republic was a "de-Christianized" or semi-Christian nation gain wider currency. The volume's fourth chapter demonstrates how little substance these claims have.

The arguments of opponents of state-supported religion during the Founding Period were also old, although not as venerable as the first three themes examined. As the fifth chapter demonstrates, revolutionary era advocates of the disestablishment of religion used the same arguments William Penn employed a century earlier, arguments which had, in turn, been formulated "even before William Penn became a Quaker." Just as Penn did not confuse the disestablishment of religion with secularism, so were his intellectual heirs in the new republic not reluctant to acknowledge that the social and political benefits of religion would and should continue after disestablishment. Many of the most ardent advocates of disestablishment during the Founding Period—Isaac Backus, for example—saw no contradiction between opposing state-sponsored religion and in considering magistrates as nursing fathers and in commending a system of divine rewards and punishments as a means of promoting the public welfare.

The most radical church-state idea during the Founding Period was James Madison's view that religion produced no social or political benefits, a conclusion 75 years in advance of a similar argument offered by John Stuart Mill in the mid-nineteenth century. Madison's view, as the sixth chapter shows, was so far outside the Founding Era consensus (as many of his other religious ideas also were) that he prudently declined to acknowledge it publicly.

The themes described in the first three chapters began to fade away in the nineteenth century. Why this happened is beyond the scope of the present volume (although some suggestions are offered) but it is ironic that themes, grounded in religious convictions nourished by centuries of reflection and experience, began to disappear during a period when religion was at its high-water mark in American history. The religion that flourished in mid-nineteenth-century America was, however, evangelical and voluntaristic and, in many areas, incongruent with the spirit of the earlier established religions which were so hospitable to the forgotten features described in this volume.

In recent times, when strict separationist ideas about the relationship between religion and government have achieved an ascendancy in academic circles and when a radical new understanding of rights as power stripped of morality has become fashionable, scholars are more than content to let what appear to be backward-looking themes from the Founding Era rest in peace and remain forgotten. Like the medium at Endor, I intend to revive the forgotten themes, for they had, like the prophet Samuel, a powerful influence in their own time. The religious mentality of the Founding generation cannot, in fact, be understood without taking them into account.

I am indebted to Professor Graham Walker of the Catholic University of America and to his colleagues in the John Courtney Murray Seminar for giving me the benefit of their wise counsel which is incorporated in several places in this volume. I also wish to thank Professor Jack Welch of the Brigham Young University Law School for convening a faculty seminar at his university which offered helpful criticism of two chapters. My learned colleague, Dr. Louis Fisher, of the Congressional Research Service, clarified my thinking about one chapter, as did Professor Jack Rakove of Stanford University, although my conclusions about Madison's religious views are distinctly different than his. Professor Daniel Dreisbach of American University gave me the benefit of his customarily trenchant observations. Finally, I wish to acknowledge my debt to Dr. Michael Novak of the American Enterprise Institute who read my work with his fine critical eye and encouraged me to publish the chapters in book form.

Chapter 1

"A Future State of Rewards and Punishments": The Founders' Formula for the Social and Political Utility of Religion

In his wise book, *The Whig Interpretation of History*, Herbert Butterfield observed that most historians were not interested in lost causes or losing arguments. Historians, Butterfield asserted, were enamored of "progress" with the result that, when re-creating the past, they focused on events and ideas that were precursors of activities and attitudes that had become dominant in their own day.[1] Butterfield's observation applies with particular force to recent American scholarship on the relationship between religion and government in the Founding Period. After World War II it became an article of faith in many quarters—in the academy, in particular—that the welfare of the republic depended upon a strict separation between religion and government. Predictably, in Butterfield's view, historians writing about religion and government in the Founding Period concentrated on advocates of the separationist view, especially on its champions, Jefferson and Madison, and more or less ignored the competing vision, endorsed by Washington and Adams and shared by large numbers of citizens, that a partnership between religion and government was necessary, not merely for

1

national happiness and prosperity, but for the survival of the nation itself. The present chapter will attempt to remedy this scholarly neglect by offering a thorough account of the partnership ideal, including an analysis, not previously attempted, of how the Founding generation assumed religion would "work" to produce the civic benefits expected from it.

Founding Era proponents of the partnering of religion and government did not, of course, foresee that in the twentieth century the writing of American history would move in a direction that would make them look misguided. Students of history themselves, they believed that more than a thousand years of human experience validated their assumptions. Accordingly, they routinely appealed to the authority of antiquity. A Connecticut minister, for example, reminded his readers that "Constantine, Theodosius, and all the first Christian emperors, made it one of their earliest cares, publicly to patronize religion. This practice hath been continued ever since."[2] "The most approved and wisest legislators in all ages," wrote a Virginian in 1784, "in order to give efficacy to their civil institutions, have found it necessary to call in the aid of religion; and in no other form of government whatever has the influence of religious principles been found so requisite as in that of a republic."[3] The next year other Virginians informed their public officials that "the wisest Legislators of antiquity are sufficiently expressive of their veneration for religion, at least as an assistant to civil Government." "Under all the Forms of civil Government," they continued, "which exist in the Christian World the political . . . effects of the Gospel have been thought worthy of legislative attention."[4] "That religion is a most valuable security to states, by its general influence on men of diverse characters and conditions, is an opinion held not only by all good and wise in the world . . . [but by] truly great minds in every age and country," wrote a Pennsylvanian two years later.[5] The next year a South Carolinian wrote in the same vein: "a transient view of the states and kingdoms, which have made the most striking figure in the history of the world, and which have been most renowned for the felicity of their government, will convince us that religion was by them always considered as a matter of great importance to civil society. The greatest politicians and most celebrated legislators of antiquity depended much on this to give sanction to their laws, and make them operate with vigour and facility."[6] The same opinion prevailed in Massachusetts, where Chief Justice Theophilus Parsons declared that civil government must "derive assistance from some superior power . . . this most manifest truth has been felt by legislators in all ages . . . in the pagan world false and absurd systems of religion were adopted and patronized by the magistrate, to remedy the defects necessarily existing in a government merely civil."[7]

Founding Era thinkers believed that the "celebrated legislators" of the past had patronized religion because it was the ideal partner of government, enabling political leaders to achieve their broadest and most fundamental objectives. The following kinds of statements, saluting religion for promoting "the civil good of society," were commonplace during the period. "We can shew," wrote a Bostonian in 1780, "that the support of public worship and the teachers of religion is founded upon the grand fundamental principle of all civil government, which is to secure the peace, safety, and happiness of the community."[8] "Let it suffice to observe," wrote a South Carolinian in 1788, "that *security of life, liberty* and *property* is the precise and specific end of the social compact. If we consider the end of civil society and the evils it was designed to remedy, we will be convinced from its very nature, that it can not reach that end, nor guard against those evils, without the aid of religion."[9]

After 1776, American political leaders frequently lectured their fellow citizens about the capacity of religion to secure the bedrock components of the "civil good of society."[10] Any list of tributes to the beneficent role of religion would begin with Washington's Farewell Address (September 19, 1796) in which the first president paid homage to "religion and morality" as the "indispensable supports" of "political prosperity" as well as thc "great pillars of human happiness."[11] It would include the Northwest Ordinance of 1787 which asserted that religion was "necessary to good government and the happiness of mankind."[12] Present as well would be these additional pronouncements of the Continental and Confederation Congresses: "true religion and good morals are the only solid foundation of public liberty and happiness" (1778); a "universal reformation" in religion would "make us a holy, that we may be a happy people" (1782); and "the practice of pure and undefiled religion . . . is the great foundation of public prosperity and national happiness" (1782).[13] At least one other official document should be added: the much admired Massachusetts Constitution of 1780 which stated that "the happiness of a people, and the good order and preservation of civil government, essentially depend upon piety, religion and morality."[14]

These testimonials to what the revolutionary generation variously called the "public utility" and the "secular and civil utility" of religion[15] are but the tip of the iceberg. From across America hundreds of citizens from all professions and denominations joined George Washington and their representatives in Congress in saluting the power of religion and in celebrating the civic dividends that it yielded. Here is a sample (only a fraction) of their statements:

Happiness

"True religion is most friendly to social and political Happiness."[16]

Virginia, 1785

"The religion such as the blessed Jesus presents to us is essential to private and to public, to temporal as well as to eternity felicity."[17]

Virginia, 1799

There is "a political religion which is essential to every good and wise government in order to its permanent and happy existence."[18]

Maryland, 1783

"Whatever state among us shall continue to make piety and virtue the standard of public honour will enjoy . . . the greatest national happiness."[19]

New Jersey, 1782

"Christian revelation . . . all its doctrines and precepts are calculated to promote the Happiness of society and the safety and well being of civil government."[20]

Pennsylvania, 1786

The American "system of dominion must receive its finishing from religion; or, that from the diffusion of virtue among the people of any community would arise their greatest secular happiness."[21]

Connecticut, 1783

The Assembly is "deeply impressed with a sense of the importance of religion to the happiness of men in civil society."[22]

Massachusetts, 1780

Prosperity

"The absolute necessity of piety and purity of morals . . . there is no other way in which you can more effectually promote the prosperity of your country, than by the practice of these."[23]

South Carolina, 1788

Religion is the "best means of promoting virtue, peace and prosperity."[24]

Virginia, 1779

"Religion has ever been found essential to the prosperity of civil government."[25]

Virginia, 1784

"It is highly necessary . . . to enact a law for the support and encouragement of the christian religion . . . for the honor, prosperity and happiness of this country."[26]

Maryland, 1785

Religion produces "true political welfare and prosperity."[27]

Connecticut, 1783

"The belief of christianity by the citizens of this state is necessary to our political prosperity."[28]

Connecticut, 1794

"There is no such thing as public prosperity without Religion."[29]

Massachusetts, 1761

"A diligent attendance on the instituted means of religion . . . is a principal means of national prosperity."[30]

Massachusetts, 1787

Chapter 1

Republicanism, liberty

"Without Religion there can be no virtue . . . without virtue there can be no liberty."[31]

Georgia, 1803

"We have the best religion in the world. There is no other so well adopted to the genius of a free and independent people, so favorable to liberty and the natural rights of man."[32]

South Carolina, 1788

The church "is one of the great bulwarks of liberty."[33]

Virginia, 1777

"The Christian religion . . . is a religion of all others most friendly to liberty."[34]

Virginia, 1801

"Christianity is the strong ground of republicanism . . . many of its precepts have for their object republican liberty."[35]

Pennsylvania, 1800

"The native tendency of the Christian religion to promote civil liberty."[36]

New York, 1793

"Statesmen . . . may plan and speculate for liberty, but it is Religion and Morality alone, which can establish the Principles upon which Freedom can securely stand."[37]

Massachusetts, 1776

"If our religion is given up, all the liberty we boast of will soon be gone."[38]

New Hampshire, 1788

Good government, good of society

"We may be fully convinced of the utility, and even the necessity of religion, to the well being, we might venture to say, to the very existence of civil society."[39]

South Carolina, 1788

Religion produces the "common good of the state."[40]

Virginia, 1779

Legislators "as they wish well to the Strength and Stability of Government, they ought to act to patronize religion."[41]

Virginia, 1784

"Christianity is generally confessed to be highly conducive to the interests of civil society."[42]

Kentucky, 1785

"Religion being the corner-stone of civil government . . . the most licentious profligate will not presume to deny."[43]

Maryland, 1785

"Christianity is necessary to the public good."[44]

Connecticut, 1794

Religion and gospel ministers are "very necessary to the well being of a christian civil society."[45]

Massachusetts, 1780

Chapter 1

Order

If "the doctrines of christianity were firmly believed, cordially embraced, and its precepts diligently practiced by all our citizens . . . perfect order . . . would then take place among us."[46]

South Carolina, 1788

"Every man in the State partakes of the Blessings of peace and order" which result from religion.[47]

Virginia, 1784

Where "shall we find a system of religion that conduces so effectually to the good order, peace and happiness of society, as the religion of Christ?"[48]

Maryland, 1785

"Impressions of religion . . . serve to maintain order in society."[49]

Maryland, 1785

Religion "establishes, perhaps more than any single thing, good order, Good morals, and happiness public and private."[50]

Connecticut, 1794

"The importance of religion to the peace and order of society is unspeakably great."[51]

Rhode Island, 1793

"The necessity of religion to public order and happiness has been generally acknowledged by discriminating minds in all countries and ages."[52]

Massachusetts, 1792

Peace

"Public worship is . . . productive of effects the most benevolent to Society. It ought to be injoined and regulated by the Legislature so as to preserve public peace, order and decency."[53]

Virginia, 1777

"Christian knowledge hath a natural tendency to correct the morals of men, restrain their vices, and preserve the peace of society."[54]

Virginia, 1784

"The design of religion . . . tends, in its own nature, to the peace and happiness of civil society."[55]

Connecticut, 1765

"Religion and virtue are the strongest bond of human society, and lay the best foundation of peace and happiness in the civil state."[56]

Connecticut, 1787

"Christianity, in its doctrines and practices, has the most natural tendency to promote the peace, safety and happiness of the community."[57]

Massachusetts, 1781

It is obvious that there is a considerable overlapping in these categories. Peace, order and safety are cognates and were often used interchangeably. Similarly, the Founding generation considered happiness and prosperity to be closely related. Some, it is true, asserted that religion promoted prosperity in the material sense. In 1780, for example, John Witherspoon declared that religion produced "opulence"[58] and, later, Daniel Webster claimed that it raised property values.[59] Many, in fact, prized religion for protecting private property. But the majority of the Founders equated prosperity and happiness and understood them in the sense of the "general welfare," mentioned in the preamble to the Constitution. There seems to have been no concerted attempt to establish a hierarchy of values among the civic goods ascribed to religion but most people would have placed order first, for without order none of the other benefits could have been realized. Demonstrably, the Founders expected religion to yield a cornucopia of social and political benefits. How, precisely, did they think it would function "to produce those effects which are confessed to be of such singular service?"[60]

The operating principle, the dynamic element, of religion that was assumed to produce its singular effectiveness was identified and encapsulated by eighteenth-century Americans in a formula—"a future state of rewards and punishments." Contained within this formula was a set of incentives/disincentives which was expected to make individuals obedient Christians as well as responsible citizens; aggregated into a larger society, these obedient citizens would enjoy—and deserve—the benefits described above.

The Founding generation was certain, in John Witherspoon's words, that "the belief or apprehension of a future state of rewards and punishments, has been as universal as the belief of a Deity, and seems inseparable from it."[61] According to a Boston pundit, "we find that a future state of rewards and punishments has been made a part of the several popular religions both of civilized and savage nations, ancient and modern."[62] A Pennsylvania pamphleteer went so far as to ascribe the fall of the Roman Empire to its repudiation of the belief in a "future state."[63]

As venerable as the belief in a future state was, it experienced a powerful revival—a kind of "great awakening"— in the Anglo-American world of the eighteenth century. Beginning in the middle of the seventeenth century, it became a principal element in a debate that preoccupied some of Britain's best thinkers, a debate that focused, in the words of a recent scholar, on "governing conduct."[64] At issue was identifying the best way to make the nation's citizens conduct themselves virtuously, to impel them to act in a moral and orderly way, that would bring goodness and stability to the nation's public life. What, it was incessantly asked, were the "real Motives, by which Mankind may be sway'd to the uniform Practice of virtue?" What were the "common and natural motives to Goodness"; the "principal Motives to duty"; the "obligations of virtue"; "the original of duty or moral obligation"; "the original principles of [the] choice" of virtue?[65]

Assessing this debate in his 1966 Jayne Lectures, Jacob Viner observed that "controversies as to what constituted the sanctions for or inducements to moral behavior and as to their comparative effectiveness" occupied many of Britain's most acute minds "from Hobbes' time [ca. 1650] on for over a century."[66] Many believed that all other methods of generating virtue paled in effectiveness before the doctrine of a future state of rewards and punishments. Called the "providential apparatus," the doctrine has been described "as one of the great governing mechanisms of the early modern European church and state. The practice associated with it is attrition: the fear of divine punishment (hell) and the hope of divine reward (heaven) are necessary to motivate people to act in accordance with moral and legal systems. Every theorist, with the important exceptions of Richard Overton and Pierre Bayle, held that belief in providentialism must underlie any stable social order."[67] Viner traced the doctrine back to Plato and Cicero and pointed out that it had been used by a "host of others."[68] In eighteenth-century Britain "the dispute over the doctrine of eternal punishment, which may superficially seem a rather arid theological debate, was in fact a strongly contested front-line behind which a deep and real conflict of ideas massed."[69]

There have been two explanations for the vigorous revival of the future state doctrine in the eighteenth century. Viner contended that its resurgence was a response to the writings of Thomas Hobbes. By his own admission Hobbes was terrified by the political and social turmoil in seventeenth-century England and became an advocate of public order at any cost. In *Leviathan* and other writings Hobbes proposed an absolute government which would control its citizens' activities by force. Hobbes's scheme minimized the role of religion in influencing human conduct. Viner asserted that in an effort to recapture its influence the British religious establishment refurbished the future state doctrine, over which it considered itself the rightful custodian, and vigorously promoted it, in opposition to the Hobbesian scheme.[70]

Influenced by the seventeenth-century revival of hedonic and Epicurean philosophy, the churchmen took the position that man, a calculating, self-interested creature, was governed by a desire to obtain pleasure and avoid pain. They argued, therefore, that to gratify his self-interest man would take those actions which would procure the highest form of pleasure—eternal bliss—and avoid the most exquisite form of pain—endless torment in hell. Since obtaining eternal bliss and avoiding eternal damnation could only be effected by obedience to the commands of the Gospel, the Christian clergy, as expositors of the Word, considered themselves as the most effective molders of virtuous conduct.

For obvious reasons, the doctrine of the future state, as it emerged in the eighteenth century, has been called "theological utilitarianism" or "otherworldly Benthamism."[71] According to Viner, the Anglican clergy, hoping to swallow its opponents, wielded it like Aaron's rod throughout the century. And not just the Anglicans employed it. Catholics, for example, argued that "the fear of divine chastisement . . . was of great use to human society in that it restrained men from committing acts of vice."[72]

The second explanation for the flourishing of the future state theory in the eighteenth century is that it was formulated, not to empower a clergy besieged by Hobbes, but to serve the needs of the modernizing, "welfare-warfare" state that emerged in the seventeenth century and that required a body of citizens who behaved with "regularity and law abidingness." With this goal in mind, John Locke advocated a version of the future state theory, called by a recent scholar "penalism," which differed in no appreciable way from clergy-sponsored "theological utilitarianism."[73] That Locke and the Anglican establishment, which feared him (unreasonably) as an apostle of atheism, could work with the same tools demonstrates the broad reach of the future state theory in the eighteenth century.

In books such as *An Essay Concerning Human Understanding* and *The Reasonableness of Christianity* Locke argued that "the Christian apparatus is the 'true ground of morality' because the law-maker is God, the author of truth, and the rewards and punishments, heaven and hell, are the greatest pleasures and pains." Locke prized the power of self-interest and contended that with "Christ's revelation of heaven and hell 'interest is come about to her [virtue] and virtue is visibly the most enticing purchase and by much the best bargain.'"[74]

By grounding virtue so firmly in calculating self-interest, Locke became a target of his former pupil, the third Earl of Shaftesbury, who was scandalized by his teacher's effort and those of the whole rewards and punishments school to make "man virtuous from a mercenary view"; those who acted virtuously because of "the Hope of future reward and fear of future punishment" were, according to Shaftesbury, no better than "Monkies under the Discipline of the Whip."[75] "By making Rewards and Punishments the principal Motives to duty, the Christian Religion in Particular is overthrown," Shaftesbury complained, "and its greatest Principle, that of Love, is rejected and expos'd."[76] Accordingly, Shaftesbury formulated a counter theory of virtuous behavior that rested on a putative "moral sense," an instinct like taste or smell, which attracted mankind, like the moth to the flame, to virtue for the sake of its intrinsic beauty. Virtue, in Shaftesbury's hands, became "disinterested" and was called by its signature term, "disinterested benevolence." The Scottish clergyman-academician, Francis Hutcheson, worked Shaftesbury's moral sense into a coherent system of moral philosophy, which became the "distinctively original idea" of the Scottish Enlightenment,[77] through whose influence it acquired a broad audience in America during the Founding Period.

If those influenced by "sentimental" moral philosophy assailed the future state doctrine because of its "interested" behavioral psychology, another group—a heterogeneous mixture of Latitudinarian ministers, deists and sceptics—attacked its theological underpinnings, specifically, its conventional understanding of hell. The "orthodox doctrine of hell," according to Daniel Walker, had reigned unchallenged in Europe since the time of Origen in the third century, A.D. The core element of this doctrine was what an eighteenth-century writer called the "*eternity* of hell torments," the perpetuity of punishment being the feature of hell that gave it its potency.[78] Toward the middle of the seventeenth century critics appeared, among them former chaplains in Cromwell's army, who denied that the punishments inflicted in hell were eternal. These dissenters alarmed religious leaders like the Bishop of Chester who, in 1677, publicly worried that efforts to mitigate the severity of hell would impair the "Credibility" of that "great Principle of religion, concerning a future state of reward and punishment."[79] The critics, however, initially had little success in arresting the "long triumph of hell," grounded, as it was, "in the firm and almost universal belief in its value as a deterrent in this life. It was thought that, if the fear of eternal punishment were removed, most people would behave without any moral restraint whatever and that society would collapse into an anarchistical orgy."[80]

By the early decades of the eighteenth century hell had begun to lose its hold on the British intelligentsia. Locke, Newton, and other "thinking men" were reported on good authority to have renounced a belief in the eternity of hell punishment, although few were prepared to admit it in public.[81] One was William Whiston, a sometime professor of mathematics at Cambridge, who in 1740 published a book attacking the eternity of hell torments as "reproachful to Christianity" and proposed a scheme of probation in the afterlife that could lead to the salvation of the damned.[82] By arguing for the restoration of the damned to good standing in heaven, Whiston revealed himself to be a universalist.

Whiston and many of the earlier opponents of the orthodox hell were pious men who could not reconcile it with a God of infinite love. Other eighteenth-century critics, like Bolingbroke, Hume and Gibbon, approached the subject from a very different perspective, that of deism and scepticism. Bolingbroke ridiculed the concept of hell as an "absurdity" that had originated with the "superstitious and idolatrous" Egyptians, who transmitted it to the Greeks, whose "luxuriant imaginations . . . improved it" and who passed it along to the post-exilic Jews from whom Christianity inherited it.[83] Hume denounced the orthodox hell as the domain of a "capricious daemon, who exercised power without reason and without humanity."[84]

Undermining hell, these writers realized, had a high probability of being socially subversive, if the British populace at large became aware of their views. The Bolingbrokes of the world and, for that matter, moral sense writers like Shaftesbury, were social and intellectual snobs who viewed the mass of the British populace as "the shallow vulgar," "the vulgar who never examine," creatures of passions and of "strong, sensual appetites."[85] This attitude was characteristic of the eighteenth-century elites, who "conceptualized the distinction" between themselves and the "mob,"and "applied it more unremittingly than ever before."[86] Fearful of arousing the destructive capacities of the "vulgar," some eighteenth-century critics of hell followed Gibbon who advised in *The Decline and Fall* that magistrates support the doctrine of a future state of rewards and punishments, even if they believed it to be false.[87] "Whatever you decide in your own mind," an advocate of Gibbon's position wrote, "the received doctrine and words must be used for the people . . . which is inclined to vice and can be deterred from evil only by the fear of punishment."[88] Bolingbroke and others included in their writings commendations of the future state as "very necessary" because "the doctrines of rewards and punishments in it had so great a tendency to enforce civil laws, and to restrain the vices of men."[89] Meliorists of hell like Whiston wanted to disabuse the vulgar of any notion that they would eventually get a free pass to eternity and, therefore, stressed that God's vengeance, which would afflict the wicked for an indeterminate, although not infinite, period after death, was not to be thought of "without Horror, Agony and Amazement."[90]

The moral sense writers were attacked for conjuring up "cobweb speculations spun in the closet" and for being "visionary," "enigmatical" and "enthusiastical."[91] Critics held it to be unrealistic to suppose that the "many, who have quick senses, strong passions, and gross intellects" could—or would want to—discern the beauty of virtue and find gratification in pursuing it for its own sake.[92] Instead of establishing virtue and order in the community at large, the moral sense theory was said to subvert them. Bishop Berkeley laid at its door the terrifying fact "that the civil magistrate daily loseth his authority, that the laws are trampled upon, and the subject [is] in constant fear of being robbed, or murdered, or having his house burnt over his head."[93] Shaftesbury, who was long dead when this attack was made, had been in his own day sensitive to these kinds of charges and had inserted into his *Inquiry concerning Virtue and Merit* the following passage: "the principle of fear of future punishment, and hope of future reward, however mercenary or servile soever it may be accounted, is yet in many circumstances a great advantage, and support of virtue."[94] Or, as he said more tersely on another occasion: "among the vulgar, a heaven and hell may prevail, where a jail and a gallows are thought insufficient."[95] On this point Francis Hutcheson's admirers were eager to correct a misconception about his own work. By stressing "a most real and intimate obligation by the moral sense to act virtuously," he did not mean, one of his early editors pointed out, that "all other obligations . . , were superseded. Nothing could be further from his thoughts; nor is it a consequence of his scheme. He was fully sensible of the importance and necessity of enforcing the practice of virtue upon mankind from all possible considerations, and especially from these awful ones of future rewards and punishments."[96] Other advocates of the moral sense employed the future state doctrine as "an after-consideration . . . an additional weight to enforce the practice of what Men were obliged to by right reason."[97] These writers, Viner observed, "were eclectic if not self contradictory."[98]

The eclecticism noted by Viner is a testimony to the compelling power of the future state doctrine, for virtually everyone who proposed an alternative system of fostering virtue incorporated it as insurance against the vulnerabilities of their own views. The process did not work in the other direction, however; the rewards and punishments camp saw no reason to augment their doctrine with "after-consider-ations" and consistently gave the British public an undiluted version of it. Viner identified the Cambridge University divinity professor, Thomas Rutherforth, as the principal eighteenth-century champion of the future state doctrine.[99] The theologian Samuel Clarke, whose writings were more influential than Rutherforth's, would have been a better choice. In his essay, "Of Future Rewards and Punishments," Clarke assessed the whole spectrum of "Arguments proper to persuade men to the practice of Virtue" and concluded that in a "corrupt and confused World . . . where the Understandings of Many are perplexed and puzzled . . . the most universally proper, and only effectual Motive, to deter men from Vice, and persuade them to their Duty is laying before them, in a clear and strong Light, the Rewards and Punishments of a future State."[100] A better choice still would have been Bishop William Warburton, who devoted the first 320 pages of his enormously influential *The Divine Legation of Moses* to proving that "the inculcating the Doctrine of a Future State of Rewards and Punishments is necessary to the Well being of Society" and that "all Mankind, especially the most Wise and Learned Nations of Antiquity, have concurred in Believing and

Teaching, that the Doctrine was of such use to Civil Society."[101] Warburton's book, which went through five editions, was an encyclopedia of the future state doctrine, covering nations ancient and modern, and was undoubtedly the source of the assertions by American writers of the antiquity of the doctrine. Warburton himself was indebted to the research of Toland and Bolingbroke, who had established that the doctrine of future rewards and punishments "began to be taught long before we have any light into antiquity, and when we begin to have any, we find it established."[102]

It is difficult in eighteenth-century Britain to estimate the proportion of future state purists to their eclectic opponents who blended the doctrine into their works. What can be said is that hardly any tract on religion or morality in eighteenth-century Britain lacked some expression of the doctrine. Even British horses were familiar with it, according to Swift's hero, Lemuel Gulliver.[103] It was, beyond contradiction, pervasive. Many, in fact, considered the doctrine to be the marrow of religion itself. To Bishop Berkeley it was one of the "great points of the faith."[104] John Brown, an important Anglican preacher popular in America, asserted that the "lively and active Belief of an all-seeing and all-powerful God, who will hereafter make them happy or miserable, according as they designedly promote or violate the Happiness of their Fellow-Creatures" was "the Essence of Religion."[105] This sentiment was broadcast through the English-speaking world by Samuel Johnson, who in his *Dictionary* defined religion as "Virtue, as founded upon the reverence of God, and expectation of future rewards and punishments."[106]

The British authors who commended the future state doctrine, whether enthusiastically or grudgingly, were a who's who of the nation's men of letters whose works, by 1776, were well-known to most literate Americans. Furthermore, moral philosophy, the arena in which the principal disputes over the future state doctrine occurred, was the "preeminent" course in eighteenth-century American colleges.[107] The new nation's leaders, therefore, were well versed in the arguments which the advocates of the future state made on its behalf. Dr. Johnson's definition was, in fact, quoted with approval in various parts of the United States as late as 1821;[108] people as diverse as Supreme Court Justice Joseph Story and the "American Farmer," J. Hector St. John de Crèvecoeur, agreed with the British luminaries that the future state was "essential" and one of the "great doctrines of religion."[109]

From 1776 onward the future state doctrine was constantly employed in the United States, although in a much different context than in Britain. In the mother country social complacency prevailed; America, however, was convulsed by revolution, which in fact was hospitable to the future state doctrine because the Americans resolved to make their new state governments republics which, the political science of the day taught, could not succeed without widespread popular virtue which was precisely what the future state doctrine was designed to supply.[110] From the beginning, therefore, religion was considered to be the handmaiden of republican government, although a few groups regarded the emphasis on the future state doctrine as excessive. Members of the emerging Universalist movement, for example, complained that the "idea, that it is necessary to the good order of civil government, that the Teachers of Religion should thunder out the doctrine of everlasting punishment, to deter men from atrocious crimes, which they may otherwise commit in secret, has long been hackneyed in the hands of men in power."[111]

Men in power in the new republican state governments wrote the future state doctrine into several of the first state constitutions, their purpose being to secure virtuous voters, elected officials and bureaucrats. The Pennsylvania Constitution of 1776 and the Vermont Constitution of 1777 required members of their Houses of Representatives to swear an oath, affirming their belief in a future state. The South Carolina Constitution of 1778 required voters to believe in a future state. The first draft of the Massachusetts Constitution of 1780 affirmed that "the knowledge and belief of the being of God, His providential government of the world, and of a future state of rewards and punishments, [were] the only true foundation of morality." The 1785 constitution of the abortive state of Franklin in western North Carolina and the 1796 constitution of Tennessee both required all officials in their "civil department" to believe in the future state.[112]

Antifederalists attacked the federal constitution of 1787 because it "disdains . . . belief of a deity, the immortality of the soul; or of the resurrection of the body, a day of judgement, or a future state of rewards and punishments."[113] They focused on Article VI, which prohibited religious tests for federal officeholders. According to the Maryland delegate, Luther Martin, some at the Philadelphia Convention would have supported a test oath, these being men who "were so unfashionable as to think that a belief of the existence of a deity, and of a future state of rewards and punishments would be some security for the good conduct of our rulers."[114] Virginia and Pennsylvania Antifederalists outdid Martin by proposing that Article VI be amended to require all officials in the executive, legislative and judicial branches at both the federal and state levels to swear to a belief in the future state doctrine.[115]

Another example of how the American Revolution created a different context than in Britain for the use of the future state doctrine was the widespread movement in the wake of the adoption of the Declaration of Independence to disestablish American churches. In Britain the established Church of England was unassailable throughout the eighteenth century but in the new American republic the egalitarian impulses unleashed by the Revolution could not abide the idea of taxing all citizens for the support of one privileged church—Congregational in New England and Anglican from Maryland southward. As a result, agitation immediately began for the abolition of religious taxes and the creation of a level playing field for all American denominations. This prospect horrified many American lay and clerical leaders, who feared that the removal of state financial support from the erstwhile established churches and a resulting reliance on purely voluntary contributions would lead to the enfeeblement of religion in the new nation. An alternative was proposed—general assessment laws which taxed all citizens for the support of religion but allowed them to channel their taxes to the churches of their choice. The proponents of these laws were obliged to make a case for them. In all states the rationale offered was the public policy benefits of religion, the wide range of civic blessings listed at the beginning of this chapter. In the years immediately following independence, the general assessment campaigns from New England to Georgia (the middle states excepted) generated the flood of endorsements of the social and political utility of religion that created the deep pool of testimonials from which public officials and Americans in general drew.

In touting the public benefits of religion, the advocacy of some Americans seemed so excessive that in 1783 Ezra Stiles lamented the scarcity of the "Christian patriot, who from his heart wishes the advancement of Christianity much less for the civil good than for the eternal welfare of immortal souls."[116] A few years later, after arguments for the "civil good" of Christianity had escalated into the equation of its positive impact on society with the militia, the judicial system and road building projects, Jefferson's former attorney general, Levi Lincoln, complained to a convocation of Massachusetts politicians that "he was pained to hear the maintenance of religious worship compared with the support of public highways."[117]

The clergymen who championed the public utility of religion were sincere, but their advocacy was transparently self-serving. Ministers of the established churches in America, in the years immediately following 1776, found themselves in precisely the position of their British brethren a century earlier, who feared that they would be marginalized by Hobbes and, later, by the moral sense theorists. If disestablishment in America succeeded or general assessment failed, the established American clergy would lose both its livelihood and status and, therefore, it appropriated the instrument honed by its British brethren—the future state doctrine —and brandished it as a unique resource whose ability to promote the public good was so manifest that the voters would see their interest in underwriting it. Although it regarded itself as the most effective dispenser of the future state doctrine, the clergy applauded its use by sympathetic civil authorities.

The campaign for passage of general assessment bills was conducted in speeches, on the floors of legislatures, in charges to juries and in newspaper articles, pamphlets and sermons. In Maryland the House of Delegates directly intervened in the public debate. Having drafted a general assessment bill in December 1784, the House prepared an "Address" to the citizens, January 8, 1785, promoting the passage of the bill, which it published in the state's newspapers.[118] The House solicited its constituents' support by declaring, in a phrase borrowed from the Massachusetts Constitution of 1780, that "the happiness of the people, and the good order and preservation of civil government, depend upon morality, religion and piety." Since the House "beheld a growing indifference to religion and things sacred, very alarming to the interests of morality, peace and good order in society," it asked the voters to provide tax support to the state's Christian ministers, the expositors of the New Testament. "Where," the House asked, "shall we find a system of religion which conduces so effectually to good order, peace, happiness of society, as the *religion of Christ?* Whatsoever things are honest, pure, lovely and of *good report*, are enforced by it under the sacred sanction of everlasting rewards and punishments." "Government," the House continued, "can have no confidence in that man who is under no religious tie, and who believes neither Heaven nor Hell, or, in other words, a future state of rewards and punishments." The future state doctrine was a mainstay of Maryland newspaper writers who supported the House's position. On March 22, for example, Philander, writing in the *Maryland Journal,* issued the following warning to his readers: "Banish religious principle and you loosen all the bonds which connect mankind together . . . you render the security arising from laws in a great measure void and ineffectual. For human laws and human sanctions cannot extend to numberless cases, in which the safety of mankind is deeply concerned. They would prove very feeble instruments of order and peace, if there were no checks upon the conduct of men from divine legislation; if no belief of future rewards and punishments were to overawe conscience, and to supply the defects of human government."[119]

At one point during the long controversy in Virginia, 1776-1786, over the public funding of religion, the House of Delegates, in the fall of 1779, came close to passing a general assessment bill which would have subsidized the state's denominations but only if they affirmed "that there is one Eternal God and a future State of Rewards and punishments."[120] The successful general assessment campaign in Massachusetts was shorter, 1778-1780, but it produced a larger crop of advocates for the public support of religion and for the future state doctrine than elsewhere in the United States. Some of the doctrine's most articulate proponents were, predictably, members of the Congregationalist establishment, who were not bashful about stressing their importance to the health of the commonwealth or claiming public funds in compensation for their efforts. A particularly frank expression of the Standing Order's view was delivered by the Reverend Samuel West on May 1, 1780. West assured the average citizen of Massachusetts "that the people are, by their religious instructions, prevented from many immoralities which they would otherwise run into. If he should find himself protected from robbers, thieves and house breakers, in consequence of religious instruction . . . will he not own it reasonable that he should pay for those instructions, which in their consequence is beneficial to him; that is, is it not right that he should pay for his protection . . . ?"[121]

The Massachusetts Constitution of 1780 had famously declared that "piety, religion and morality" produced "the happiness of a people, and the good order and preservation of civil government." The ministers and their allies were eager to show how this was done. The Reverend Phillips Payson in his Election Sermon of May 27, 1778, composed against the background of the flawed and popularly rejected state constitution of February 28, 1778, asserted that the "importance of religion to civil society and government is great indeed . . . the fear and reverence of God, and the terrors of eternity, are the most powerful restraints on the minds of men . . . let the restraints of religion once be broken down, as they infallibly would be by leaving the subject of public worship to the humors of the multitude, and we might well defy all human wisdom and power to support and preserve order and government in the state."[122] The preacher of the May 30, 1780, Election

Sermon, Simeon Howard, spoke during the campaign to ratify a newly drafted constitution to replace the failed instrument of 1778. Howard addressed the problem that had preoccupied the British experts, with whom he was obviously familiar, that of identifying the "principle" that "effectually promotes" virtue. Like the British future state purists, Howard came out four square for the efficacy of "self-love," dismissing the sentimentalist school's "regard to the intrinsic amiableness and excellency of virtue." Suppose, Howard continued, " a man to be habitually under the influence of this principle, that is, to believe and duly consider God as his ruler and judge, who will hereafter reward virtue and punish vice with happiness and misery respectively, unspeakably greater than any to be enjoyed in this world, and he may then, upon rational principles, and in consistency with his self love, forego the greatest temporal good, and expose himself to the greatest temporal evil, in the cause of virtue; and we may reasonably expect that he will. Virtue will be his chief good. The fear of God, therefore, is the most effectual and the only sure support of virtue in the world."[123] Since Howard subscribed to the truism that virtue created happiness, it followed that religion, in the form of the future state theory, produced virtue which produced public happiness, as the 1780 Constitution said that it did.

No member of the Massachusetts establishment was more indefatigable in expounding the future state doctrine than the aforementioned Reverend Samuel West, who, writing over the signature of Irenaeus, conducted a newspaper controversy with Philanthropos, a formidable, but never satisfactorily identified foe of general assessment, which lasted from March 1780 into the winter of 1781, spread over four Boston newspapers, and produced a score of articles on both sides. Irenaeus took it for granted that "the government both of church and state is founded upon and presupposes the belief of the being and attributes of God and of a future state of rewards and punishments."[124] On November 27, 1780, he lectured his opponent on the value of the future state doctrine. He began by stipulating that "all those doctrines and parts of worship" in the state's Christian churches were "really necessary for the well-being of civil society." Then he began in earnest:

> Among which perhaps no one is of greater importance to promote the peace and safety of the community than the doctrine of a future state of reward and punishment; for we shall find that persons are often restrained from gross immoralities by the fear of future miseries, when civil penalties prove insuffi-

cient for that purpose. A doctrine of such amazing importance to promote the civil good of society ought to be very strongly impress'd upon the minds of men in order to render it beneficial to society. Hence the necessity of teachers of religion warmly to enforce the doctrine upon the minds of their hearers with such arguments and authorities as will appear to be weighty, and be likely to convince the minds of those upon whom they are urged.

We find that a future state of rewards and punishments . . . when it has been taught and impressed upon the minds of any people according to the received standard of their religious belief, it has undoubtedly produced beneficial effects to society. Thus a Mahometan is excited to the practice of good morals in hopes that after the resurrection he shall enjoy the beautiful girls of paradise to all eternity. He is afraid to commit murder, adultery, & theft lest he be cast into hell, where he must drink scalding water and the scum of the damned & have nothing to breathe but terrible hot and suffocating air.

West continued with his exposition, arguing that since the "belief of a future state of rewards and punishments" was "absolutely necessary for the well being of civil society" it ought to be taught "according to the sacred oracles of the new testament," which was the province of the Christian minister who, accordingly, "had a much greater right to have a maintenance secur'd to him by a Christian legislature."[125]

Philanthropos, whose arguments were not, as West's were, saturated with economic self-interest, agreed with his opponent that "no person who is acquainted with christianity, can reasonably deny that it is conducive to the peace, safety and happiness of civil society."[126] Nor was the Massachusetts Baptist leader, Isaac Backus, a fervent opponent of any form of public funding for the state's churches, reluctant to acknowledge the social and political utility of religion. In his important 1778 pamphlet, *Government and Liberty Described and Ecclesiastical Tyranny Exposed,* Backus asserted that "I am as sensible of the importance of religion and the utility of it to human society as Mr. Payson is. And I concur with him that the fear and reverence of God and the terrors of eternity are the most powerful restraints on the minds of men." In a newspaper article two years later Backus emphasized that he "*fully concurred*" with these sentiments.[127] Elsewhere in the new states other "dissenting"denominations subscribed to Backus's position. Presbyterians in Virginia, for example, asserted that it was "absolutely necessary to the existence and welfare of every political combination of men in Society, to have the support of Religion and its solemn institutions . . . on this

Account it is wise policy in Legislators to seek its alliance and solicit its aid in a civic view, because of its happy influence upon the morality of the Citizens."[128] The point is that neither differences in doctrine nor economic interests prevented a consensus from forming among American churches that religion had—and should have—a positive impact on the nation's public life.

The nation's politicians, from right to left, subscribed to this consensus. An arch-conservative like Theophilus Parsons and an ardent liberal like Thomas Paine might agree about the virtues of the future state doctrine, when they could concur on nothing else. According to Parsons, Christianity made a constructive contribution to civil society because it was able to "furnish the most efficacious sanctions, by bringing to light a future state of retribution."[129] Paine contended that those who made "their fellow mortals happy . . . will be happy hereafter; and that the very wicked will meet some punishment."[130] Between these two poles men of all shades of opinion endorsed the future state doctrine. The friction between Benjamin Franklin and John Adams during the Revolution is well documented but both statesmen agreed about the value of the future state.[131] In his *A Defence of the Constitutions of Government of the United States of America* (1787) Adams addressed the persistent eighteenth-century problem of the creation of virtue. "What stronger motive to virtue," he asked, "and to the preservation of liberty can the human mind perceive, next to those of rewards and punishments in a future life, than the recollection of a long line of ancestors" who have served the republic well?[132] As president, in 1799, he issued a fast day proclamation that asserted that there was no truth "more clearly taught in the Volume of Inspiration, nor any more fully demonstrated by the experience of all ages, than that a deep sense and full acknowledgment of the governing providence of a Supreme Being and of the accountableness of men to Him as the searcher of hearts and the righteous distributor of rewards and punishments are conducive equally to the happiness and rectitude of individuals and the well being of communities."[133] Benjamin Rush, a friend of both Adams and Franklin, seemed to be echoing Irenaeus, when he wrote in 1786 that "such is my veneration for every religion that reveals the attributes of the Deity, or a future state of rewards and punishments, that I had rather see the opinions of Confucius or Mohammed inculcated upon our youth than see them grow up wholly devoid of a system of religious principle."[134] Was there an important Founder who dismissed the future state doctrine? Certainly not Jefferson, about whom more later. The only possible candidate would be James

Madison but, if he excluded the future state doctrine from his political calculations, he would be the exception that proved the rule.

One of the striking aspects of the Founding generation's repeated use of the
future state doctrine is the absence of explication of its full dimensions. Americans
habitually used the bare formula, a future state of rewards and punishments, on the
assumption that their countrymen knew what it meant. Perhaps the profusion of
British works on moral obligation, which explained the doctrine and its
alternatives, precluded the necessity of Americans attempting to expound it. Its
code-like quality may explain why scholars have overlooked its surpassing
importance. There was, nevertheless, one systematic American exposition of the
doctrine, in an important, but long neglected work, which, though principally a
rehash of the British literature, emphasized certain points that gave it a distinctive
American flavor. It is to this work, which fleshes out the future state formula and
explains in detail how Americans believed that it would produce public benefits,
that we now turn.

The work, an 87-page tract, entitled *An Essay on the Influence of Religion in
Civil Society* (Charleston, 1788), was written by a Presbyterian minister, Thomas
Reese, since 1773 pastor at a church in Salem in rural South Carolina. Reese was
no country bumpkin. He was considered the "most finished writer of the day"
among southern Presbyterians. In recognition of his learning, Princeton in 1794
awarded him an honorary degree. One of South Carolina's political leaders,
David Ramsay, thought that Reese's *Essay* "would have been reputable to the pen
of Warburton: but coming from the woods of Carolina . . . it fell still-born from
the press in Charleston."[135] The comparison to Warburton was apt, for like the
English bishop Reese argued with unremitting energy that mankind was "so
formed as to be greatly influenced by whatever works upon our hopes or our fears
. . . it is by taking hold on these that religion produces those salutary effects of
which we now speak; thus restraining men from vice by the dread of punishment,
and alluring them to virtue by the hope of reward." Reese laid so much stress on
this point that at the end of his work he apologized to his readers for "taking so
much pains to prove what very few either doubt or deny."[136]

To what extent Reese was indebted to John Witherspoon for his partiality to
the future state doctrine is unclear. Reese graduated from Princeton in 1768, the
year Witherspoon became president of the college. He received a master's degree
the next year (often a formality) and prepared for the ministry in the following
years. What can be said is that Reese, in common with other Princeton graduates,

immersed himself in Witherspoon's *Lectures on Moral Philosophy*, which conveyed all the particulars of the British dispute about the relative merits of the moral sense and the future state of rewards and punishments as catalysts of virtuous conduct and of "moral obligation."[137] Witherspoon himself had been a principal protagonist in the acrimonious quarrels in the Church of Scotland over this and related issues and held Hutcheson and other partisans of the moral sense doctrine in contempt, stigmatizing them as "paganized Christian divines." In the "last of his great doctrinal sermons" delivered before leaving Scotland, Witherspoon lamented that "an unsubstantial theory of virtue was being preached instead of 'the great and operative views of the gospel.'"[138] Nevertheless, Witherspoon gave the moral sense theory fair play in his *Lectures*, although his sympathies were clearly on the side of the future state doctrine, which, he argued, was "absolutely necessary to reclaim men from vice and impiety."[139]

It was, then, from Witherspoon that Reese apparently acquired his distaste for the moral sense theory, disparaging it as one of those "fine-spun systems, however much they may display the ingenuity of their authors, have but very little tendency to promote virtue, and reform the manners of the people; and therefore can be of little service to society. It is not easy to see how the moral sense . . . can properly establish the sanction of future reward and punishment. This we have shewn is of the greatest moment to civil government; and hence arises the singular utility of religion." Reese conceded that the moral sense theory might "have its weight with men of elegant minds and delicate sentiments"[140] but suggested that in America these individuals were few and far between. And they were—with one major exception: the Master of Monticello.

As a young man Jefferson encountered a passage criticizing the future state theory in the writings of his favorite author at the time, Bolingbroke, which he judged to be of sufficient importance to copy into his Literary Commonplace Book.[141] By 1776 Jefferson had become enamored with the moral sense theory, possibly through the influence of Shaftesbury, whose books he admired, but more likely through the writings of the Scottish jurist, Lord Kames, who refined Hutcheson's theories.[142] In notes for a speech in the Virginia Assembly in 1776 concerning state funding for religion, Jefferson countered the contentions of friends of Virginia's religious establishment that a "Belief of Future State [is] necess[ary]" by denigrating the doctrine with Bolingbroke's argument that it was unknown to the Jewish patriarchs and had insinuated itself into Christianity through the corrupt channels of Egyptian and Greek superstition.[143] Over time

Jefferson formed a better opinion of the future state doctrine, as he did of the value of religion itself. In 1803 he declared that Jesus himself had "taught, emphatically, the doctrine of a future state: which was either doubted or disbelieved by the Jews: and wielded it with efficacy, as an important incentive, supplementary to other motives to moral conduct."[144] This estimate of the future state doctrine Jefferson repeated in a letter to Thomas Law, June 13, 1814, in which he affirmed his allegiance to the moral sense theory but addressed its shortcomings. It was true, Jefferson conceded, that in some men the moral sense was "wanting." This deficiency could be remedied by publicizing "the prospects of a future state of retribution for evil as well as the good while done here."[145] By 1822 Jefferson offered a definition of Christianity that was similar to the one in Johnson's *Dictionary*: "that there is one God, and he is all-perfect: that there is a future state of rewards and punishments: that to love God with all thy heart, and thy neighbor as thyself, is the sum of religion."[146]

In shoring up the moral sense with the future state doctrine Jefferson was employing what Viner called the eclectic strategy of Shaftesbury, Hutcheson and other members of the British moral sense school. Unlike the British thinkers, Jefferson sought no converts to the moral sense, never sharing his thoughts on the subject with the public, which was not, in any case, in sympathy with him on this issue. The pure future state theory was what suited the palates of Jefferson's fellow Americans. By subscribing to the moral sense the third president remained, as he once described himself, a sect of one—or of at most a few.

Like Shaftesbury and his followers, Jefferson objected to the future state theory because it was grounded in self-interest. "Self love," Jefferson protested, "is no part of morality."[147] British supporters of the future state doctrine, as we have seen, rejected this view and explicitly made self-interest the pivot of their system. Americans followed suit. "The whole of what is urged . . . under the notion of motive," Reese wrote, "may be resolved into the principle of self-love." Religion, he argued, "affords the necessary assistance" to virtue, "for by inculcating a future retribution, and thus exciting the hopes and fears of men, she opposes *self-love* to *self-love*."[148] What Reese meant was that religion trumped the lure of temporal gratifications with its ineffably sublime or horrific recompenses of eternal pleasure or pain for good or bad behavior.

Reese raised the question of "whether the hope of reward or the dread of punishment, most influences the actions of men."[149] Although a handful of Americans denounced those who would "manage the human mind by the inferior and precarious handle of fear,"[150] it is clear that the overwhelming majority of Americans regarded divine punishment—the terrors of eternity—as the more effective method of governing human conduct. To hold out to men the prospect that they could gain the reward of eternal bliss by good works was too close to Arminianism to be palatable in a land where Calvinism was still strong and depravity was still considered to be the common denominator of the human condition. The threat of punishment, therefore, was considered to be the surest method of inducing socially responsible behavior.

Reese's *Essay* reveals that a sensitivity to social status was not absent from American future state advocates but that it was far removed from the outspoken and virulent class consciousness of British proponents. Bishop James Madison of Virginia, for example, in asking if man can "look intently forward to a state of future rewards and punishments, and not be urged by the most irresistible motives, to love and practice virtue" fixed his gaze on the "great bulk of mankind, who are incapable of abstract speculation, and whose moral feelings can not be supposed to receive much cultivation." "It is chiefly this view of religion," the Bishop remarked, "which is addressed to their hopes and fears, that can secure a faithful discharge of their social duties."[151] Reese remarked that the "gross of the common people" did not think much and were not disposed to examine topics like the obligations of morality which to them appeared "not a little intricate and perplexed." Possessing "quick senses, strong passions, and gross intellects," ordinary citizens were creatures of self-interest and could only be reached by a potent religion "which is calculated to operate upon the bulk of the common people in every society."[152] This tone even surfaced in Washington's Farewell Address, when the departing president conceded that the "influence of refined education on minds of peculiar structure" might eliminate the need for the kind of religious precepts that were required to produce morality in the general population.[153] Behind none of these statements, however, lurked the class condescension that informed British advocates of the future state. In the United States denunciations of the common man as vulgar were very rare. And statements from Americans about men being "ungovernable beasts" who needed a "strong chain"—in the seventeenth century the talk was of the "double chain" of law and religion—"to keepe them downe"—were directed more at the general human condition than at a particular social stratum.[154] As Bishop Madison wrote on another occasion, "those awful sanctions, which religion annexes, touch the hearts of an entire nation, the poor, the simple, the unlettered, as well as the learned and the wise."[155]

The presumption of widespread human depravity posed a challenge for the architects of the new American republican governments, who could not count on the coercive apparatus of European states to assure the durability of their experiments. In European governments, John Witherspoon observed, "a principle of honour, and the subordination of ranks, with the vigor of despotic authority, supply the place of virtue, by restraining irregularities and producing public order."[156] But the new American states did not have these resources. "We have," said John Adams, "no government armed with power of contending with human passions unbridled by morality and religion."[157] "In America," declared the citizens of Surry County, Virginia, "where liberty flourishes in its most luxuriant state . . . where much is left to the [peoples'] discretion, much to their caprice; the aid of religion will be more necessary and its influence more decisive, than in the Monarchies of Europe where the Governments have more energy."[158]

Was the new republic really as vulnerable as these statements imply? On paper the criminal codes in the new states looked strong enough to maintain order and to lessen the need for the discipline imposed by the future state doctrine. But the Founders were skeptical about the effectiveness of the criminal justice system. From the rural south to the cities of New England men complained about its "great deficiency." "Human laws and punishments," declared the residents of Southampton County, Virginia, in 1785, "were insufficient to restrain men within proper bounds," a view shared by the Boston Town Meeting, which asserted in 1780 that "human Laws were feble barriers opposed to the uninformed lusts of Passions of mankind."[159] One major problem was "secret offenses," for if miscreants could "conceal their guilt from the eye of men, they are sure to escape that punishment which is the sanction of human laws."[160] Reese complained that "civil society not only cannot punish secret crimes, but, in some cases, cannot adequately punish even such as are apparent and can be clearly proven."[161] Judge Parsons of Massachusetts concluded that civil government, "availing itself only of its own powers, is extremely defective." The rule of law needed, in his opinion, to be reinforced by "some superiour power, whose laws extend to the temper and disposition of the human heart and before whom no offense is secret."[162] This was also the view in Connecticut, where it was said that "human laws always prove weak and inefficient unless aided, in some form or other, by religion"; to accomplish its purposes law must be backed by a religion which could "make men accountable to an omniscient judge, and call to its aid those awful motives, which are drawn from a future state of rewards and punishments."[163] Another problem with human law was that it did not extend its reach to what the Founding generation called "imperfect obligations," a concept borrowed from moral philosophy, which included hospitality, charity, gratitude, benevolence and "good neighbourhood."[164] Civil laws could not "punish the neglect of them; but the laws of God extend to them; and religion strongly exacts them as duties of perfect obligation."[165]

To support the law and society adequately, religion, it was incessantly asserted, must be "awful." Its deterrent, the fear of future punishment, must have the maximum potency, which meant that hell must be horrific. American advocates of the future state emphasized, therefore, without apology the terrifying aspects of the Christian hell. In the first place they stressed that malefactors, though they might escape the observation of men, could not elude the vigilance of God whose "all seeing eye" made Him "omniscient" and capable of penetrating the "inmost recesses" of the human heart. They exulted that, unlike the deities of "infidel" systems, the god of Christianity was "vindictive" and would let no sinner escape his condign punishment.[166] As on so many other topics, Reese captured his contemporaries' view of hell. "Christianity," he wrote, "exhibits the most terrible and striking picture of that punishment which will be inflicted on the wicked." Heathen writers, including geniuses like Homer and Virgil, who had "tried their strength and exerted the whole force of their talents, in describing a future state" were no match for the gospel writers. "What are these," Reese continued, "when compared to the descriptions which the pen of inspiration gives us of hell, the seat of enraged justice and burning vengeance, and of those eternal pains which the enkindled wrath of the almighty inflicts upon the wicked ghosts, who are condemned to those gloomy mansions of endless horror and despair. . . . What gloomy and dreadful images are these! How awfully grand and striking! How well accommodated to awaken our fears, to deter us from evil, and to stimulate us to the practice of piety and virtue, without which we can not expect to escape."[167]

As with British future state proponents, Americans believed that the success of hell as an incentive to virtue was its perpetuity. Writers in both nations subscribed to the ancient axiom that a sin, however small, against an infinite being, God, was an infinite evil that deserved an infinite punishment, which would, accordingly, be "everlasting, eternal, forever and ever, etc."[168] The Universalists, who appeared in the United States in the 1780s, rejected the eternity of hell punishment and on that account were widely denounced as "a bane to civil society," who would plunge the state into an orgy of wickedness. In Massachusetts it was claimed that "little boys in your streets are already caught in the [universalists'] snare and say 'we may swear and curse and lie and quarrel and do what we will that is bad without any danger of going to the devil in everlasting burnings.'" [169]

The Universalists refuted these calumnies, as had their British progenitor Whiston, whom they cited with respect, with arguments that stressed the value of future punishment. Universalism, wrote Charles Chauncy, would not let men "live as we list" because it taught that, although all would finally be saved, those who sinned on earth would suffer in a future life "positive torments . . . awfully cruciating and yet awfully protracted in their continuance" such as no rational person would risk enduring for the sake of transient licentiousness in this life.[170]

Although there are questions about how enthusiastically the Universalists preached future torments, there is no doubt whatever about the practices of their orthodox countrymen. The terrors of eternity were for them a staple of childhood education. Critics cited children to whom their mothers "constantly kept preaching damnation without end, for every sin."[171] Others mentioned children being compelled "to repeat that hymn of Watts's, which represents God with his 'great book' in which he 'writes every lie that children tell,' and ends with 'every liar shall have his portion in the lake which burns with brimstone and fire.'"[172] Writing about the state of American religion in 1790 Noah Webster observed that preaching perdition, far from being a tactic of revivalists, was the practice of the most conventional divines, who "thunder from the pulpit the terrors of infinite wrath against the vices that stain the characters of men."[173] The effectiveness of this kind of preaching was denounced by "Tacitus" in an indignant article in the *Maryland Journal,* April 1, 1785, who railed against the cynicism of the state's political leaders for using the future state doctrine to manipulate the common people. "Would it not be inconsistent with humanity," Tacitus fumed, "would it not be cruel to them to be terrified day and night with the fearful apprehension of endless misery, while in your great wisdom, you are well assured there is no such thing to be feared"— a charge similar to one leveled by Chauncy, who claimed that a "considerable number" of American ministers did "not believe the eternity of hell torments . . . but, for political reasons, suffer it to pass among them, that they do believe it."[174] Reflecting in 1830, on the effect on the American population of a constant diet of the future state doctrine, a Massachusetts writer charged that its "whole bearing . . . is, and ever has been, rather to keep them from sinning . . . the aim from the beginning should be, not to lay the foundation of religion in terror to evil doers, but in its encouragements and rewards to those who do well."[175]

What kind of person was actually produced in America by the unremitting exposure to the future state document with its single-minded emphasis on punishment? Was he the traumatized automaton that Shaftesbury caricatured as "a tiger strongly chained," "a monkey under the discipline of the whip," someone who was intimidated into proper behavior, whose "obedience is servile, and all of which is done through it merely servile"?[176] Or was he someone who, according to other advocates of the moral sense, could not rise above a "low, popular, interested kind of virtue"?[177] In the new American republic the future state doctrine confuted its critics and created what later generations would have called bourgeois virtue—that solid, if unspectacular, morality which made civilized living possible. Religion, said Timothy Dwight, provides "cogent motives to duty, and excitements to decent, amiable and useful conduct . . . it makes good men and good men must be good citizens."[178]

Here was the secret of religion's public utility: it made good citizens. The scriptural commandments, especially those stressing good neighborliness, justice and peace, translated in the public sphere into those baseline civic virtues without which a decent society could not function. In describing the relationship between religion and the "civil laws" Reese went to the heart of the matter: the "language of both coincides."[179] From across the new republic advocates of the future state doctrine praised it for making "dutiful subjects," "good members of society," "better members of society," "better members of the commonwealth" and—repeatedly— "good citizens."[180] Reese said it all, when he wrote, at the conclusion of his tract, that "if you be good Christians, you can never fail of being good citizens."[181]

Some Americans during the Founding Period viewed religion's impact on society horizontally. They described the nation's good Christian citizens as the "great Cement of civil society" through whose conduct religion became the "floor of society and government."[182] There was nothing peculiarly American about this idea; expressions of it can be found a hundred years earlier in English sermons: "Religion is both the Foundation and Cement of every humane Society . . . this alone can unite all the parts and give firmness and solidity to the whole."[183] Although horizontal references to religion as a foundation, a prop, a support, of society, held together by "that divine cement, the religion of Jesus,"[184] were plentiful in the new republic, Americans also conceived of religion as acting on society vertically, creating an inverted pyramid of virtue. The individual, on whom the future state doctrine operated to create an orderly, good citizen, was at the base of the pyramid. As dutiful individuals increased in ascending numbers, they created a density that became a corporate society, expanding in breath as it reached toward God, who acted on citizens in their corporate capacity in predictable and well understood ways. The Puritans described the transactions between God and the citizens at large as the national covenant, a legalistic agreement in which God rewarded "the obedience of His chosen covenanted people with prosperity and their disobedience with adversity."[185]

Other Protestant denominations, the Anglicans, for example, who did not codify the relationship between God and nations into a legalistic covenant, nevertheless, subscribed to the idea that there was a reciprocal relationship between God and the people of a given state, in which faithfulness would be rewarded, apostasy punished. This was, in fact, a cliche with Church of England preachers in both England and America; as an obscure English rector said in 1704, "by a People's being truly religious, themselves and the Prince are made happy and prosperous." The proof text here was almost always Proverbs 14:34, which was also a perennial favorite throughout America, in New England as well as in the southern states. Declared the English preacher in 1704: "So true is that of the wise Solomon, Righteousness exalteth a nation, raiseth it to highest degree of Prosperity and Glory, and establisheth it upon the sure and lasting Foundations of peace and happiness." [186] Preaching in the King's Chapel in Boston in 1761, the Anglican Henry Caner spoke in the same vein, reminding his audience that Solomon made "a very high Sense of Religion . . . the principal if not the only Ingredient of public Happiness. Righteousness (says he) exalteth a Nation." From religion, Caner continued, "every Instance of public Happiness arises. Tis that alone which can conciliate the Favour of God, from whom is derived all Wisdom, Strength, and Policy, and Power, and Riches, and Peace, and Protection, and whatever else it is, that any Way contributes to public Prosperity."[187] The wisdom of Solomon on the social and political benefits of religion echoed throughout the land, from Quaker meeting houses to Puritan pulpits.

The point is that Americans of all religious persuasions during the Founding Period took what might be described as a macro and a micro view of the impact of religion on society. At the macro level, they believed that God tangibly exalted nations that were obedient to him; at the micro level, they perceived that religion, operating through the future state doctrine, transformed otherwise sinful individuals, creating good citizens who made an orderly society possible and who, when aggregated, made it prosperous. As he so often did, Reese captured the sentiments of his countrymen on this point: "religion . . . must ever be productive of good to society, as far as it prevails. The more strongly men are influenced by its motives, and the more perfectly they are conformed to its precepts, the better members of civil society they will be and the greater number of such in any state, other things being equal, the higher it will rise in the scale of political glory and happiness. Righteousness exalteth a nation."[188]

Overshadowed by the broad, glorious objectives expected to be achieved by the future state doctrine was a specific one, whose importance was, in some eyes, second to none: the preservation of the integrity of the judicial process by guaranteeing the sanctity of oaths. The Founding generation esteemed oaths. Many believed that they were the true "cement of society."[189] Since oaths were "one of the principal instruments of government," they must be backed by the strongest sanction, the "fear and reverence of God, and the terrors of eternity."[190] Lecturing his readers in the *Virginia Gazette*, September 11, 1779, on the importance of truth telling under oath, a "Social Christian" wrote as follows: "I may again appeal to the same tribunal of common sense whether he who acknowledges the divinity of the scriptures and believes a future state of rewards and punishments, or he who disregards both, [is] the most likely to prevaricate or temporize."[191]

Blackstone was considered by the Founding generation to be the oracle of the law and, therefore, his opinion on the relationship of the future state doctrine and the sanctity of oaths was considered authoritative. The Maryland House of Delegates, in its Address of January 8, 1785, quoted him at length on the subject:

"The preservation of christianity, as a national religion, is (abstracted from its own intrinsic truth) of the utmost consequence to the civil state, which a single instance will sufficiently demonstrate. The belief of a future state of rewards and punishments, the entertaining just ideas of the moral attributes of the Supreme Being, and a firm persuasion that he superintends, and will finally compensate, every action of human life (all which are clearly revealed in the doctrines, and forcibly inculcated by the precepts, of our Saviour Christ) are the grand foundation of all judicial oaths, which call God to witness the truth of those facts, which perhaps may only be known to him and the party attesting; all moral evidence, therefore, all confidence in human veracity, must be wrecked by irreligion, and overthrown by Infidelity."[192]

In the North Carolina Ratifying Convention, July 30, 1788, James Iredell made the customary linkage between the future state and oaths: an oath "is considered a solemn appeal to the Supreme Being, for the truth of what is said, by a person who believes in the existence of a Supreme Being and in a future state of rewards and punishments, according to that form which will bind his conscience most."[193] Washington spoke in the same vein in his Farewell Address: "where is the security for property, for reputation, for life, if the sense of religious obligation desert the oaths, which are the instruments of investigation in Courts of Justice."[194] As late as 1829, in the constitutional convention of that year, Virginians attempted to amend their fundamental law to prevent "all persons who disbelieved in God or a future state of rewards and punishments" from being "received as witnesses in any Court of law in the Commonwealth."[195]

The Massachusetts Constitutional Convention of 1820 furnished the best example of the staying power of the future state doctrine. In fact, one of the best statements of the doctrine on record was delivered by a Boston delegate, Warren Dutton, in a speech of December 21, 1820. "No nation," declared Dutton, "had yet been found without some notion of a future state of reward and punishment, and that all lawgivers have availed themselves of this belief to give, in some form or other, sanction and authority to their civil institutions." It, therefore, became, Dutton continued, the "the duty of the State to establish the Christian religion, because it aided the highest and best purposes of the State—its tendency was to make better subjects and better magistrates, better husbands, parents and children. It enforced the duties of imperfect obligations which human laws could not reach—it inculcated all the domestic and social virtues, frugality and industry, prudence, kind and charitable feeling—it made men just and honest in their dealings as individuals, and by diffusing the sentiments of equity and benevolence, its tendency was to make states and communities just toward each other. It applied itself to the source of all action, the thoughts and interests of the heart. It entered the secret chambers of the soul and there performed its work silently and invisibly, but effectually. It suppressed the rising sin, it extinguished the embryo transgression. It subdued and controlled the bad passions of men, by its powerful influence upon their hopes and fears. Are not these civil benefits; are not these effects good for the State?"[196]

The passage of years did not change the target of the future state doctrine; it was still those whom Reese called the "gross of the common people." Writing in 1820 in support of the Massachusetts Convention's efforts to preserve the state's system of religious taxation, the influential Boston minister, William Ellery Channing, declared that "religious instruction is particularly needed for those classes of society who can least afford to provide it for themselves, and whose hard and unequal lot begets discontents and temptations which only religion can subdue."[197] A decade later this attitude was still popular: as described by a critic, its advocates insisted that "fear . . . must govern the common people, and no fear is strong enough but the fear of literal and everlasting burnings, which ought, therefore, whether true or not, to be the exoteric faith."[198]

The disestablishment of religion in Massachusetts in 1833 was a turning point for the future state doctrine. To be sure, dignitaries in various states still commended it[199] and the Universalists were still assailed as "licentious" for diluting its full force.[200] In *On Liberty* John Stuart Mill cited the refusal of a London court in 1857 to accept the testimony of a certain Baron de Gleichen, who repudiated the future state doctrine, as a sign of its continuing influence.[201] Scattered references of this sort cannot, however, conceal that in the United States the Massachusetts action of 1833 paved the way for the disappearance of the future state doctrine from the range of options in public policy discourse. As long as Americans campaigned for public funding of religion, so long were they obliged to convince taxpayers that their money would produce public benefits. After 1833 religion all across America relied on voluntary financial support. Campaigns for public funding ceased and with them the high energy advocacy of the public utility of religion, powered by the future state doctrine.

Viner argues that guilt by association may also have contributed to the doctrine's demise, postulating that as a species of theological utilitarianism, based on the pain-pleasure calculus, its reputation suffered as it came to be associated in the public mind with Bentham's "completely irreligious hedonic utilitarian-ism."[202] A more compelling explanation for the doctrine's difficulties is that it was incompatible with the optimistic democratic society that began to flourish in the United States in the 1830s. As writers such as Nathan Hatch have argued, the Age of Jackson or the Age of Common Man, as it was once called, was inhospitable to Calvinism, with its seemingly capricious and undemocratic doctrine of election and with its assumption that mankind was depraved and needed to be kept in order by divine intimidation.[203] The bumptious, boisterous republican citizen of the 1830s simply did not see himself in this purported picture of reality. The future state doctrine, therefore, was out of synch with the spirit of the times. As one of its critics wrote in 1830, "the age which has demolished dungeons, rejected torture, and given so fair a prospect of abolishing the iniquity of the slave trade, cannot long retain among its articles of belief, the gloomy perplexities of Calvinism, and the heart-withering perspective of cruel and never-ending punishments."[204] As the nineteenth century progressed, Calvinism lost its grip on the American public and the future state doctrine faded with it. Another sentiment that emerged in the Jacksonian Era may also have been detrimental to the future state doctrine. Professor Philip Hamburger has recently argued that a fear of ecclesiastical authority, fueled principally by nativist suspicions of the growing power of the Catholic Church, began to have an impact in Jacksonian America.[205] That fear may have made Americans wary of all proposals to inject religion into public life.

Where does the future state doctrine stand today? During the 2000 presidential campaign both major party candidates endorsed programs that have come to be called "faith based initiatives," which envisioned that the federal government would resume the practice of governments stretching back to the dawn of time by entering into partnerships with religion to promote public policy goals. Both parties proposed—or at least implied—that financial support and encouragement would be offered to religious groups to address the social pathologies that afflict portions of the population with the intention of creating better citizens who, it was assumed, would strengthen the fabric of society and promote its well-being. In achieving these traditional objectives, no mention was made of employing the venerable future state doctrine. What was once considered a vital tool to assure the health of society has, evidently, vanished.

NOTES

1. Herbert Butterfield, *The Whig Interpretation of History* (London: G. Bell and Sons, 1968), 11-12, 42-45.

2. Edward Dorr, *The Duty of Civil Rulers, to be nursing Fathers to the Church of Christ* (Hartford: Thomas Green, 1765), 11.

3. James H. Hutson, *Religion and the Founding of the American Republic* (Hanover, N. H.: University Press of New England, 6th ed., 2002), 64.

4. Surry County petition to the Virginia General Assembly, November 14, 1785, Virginia Religious Petitions, Library of Virginia.

5. [Nicholas Collin], "An Essay on the Means of Promoting Federal Sentiments in the United States," in *Friends of the Constitution Writings of the "Other" Federalists*, ed.

Colleen A. Sheehan and Gary L. McDowell (Indianapolis: The Liberty Fund, 1998), 415-16.

6. Thomas Reese, *An Essay on the Influence of Religion in Civil Society* (Charleston: Markland & M'Iver, 1788), 3-4.

7. *Barnes v. First Parish in Falmouth*, 6 Mass. 401 (1810), 405-6.

8. Irenaeus, *Boston Gazette*, October 23, 1780.

9. Reese, *An Essay*, 5-6.

10. Irenaeus, *Boston Gazette*, October 23, 1780.

11. Hutson, *Religion and the Founding*, 79.

12. Hutson, *Religion and the Founding*, 57.

13. Worthington C. Ford and Gaillard Hunt, eds., *Journals of the Continental Congress, 1774-1789* (Washington, D.C.: Library of Congress, 34 vols., 1904-1937), 10, 1001; 22, 138; 23, 647.

14. Broadside Collection, Rare Book and Special Collections Division, Library of Congress.

15. Lunenberg County Petition to the Virginia General Assembly, November 3, 1779, Amelia County Petition to same, November 8, 1784, Library of Virginia; *Barnes v. First Parish*, 411; Ezra Stiles, *The United States Elevated to Glory and Honor* (1783), in *The Pulpit of the American Revolution*, ed. John W. Thornton (New York: Burt Franklin, 1970), 503.

16. Surry County Petition, November 14, 1785, to the Virginia General Assembly, Library of Virginia.

17. Bishop James Madison, *An Address to the Members of the Protestant Episcopal Church in Virginia* (Richmond: T. Nicholson, 1799), 16-17.

18. Theophilus, *Maryland Journal*, September 23, 1783.

19. Jeffrey Hays Morrison, "John Witherspoon and 'The Public Interest of Religion,'" *Journal of Church and State* 41 (Summer 1999): 564.

20. Benjamin Rush, *A Plan for the Establishment of Public Schools* (1786), in *Essays on Education in the Early Republic,* ed. Frederick Rudolph (Cambridge, Mass.: Harvard University Press, 1965), 10-11.

21. Ezra Stiles, *United States Elevated*, 487.

22. Massachusetts General Court, Message, November 8, 1780, *Independent Ledger* (Boston), November 20, 1780.

23. Reese, *An Essay*, 86.

24. Hutson, *Religion and the Founding*, 64.

25. Hutson, *Religion and the Founding*, 61.

26. Maryland House of Delegates, Address to the People, January 8, 1785, *Maryland Journal and Baltimore Advertiser,* January 18, 1785.

27. Ezra Stiles, *United States Elevated*, 403.

28. Jonathan Edwards, Jr., *The Necessity of the Belief of Christianity by the Citizens of the State*, in *Political Sermons of the American Founding Era 1730-1805,* ed. Elliot

Sandoz (Indianapolis: Liberty Press, 1991), 1212.

29. Henry Caner, *Joyfulness and Consideration; or, the Duties of Prosperity and Adversity* (Boston: Green & Russell, 1761), 14-15.

30. Sandoz, *Political Sermons,* 877.

31. Hutson, *Religion and the Founding,* 62.

32. Reese, *An Essay,* 81.

33. Mecklenberg County Petition to the Virginia General Assembly, May 29, 1777, Library of Virginia.

34. Thomas Jefferson, 1801, Hutson, *Religion and the Founding,* 84.

35. Hutson, *Religion and the Founding,* 62.

36. Sandoz, *Political Sermons,* 1160.

37. John Adams to Zabdiel Adams, June 21, 1776, *Adams Family Correspondence,* ed. Lyman Butterfield (Cambridge, Mass.: Harvard University Press, 1963), 2, 21.

38. Sandoz, *Political Sermons,* 965.

39. Reese, *An Essay,* 5, 73-74.

40. Social Christian, *Virginia Gazette,* September 18, 1779.

41. Amelia County Petition to the Virginia General Assembly, November 8, 1784, Library of Virginia.

42. George Muter to James Madison, January 6, 1785, *The Papers of James Madison,* ed. Robert Rutland and William Rachal (Chicago: University of Chicago Press, 1973), 8, 219.

43. A Marylander, *Maryland Journal and Baltimore Advertiser,* February 8, 1785.

44. Sandoz, *Political Sermons,* 1211.

45. Irenaeus, *Boston Gazette,* November 27, 1780.

46. Reese, *An Essay,* 72.

47. Amelia County Petition to the Virginia General Assembly, November 8, 1784, Library of Virginia.

48. Maryland House of Delegates, Address, January 8, 1785.

49. Philander, *Maryland Journal,* March 22, 1785.

50. Hutson, *Religion and the Founding,* 62.

51. Sandoz, *Political Sermons,* 1183.

52. Sandoz, *Political Sermons,* 1107.

53. Caroline County Petition to the Virginia General Assembly, 1777, Library of Virginia.

54. Hutson, *Religion and the Founding,* 66.

55. Dorr, *Duty of Civil Rulers,* 20.

56. Sandoz, *Political Sermons,* 919.

57. Philanthropos, *Boston Gazette,* January 8, 1781.

58. Morrison, "John Witherspoon," 562.

59. Daniel Webster, Speech, January 8, 1821, *Journal of Debates and Proceedings in the Massachusetts Constitutional Convention 1820-1821* (New York: DaCapo Press, 1970),

593.

60. Reese, *An Essay,* 4.

61. Jack Scott, ed., *An Annotated Edition of Lectures on Moral Philosophy by John Witherspoon* (Newark: University of Delaware Press, 1982), 92.

62. Irenaeus, *Boston Gazette,* November 27, 1780.

63. Nicholas Collin, "An Essay," 417.

64. James Tully, "Governing Conduct," in *Locke Volume II,* ed. John Dunn and Ian Harris (Cheltenham, U.K.: Edward Elgar Publishing Limited, 1997), 289-348.

65. John Brown, *Essays on the Characteristics of the Earl of Shaftesbury,* ed. Donald D. Eddy (Hildesheim: G. Olms, 1969), 206; Paul C. Davies, "The Debate on Eternal Punishment in Late Seventeenth and Eighteenth Century England," *Eighteenth Century Studies* 4, no. 3 (Spring 1971): 267-68; Scott, *Witherspoon,* 92; Francis Hutcheson, *A System of Moral Philosophy* (New York: A. M. Kelly, 1968), xxxviii; *The Works of the late Right Honorable Henry St. John, Lord Viscount Bolingbroke* (London, 1777), 5: 222.

66. Jacob Viner, *The Role of Providence in the Social Order* (Philadelphia: American Philosophical Society, 1972), 62.

67. Tully, "Governing Conduct," 317.

68. Viner, *The Role of Providence,* 73.

69. Davies, "The Debate," 276.

70. Viner, *The Role of Providence,* 74-75.

71. Viner, *The Role of Providence,* 70-71; Davies, "The Debate," 266.

72. Walter Rex, *Essays on Pierre Bayle and Religious Controversy* (The Hague: M. Nijhoff, 1965), 54.

73. Tully, "Governing Conduct," 291, 326, 348.

74. Tully, "Governing Conduct," 323, 335.

75. Brown, *Essays,* 212; for the full quotation, see Shaftesbury, *An Inquiry concerning Virtue and Merit,* in *Characteristics of Men, Manners, Opinions, Times, etc.,* ed. John M. Robertson (Gloucester, Mass.: 1963), 267.

76. Davies, "The Debate," 267.

77. Frank D. Balog, "The Scottish Enlightenment and the Liberal Political Tradition," in *Confronting the Constitution,* ed. Allan Bloom (Washington, D. C.: AEI Press, 1990), 193.

78. Daniel P. Walker, *The Decline of Hell: Seventeenth-Century Discussions of Eternal Torment* (Chicago: University of Chicago Press, 1964), 4, 96.

79. Davies, "The Debate," 260.

80. Walker, *The Decline,* 4.

81. Walker, *The Decline,* 96.

82. Walker, *The Decline,* 100.

83. *Works of Bolingbroke,* 5: 240, 313, 518.

84. Davies, "The Debate," 271.

85. David Berman, ed., *Alciphron, or, The minute philosopher* (London: Routledge, 1993), 30; *Works of Bolingbroke,* 5: 352; Brown, *Essays,* 208.

86. Ian Watt, "The Ironic Tradition in Augustan Prose from Swift to Johnson," in *Restoration and Augustan Prose,* no editor indicated (Los Angeles: U.C.L.A. Press, 1956), 21.

87. Edward Gibbon, *The Decline and Fall of the Roman Empire* (New York: Modern Library, 1932), 1, 639.

88. Walker, *The Decline,* 159.

89. *Works of Bolingbroke,* 5: 238, 322.

90. Davies, "The Debate," 268.

91. Brown, *Essays,* 206, 208; Berkeley, *Alciphron,* 64, 73.

92. Berkeley, *Alciphron,* 74.

93. Walker, *The Decline,* 173.

94. Walker, *The Decline,* 71.

95. Reese, *An Essay,* 32.

96. Hutcheson, *A System,* xvii.

97. Davies, "The Debate," 265.

98. Viner, *The Role of Providence,* 61.

99. Viner, *The Role of Providence,* 71, 73.

100. *The Works of Samuel Clarke, D.D.* (London, 1738), 2, 37-38.

101. William Warburton, *The divine legation of Moses demonstrated* (London, 1742), 85.

102. *Works of Bolingbroke,* 5: 237.

103. Davies, "The Debate," 265.

104. Berkeley, *Alciphron,* 65.

105. Brown, *Essays,* 210.

106. Davies, "The Debate," 257.

107. Norman Fiering, *Jonathan Edwards's Moral Thought and Its British Context* (Chapel Hill: University of North Carolina Press, 1981), 4.

108. Reese, *An Essay,* 4; *The Christian Disciple and Theological Review* (Boston, May-June 1821): 177.

109. Hutson, *Religion and the Founding,* 64; Albert E. Stone, ed., *Letters from an American Farmer and Sketches of Eighteenth-Century America by J. Hector St. John de Crèvecoeur* (New York: Penguin Books, 1986), 128.

110. Theorists such as Montesquieu, of course, made a distinction between "political" virtue, which was considered to consist of the sacrifice of personal interests to the public good, and "Christian" or "moral virtue." Technically, the former was considered indispensable for republican government but writers tended to conflate the two kinds of virtue and most Americans, if they made the distinction at all, would have argued that both kinds of virtue were necessary for the republic to succeed. The future state doctrine was assumed to produce Christian or moral virtue. Anne Cohler, Basia Miller, and Harold

Stone, eds., *The Spirit of the Laws* (Cambridge: Cambridge University Press, 1989), xli.

111. James Sullivan, *An Appeal to the impartial public by the Society of Christian Independents* (Boston: Benjamin Edes & Son, 1785), 17.

112. For Pennsylvania, Vermont, South Carolina and Tennessee, see William Swindler, ed., *Sources and Documents of United States Constitutions* (Dobbs Ferry, N.Y.: Oceana Publications, 1979), 8, 280, 471; 9, 146, 491. For the draft of the Massachusetts Constitution, see Charles F. Adams, ed., *The Works of John Adams* (Boston: Little & Brown, 10 vols., 1850-1856), 4, 221; for the state of Franklin, see Stephen A. Marini, "Religion, Politics, and Ratification," in *Religion in a Revolutionary Age*, ed. Ronald Hoffman and Peter J. Albert (Charlottesville: The University Press of Virginia, 1994), 206.

113. Isaac Kramnick and R. Laurence Moore, *The Godless Constitution: The Case Against Religious Correctness* (New York: W.W. Norton & Company, 1996), 35.

114. Max Farrand, ed., *The Records of the Federal Convention* (New Haven, Conn.: Yale University Press, 4 vols., 1966), 3, 227.

115. John P. Kominski and Gaspare J. Saladino, eds., *The Documentary History of the Ratification of the Constitution* (Madison: State Historical Society of Wisconsin, 1990), 9 (Va. 2), 779.

116. Ezra Stiles, *The United States Elevated*, 495.

117. Levi Lincoln, speech, December 26, 1820, *Journal of Debates and Proceedings in the Massachusetts Constitutional Convention 1820-1821* (New York: DaCapo Press, 1970), 423.

118. *Maryland Journal and Baltimore Advertiser*, January 18, 1785.

119. Philander, To the Rulers of the State of Maryland, *Maryland Journal and Baltimore Advertiser*, March 22, 1785.

120. Thomas E. Buckley, S.J., *Church and State in Revolutionary Virginia* (Charlottesville: University Press of Virginia, 1977), 57.

121. *Independent Ledger* (Boston), May 1, 1780.

122. Phillips Payson, *A Sermon preached before the Honorable Council . . . at Boston, May 27, 1778*, in *The Pulpit of the American Revolution*, ed. John W. Thornton (New York: Burt Franklin, 1970), 339-40.

123. Simeon Howard, *A Sermon*, Thornton, 370-71.

124. Irenaeus, *Boston Gazette*, October 23, 1780.

125. Irenaeus, *Boston Gazette*, November 27, 1780.

126. Philanthropos, *Boston Gazette*, January 8, 1781.

127. William McLoughlin, *Isaac Backus on Church, State, and Calvinism* (Cambridge, Mass.: Harvard University Press, 1968), 358; *Independent Ledger* (Boston), June 26, 1780.

128. Hanover Presbytery Petition to the Virginia General Assembly, November 12, 1784, Library of Virginia.

129. *Barnes v. First Parish*, 406.

130. Norman Cousins, ed., *In God We Trust: The Personal Philosophies of the Founding Fathers* (New York: Harper & Row, 1988), 443.

131. For Franklin, see A. Owen Aldridge, "Natural Religion and Deism in America before Ethan Allen and Thomas Paine," *William and Mary Quarterly* 54, no. 4 (October 1997): 848.

132. John Adams, *A Defence of the Constitutions of Government of the United States of America* (Aachen, Germany: Scientia Verlag, 1979), 3, 333.

133. Hutson, *Religion and the Founding,* 82.

134. Rush, *Establishment of Public Schools,* 10.

135. James McLachlan, ed., *Princetonians 1748-1768 A Biographical Dictionary* (Princeton, N.J.: Princeton University Press, 1976), 652-53.

136. Reese, *An Essay,* 4, 73.

137. Reese, *An Essay,* 19.

138. Dumas Malone, ed., *Dictionary of American Biography* (New York: Charles Scribner's Son, 1936), 20, 436.

139. Scott, *Witherspoon,* 92.

140. Reese, *An Essay,* 19.

141. Douglas L. Wilson, ed., *Jefferson's Literary Commonplace Book* (Princeton, N.J.: Princeton University Press, 1989), 47.

142. Jean Yarborough, *American Virtues: Thomas Jefferson on the Character of a Free People* (Lawrence: University Press of Kansas, 1998), 27-54.

143. Julian P. Boyd, ed., *The Papers of Thomas Jefferson* (Princeton, N.J.: Princeton University Press, 1950), 1, 537.

144. Dickinson W. Adams, ed., *Jefferson's Extracts from the Gospels* (Princeton, N.J.: Princeton University Press, 1983), 334.

145. Adams, *Jefferson's Extracts,* 357.

146. Adams, *Jefferson's Extracts,* 405.

147. Adams, *Jefferson's Extracts,* 356.

148. Reese, *An Essay,* 16.

149. Reese, *An Essay,* 10.

150. Sandoz, *Political Sermons,* 1111.

151. Madison, *An Address,* 16-17.

152. Reese, *An Essay,* 15, 20.

153. Hutson, *Religion and the Founding,* 79.

154. Collin, "An Essay," 416-17; Mark N. Brown, ed., *The Works of George Saville Marquis of Halifax* (Oxford: Clarendon Press, 1989), 199.

155. Sandoz, *Political Sermons,* 1318.

156. Morrison, "John Witherspoon," 564.

157. James H. Hutson, ed., *Religion and the New Republic* (Lanham, Md.: Rowman & Littlefield, 2000), 177.

158. Hutson, *Religion and the Founding,* 61.

159. Reese, *An Essay*, 9; Southampton County Petition to the Virginia General Assembly, December 10, 1785, Library of Virginia; Oscar Handlin, ed., *Popular Sources of Political Authority Documents on the Massachusetts Constitution of 1780* (Cambridge, Mass.: Harvard University Press, 1966), 784.

160. *Barnes v. First Parish*, 405.

161. Reese, *An Essay*, 8.

162. *Barnes v. First Parish*, 405.

163. Asabel Hooker, Connecticut Election Sermon, 1805, 27-28.

164. *Barnes v. First Parish*, 405; Reese, *An Essay*, 11.

165. Reese, *An Essay*, 11.

166. Sandoz, *Political Sermons*, 1194, 1318-19; Reese, *An Essay*, 13.

167. Reese, *An Essay*, 29-30.

168. Fiering, *Edwards's Moral Thought*, 220; *Works of Bolingbroke*, 5, 503; John Cleaveland, *An Attempt to Nip in the Bud, the Unscriptural Doctrine of Universal Salvation* (Salem: E. Russell, 1776), 12.

169. Cleaveland, *An Attempt*, 26, 44.

170. Charles Chauncy, *The Mystery Hid from Ages and Generations* (New York: Arno Press, 1969), 351-52, 354.

171. Elhanan Winchester, *The Universal Restoration* (Boston: Benjamin B. Mussey, 1831), 186.

172. *The Christian Examiner and General Review*, July 1830, 295.

173. Frederick Rudolph, *Essays on Education in the Early Republic* (Cambridge, Mass.: Harvard University Press, 1965), 63.

174. Chauncy, *The Mystery Hid*, 354.

175. *The Christian Examiner and General Review*, July 1830, 294-95.

176. Shaftesbury, *An Inquiry*, 267.

177. Berkeley, *Alciphron*, 65.

178. Hutson, *Religion and the Founding*, 62.

179. Reese, *An Essay*, 17.

180. Amherst County Petition to the Virginia General Assembly, December 5, 1777, Library of Virginia; Irenaeus, *Boston Gazette*, October 23, 1780; Social Christian, *Virginia Gazette*, September 18, 1779; James Sullivan, *An appeal to the impartial public*, 25-26; Maryland House of Delegates, Address, January 8, 1785; *Barnes v. First Parish*, 411.

181. Reese, *An Essay*, 86.

182. Hutson, *Religion and the Founding*, 61; John Witte, Jr., "'A Most Mild and Equitable Establishment of Religion': John Adams and the Massachusetts Experiment," *Journal of Church and State* 41 (Spring 1999): 234.

183. Joseph Brett, *A Sermon preach'd in the Cathedral Church of Norwich, upon March the 8th, 1703-4, being the Anniversary Day of her Majesty's Happy Inauguration* (Norwich: Widow Oliver, 1704), 9-10. British Library.

184. Hooker, *Election Sermon*, 32.

185. Edmund S. Morgan, *Roger Williams, the Church and State* (New York: Harcourt, Brace & World Inc., 1967), 82.

186. Brett, *A Sermon*, 8, 13-14.

187. Henry Caner, *Joyfulness and Consideration*, 14-15.

188. Reese, *An Essay*, 72-73.

189. Witte, "Establishment of Religion," 222.

190. Payson, *A Sermon*, 339.

191. Social Christian, *Virginia Gazette*, September 11, 1779.

192. Maryland House of Delegates, Address, January 8, 1785.

193. Jonathan Elliot, ed., *The Debates in the Several State Conventions on the Adoption of the Federal Constitution* (New York: Burt Franklin, 1968), 4, 196-98.

194. Hutson, *Religion and the Founding*, 79.

195. Hutson, *Religion and the New Republic*, 57, note 12.

196. *Massachusetts Constitutional Convention 1820-1821*, 369.

197. William Ellery Channing, *Religion a Social Principle* (Boston: Russell & Gardner, 1820), 14.

198. *Christian Examiner* 8 (May 1830), 248.

199. Daniel L. Dreisbach, ed., *Religion and Politics in the Early Republic: Jasper Adams and the Church-State Debate* (Lexington: University of Kentucky Press, 1996), 56.

200. Ernest Cassara, *Hosea Ballou: The Challenge to Orthodoxy* (Boston: Beacon Press, 1961), 150.

201. John Stuart Mill, *On Liberty* (New York: P.F. Collier and Sons [Harvard Classics], 1909), 232. As late as 1873 Pennsylvania adopted a new constitution which debarred from public office individuals who did not believe in the future state.

202. Viner, *The Role of Providence*, 74.

203. Nathan Hatch, *The Democratization of American Christianity* (New Haven, Conn.: Yale University Press, 1989).

204. *Christian Examiner* 8 (May 1830), 249.

205. Philip Hamburger, *Separation of Church and State* (Cambridge, Mass.: Harvard University Press, 2002), 193-251.

Chapter 2

"Nursing Fathers": The Model of Church-State Relations in America from James I to Jefferson

On April 15, 1775, four days before hostilities between British and American troops began at Lexington and Concord, the Massachusetts Provincial Congress proclaimed May 11 as a day of fasting and prayer throughout the colony. The fast day proclamation accused the British ministry of inciting the "Powers of Earth and Hell" to harass the Congregational Church in Massachusetts. Those, it asserted, "who should be Nursing Fathers become its Persecutors."[1] "Nursing Fathers?" Where did this peculiar phrase, more appropriate for an aberration in biology than statecraft, come from? And what did it mean?

Those familiar with colonial Massachusetts would assume, correctly, that the phrase had theological roots. It comes from the prophet Isaiah and in 1775 had been in use for more than two hundred years by British and American religious and political leaders (including two kings of England) to express their conviction that the government of any state must form a nurturing bond with religious institutions within its jurisdiction, that it must, in fact, become the "nursing father" of the church.

After the Declaration of Independence in 1776, substantial numbers of American citizens continued to use the nursing fathers metaphor to articulate their view about the proper relationship between government and religion, a view at polar opposites to Thomas Jefferson's assertion in 1802 that there should be a "wall of separation" between church and state.[2] Jefferson's phrase was an arresting one, but it languished, as a scholar has recently demonstrated, in relative obscurity until after World War II, when the Supreme Court embraced it in the *Everson* case (1947).[3] It is, therefore, no exaggeration to say that Jefferson's "wall" formulation has had a short and controversial run of only fifty years compared to the two hundred and fifty years in which the nursing fathers metaphor dominated the church-state dialogue in the Anglo-American world.

"Nursing fathers" appears in the 23rd verse of the 49th chapter of the book of Isaiah, which in the King James version of the Bible (1611) reads: "And kings shall be thy nursing fathers, and their queenes thy nursing mothers: they shall bow downe to thee with their face toward the earth, and licke up the dust of thy feete, and thou shalt know that I am the LORD; for they shall not be ashamed that waite for me."

Isaiah was a favorite book of the seminal thinkers of the Protestant Reformation of the sixteenth century, many of whom wrote commentaries on it: Zwingli (1529), Luther (1532), Munster (ca. 1540), Brenz (1550), Castiello (1551), Calvin (1551, 1552, 1559), Musculus (1557), and Bullinger (1567).[4] Most of these savants thought Isaiah 49:23 deserved only a few perfunctory remarks. For Luther the verse meant little more than that "queens and wives of important men are to be converted to the Gospel."[5] John Calvin, however, was impressed by the possibility that the nursing father metaphor in verse 23 could promote the mission of the newly reformed churches. By giving the verse a militantly sectarian interpretation, he excited the imagination of English-speaking reformers who, beginning in the 1560s, appropriated the metaphor and broadcast it across the British Isles.

Calvin published a Latin edition of his *Commentary* on Isaiah in 1551 and a French one the following year. In 1559 he brought out a new Latin edition, so extensively revised that he claimed it "ought justly to be reckoned a new work."[6] Another Latin edition appeared in 1570, a French one in 1572, and other reprintings followed.

Calvin's extensive comments on chapter 49, verse 23, bristled with the belligerence of the early reformers, locked in a lethal struggle with the Church of Rome. Princes who defended the true, reformed religion "obtained," Calvin declared, "this highest pinnacle of rank, which surpasses dominion and principality of every sort, to be 'nursing-fathers' and guardians of the Church." "The Papists," he continued, "have no other idea of kings being 'nursing fathers' of the Church than that they have left to their priests and monks very large revenues, rich possessions and prebends, on which they might fatten, like hogs in a sty." For the Protestant prince "'nursing' aims at an object quite different from filling up those insatiable gulls"; rather it was "about removing superstitions and putting an end to all wicked idolatry, about advancing the kingdom of Christ and maintaining purity of doctrine, about purging scandals and cleansing from the filth that corrupts piety and impairs the lustre of Divine majesty." Of course, Protestant princes would "supply the pastors and ministers of the Word with all that is necessary for food and maintenance," but material support was incidental to a higher spiritual obligation. To "shew themselves to be 'nursing fathers'" they must, above all, be "protectors of believers, and shall bravely defend the doctrine of the Word."[7]

It was Calvin's habit to work ideas from his numerous biblical commentaries into the multiplying and progressively expanding editions of his *Institutes of the Christian Religion*. In 1559 he introduced "nursing fathers" into book four of the *Institutes*. There Calvin noted that "Isaiah, when he predicts that 'Kings shall be nursing-fathers, and queens nursing mothers' to the Church, does not depose them from their Thrones, but rather establishes them by an honourable title, as patrons and protectors of the pious worshipers of God."[8] This rather economical treatment of the passage would, no doubt, have encouraged contemporary readers to seek a fuller exposition of Calvin's views on Isaiah 49:23 by turning to his popular *Commentary*.

Confident, apparently, of obtaining an English audience, Calvin dedicated the first edition of his *Commentary* to the young Protestant king, Edward VI. Lamenting that the "Roman Antichrist, far and wide usurping and tyrannizing over the sanctuary of God, tears, crushes, and tramples under his feet all that belonged to God," Calvin urged Edward to devote himself to the promotion of "pure doctrine": "I expressly call upon, or rather, God himself addresses you by the mouth of his servant Isaiah, charging you to proceed, to the utmost of your ability and power, in carrying forward the restoration of the Church. You daily read and hear that this duty is enjoined on you. More especially Isaiah, as I have said, calls *Kings the nursing fathers of the Church*, (Is. xlix. 23) and does not permit them to withhold that assistance which her afflicted condition demands."[9]

When Queen Mary, a Catholic, ascended the English throne in 1553 she attempted to compel the country to return to Rome. According to Calvin, the "oppression of pure doctrine, which raged with prodigious violence for a short period" claimed as one of its victims his *Commentary* which was "banished" from the realm.[10] Protestant fortunes revived in 1559, when Elizabeth became queen. Calvin dedicated his expanded 1559 edition of the *Commentary* to the new monarch, urging her to lay aside "all other kinds of business, a vast number of which, I have no doubt, will crowd upon you at the commencement of your reign" and concentrate with "invincible determination" on purifying the nation's religion. Entreated Calvin: "You ought to be stimulated, venerable Queen, by a sacred regard to Duty; for the Prophet Isaiah demands not only from *Kings* that they be *nursing fathers*, but also from *Queens* that they be *nursing mothers*. (Isa. xlix. 23.) This duty you ought to discharge . . . by removing the filth of Popery."[11]

Whether Elizabeth read Calvin's *Commentary* is unknown, but the Geneva reformer's writings enjoyed a great vogue among her subjects. An English translation of his *Institutes of the Christian Religion* went through seven printings between 1561 and 1599. A translation of Calvin's sermons on Job was reprinted five times in ten years.[12] Both Elizabethan Puritan leaders and their opponents in the Anglican hierarchy appealed to Calvin's authority in theological disputes. The Puritan Thomas Cartwright, for example, arguing with the future archbishop of Canterbury, John Whitgift, exclaimed that "we receive M. Calvin and weigh of him, as one of the notoblest instruments that the Lord hath stirred up for the purging of His Churches, and of the restoring of the plain and sincere interpretation of the Scriptures, which hath been since the Apostles' times."[13]

Calvin was personally acquainted with many of the Elizabethan Anglican leaders, who, during the Marian persecutions, fled to the European continent and found refuge in Switzerland and neighboring countries. These English exiles, it has been said, "came under the spell of Calvin's genius."[14] One of them, John Jewel, became bishop of Salisbury upon Elizabeth's accession and began the administration of his diocese with "decided leanings to Calvinism." Jewel certainly knew Calvin's *Commentary* on Isaiah, for in 1562 he incorporated the nursing father metaphor into his *Apology for the Church of England*, a book that was "immediately adopted on all sides as the literary exposition of England's ecclesiastical position" and soon was considered so "authoritative" that it was chained to lecterns in churches throughout England.[15] By using the nursing father metaphor to describe the obligation of civil authorities to the church, Jewel embedded the concept in the consciousness of Anglicans, who habitually employed it during the following centuries; from luminaries like Richard Hooker[16] to the humblest parish curate it became a mainstay of the church's vocabulary.

A "Christian prince," Jewel declared, "hath the charge of both tables committed to him by God, to the end he may understand that not temporal matters only but also religious and ecclesiastical causes pertain to his office: besides also that God by his prophets often and earnestly commandeth the king to cut down the groves, to break down the images and altars of idols, and to write out the book of the law for himself; and besides that the prophet Isaiah saith 'a king ought to be a patron and nurse of the church' . . . we see by histories and by examples of the best times that good princes ever took the administration of ecclesiastical matters to pertain to their duty."[17] The prophetic commission to the king as nursing father served, in Jewel's view, two purposes: it trumped the Church of Rome's pretensions, based on a theory of papal supremacy, to control English ecclesiastical affairs and it authorized the English monarchy to impose its own brand of uniform religious truth throughout the realm. In response to attacks by Catholic theologians, Jewel issued a *Defense of the Apology* in 1567, which, like Calvin, he dedicated to Queen Elizabeth as the "nource" of the church.[18]

Neither Jewel's influence nor the appearance in 1560 of the popular, English language Geneva Bible, which translated Isaiah 49:23 as "Kings shall be thy nourcing fathers, and Queenes shall be thy nources," were sufficient to supplant a rival translation of the nursing father metaphor. Other authors, evidently uneasy about the propriety of a word picture of a suckling male, rendered it "foster fathers." The Latin phrase Calvin used in his *Commentary* on Isaiah and in his *Institutes* which Jewel[19] and the Geneva Bible translated as nurse and nourcing fathers, he (or his typesetters) spelled variously as "Ecclesiae nutritios," "Ecclesiae nutricios," "Ecclesiae nutricii," and "nutritii tui."[20] "Nutritios" and its variant spellings were derived from the Latin feminine noun, nutrix, which a standard Latin-English dictionary translates as "a nurse, foster mother."[21] Therefore, Thomas Norton, the translator of the frequently reprinted 1561 English edition of the *Institutes*, was on solid ground in rendering Calvin's "Ecclesiae nutritios" as "fosterfathers of the church."[22] William Allen in his *An Apologie . . . of two English colleges* (1581) employed the same locution. "Kings," wrote Allen, "are called by the Prophete [Isa. 49.23] her *foster fathers*, as Queenes be also named her nources: because it belongeth to the earthly power that God hath given them, to defend the lawes of the Church, to cause them to be executed, and to punish rebels and transgressors of the same."[23]

The royal prestige of James I secured the victory of the nursing fathers metaphor. In the course of his celebrated campaign to persuade the Dutch government to expel from its dominions the "wretch Heretique," Conrad Vorst (Conradus Vorstius), a reputed Socinian whom it had appointed to succeed the famous Arminius on the theological faculty at the University of Leiden, James issued his widely read *Declaration against Vorstius* (1610). In this polemic James declared "that it is one of the principal parts of that duetie which appertaines unto a Christian King, to protect the trew Church within his owne Dominions, and to extirpate heresies, is a maxime without all controversie." "Those honorouable Titles . . . Nutritius Ecclesiae, Nursing father of the Church," James asserted, "doe rightly belong unto every Emperour, King, and Christian Monarch."[24]

That Charles I, in whom his admirers believed "God had particularly made good his promise to our Part of his Church, that Kings should be its Nursing Fathers," also called himself "an indulgent nursing father"[25] gave the metaphor the cachet of a second royal patron. The incessant use of the metaphor by the Anglican hierarchy to compliment the Stuart kings[26] and their successors— William III, for example, was extolled as "a Nursing Father to Zion the Church of God"[27]—put it in general circulation and secured it a place in the vocabulary of political controversy. The metaphor was used by two of the seventeenth century's most celebrated intellectual antagonists, political philosophers Robert Filmer and John Locke,[28] and through Locke's *Second Treatise of Government* it came to the attention of a wide American audience. That it retained its vitality among eighteenth-century thinkers is attested by Edmund Burke, who referred to the civil magistrate as a "Nurse and Increasor of Blessings."[29]

Puritan opponents of the Church of England under Elizabeth and the Stuarts differed among themselves on many issues, on none more important than church government. Some Puritans favored a Presbyterian form of church government, others a Congregational one. Congregationalists were split between those who regarded themselves as a loyal opposition within the Church of England—the settlers of Massachusetts Bay belonged in this camp—and those "separatists" who utterly renounced the Church. Both wings of the Congregational movement subscribed to the Anglican interpretation of the ecclesiastical role of civil authority, as articulated by James I, that the ruler was obliged to establish true religion in his realm and both appropriated the "nursing father" metaphor to convey this understanding.

The separatist position received its clearest formulation in the "Confession of 1596," a document issued in Amsterdam by men who had been driven out of England by political authorities who had executed their leaders and brutally persecuted their flocks. The authors of the "Confession," nevertheless, asserted that "it is the office and Duty of Princes and Magestrates . . . to suppress and root out by their authoritie all false ministries, voluntarie Relligions, and counterfeyt worship of God, to destroy the Idoll Temples, Images, Altares, Vestments, and all other monuments of Idolatrie and superstition" and to confiscate all church property of "anie false ministeries . . . And on the other hand to establish & mayntein by their lawes every part of Gods word his pure Relligion and true ministerie . . . they accompt it a happie blessing of God who granteth such nourcing Fathers and nourcing Mothers to his Church."[30]

The religious dynamics of the English Civil War compelled the mainstream, non-separating congregationalists, now called independents, to temper some of their earlier doctrinal zeal. On January 31, 1648, the day after the execution of Charles I, one of the most learned independent ministers, Dr. John Owen, delivered a famous sermon in Parliament on the limits of religious toleration. According to Owen, Scripture commanded "kings and queens to serve the Lord, in promoting the kingdom of the Lord Jesus Christ. And it is promised, Isa. xlix. 23 that 'they shall be nursing-fathers and nursing-mothers to the church' of Christ, even then when she shall 'suck the breasts of kings' (earthly things are the milk of kingly breasts)."

Among the "earthly things" the nursing fathers were required to supply Owen listed the following: the "providing or granting of places requisite for the performance of that worship which in the gospel is instituted"; "protection, as to peace and quietness in the use of the ordinances of the Lord Jesus Christ; from violent disturbers"; and "supportment and provision [for the gospel ministry] as to earthly things, where regularly failing." Owen was as confident as the authors of the 1596 Confession that "it was the duty of the magistrate," as nursing father "not to allow any public places for (in his judgment) false and abominable worship; as also, to demolish all outward appearances and demonstrations of such superstitious, idolatrous, and unacceptable service."[31] Those publicly and obstreperously propagating "uncouth" religious opinions were to be suppressed. But out of respect for the welter of protestant religious opinions that had surfaced during the Civil War, Owen would permit the magistrate to allow the public airing of a variety of religious views (at least on matters indifferent) and would offer a wide latitude for the expression of religious opinions in private.

This was a position that many Presbyterians, especially those in Scotland, were not prepared to countenance. John Knox, the great pillar of Scottish Presbyterianism, was a disciple of Calvin who carried his preceptor's view on church-state relations directly from Geneva to the court of Queen Mary at Edinburgh. In an interview which the Reformer called "the first reasoning betwixt the queen and John Knox," September 4, 1561, Knox lectured the young monarch in the following manner: God "subjects people under princes, and causes obedience to be given unto them; yea, God craves of kings that they be as it were foster-fathers to his Church, and commands queens to be nurses to his people."[32] Knox's use of foster fathers gave the term as much prestige in Presbyterian circles as Jewel's simultaneous use of nursing fathers had done in the Anglican community. The metaphor eventually achieved a higher status among Presbyterians because it was incorporated by reference into the Westminster Confession of 1646,[33] for the past three centuries the basic creed of the denomination.

The English Civil Wars did not make Presbyterians as malleable as the independents, a point vividly illustrated by one of the classics in the literature of Presbyterian apologetics, Samuel Rutherford's *Lex Rex*. Writing in 1644, Rutherford championed the nursing father metaphor (which in Scotland had by now supplanted Knox's foster fathers). He began his book with the strong, if conventional, assertion that "Kings and all Magistrates are Gods, and Gods deputies and lieutenants upon earth" as well as "nursing fathers of the Church." Later in his work Rutherford tackled the question of whether kings were fathers "univocally, or only analogically." He concluded "that though the Word warrant us to esteem King's fathers, Esa. 49. 23 . . . yet they are not essentially and formally fathers by generation . . . and yet are they but fathers metaphorically." Rutherford, in fact, preferred the term "Nurse-father" and applied it to kings, judges and other civil officials. He took an uncompromising view of the role of the nurse-father, who was not only "appointed for Civill Policy, but for the maintenance of true religion, and for the suppression of idolatrie and superstition." "The King," Rutherford declared, "hath a chiefe hand in Church affaires, when he is a Nurse-Father, and beareth the Royall Sword to defend both the Tables of the Law." Rutherford made Henry VIIII a posthumous "Nurse-father" because he had defended the faith "by his Sword."[34]

In 1652 a heated exchange occurred between an anonymous defender of the mainstream conception of the nursing father metaphor and Roger Williams, who was in England at the time defending Rhode Island's interests. In a pamphlet, *The Examiner Examined*, which contained a long subtitle, asserting that the civil magistrate was obliged to "advance the true Religion" and quoting, in justification, the text from "Esay 49.22,23," the anonymous advocate posed as his "Question 1"[35] the following proposition: "Whether a Magistrate that knowes the Doctrine of Salvation by Christ Jesus, doe fulfill the Office of a Nursing Father, if he doe not cause this saving Food to be given to his Children; and Poyson, that is contrary Doctrine to be kept from them." In an impassioned rejoinder, *The Examiner Defended*, Williams employed his distinctive, anti-typological exegetical approach to argue that "this Prophesie of Kings and queens being nursing fathers and nursing mothers to the Saints" applied only to the Jews of the Old Testament. "Consequently," he asked, "whether all those bloody persecutors (Papists and Protestants), who have used to drawn this shaft out of the Quiver of Scripture, whereby to pierce the tender heart of Jesus; yea and all that give a power to the Civil magistrate in Spirituals from this Scripture, Have not most ignorantly profaned the prophecy, and that to usurpation over the temple of God, the Consciences of Gods own people; and to bloody violence against their Bodies, although under a cloak of providing wholesome food for their children and prohibiting poyson, etc." After offering several more objections to the popular interpretation of Isaiah 49:23 Williams concluded by asking whether it "was not this very Doctrine that cost the late King Charles his Crown, and Life? Who being flattered and bewitched into this dream of a Nursing father, and a judge of wholesome food and poyson for his people; he forced poyson for food on the Scotch Nation . . . and prosecuting those fatal Wars, which (by a naked Hand from heaven) justly pluckt up root and branch, both Ceremonies, Bishops, and king together."[36]

A few years later an equally eminent advocate of liberty of conscience, John Milton, attacked the conventional understanding of Isaiah 49:23. Milton's eye was apparently caught by a passage in a precis of Protestant theology, *Compendium Theologiae Christianae* (Basel, 1626) by the Swiss theologian, Johannes Wolleb (Wollebius), which "caused a considerable sensation" in London in the

1650s, when it appeared in an English translation.[37] In his *Abridgement of Christian Divinitie*, as the translation was called, Wolleb asserted that "Magistrates are the Churches nursing-fathers, as they are keepers of the two Tables of the law, as they preserve Churches and Schools, and defend the Truth." In reply, Milton declared that "churches do not need the supervision of magistrates," or of kings, acting as "foster-fathers" (apparently, a deliberate substitution by Milton for what he considered the excessive Anglican, royalist usage of "nursing fathers.") "The magistrate," Milton insisted, "should protect religion, not enforce it . . . since Christ's kingdom is not of this world, it does not stand by force and constraint, the constituents of worldly authority. So the gospel should not be made a matter of compulsion, and faith liberty and conscience cannot be."[38]

Americans in 1776 were unacquainted with—and could not have been influenced by—Williams's polemic against the nursing fathers; like his other theological writings it had long been forgotten, if, in fact, it had ever been known in the colonies. Nor is it likely that they would have been aware of Milton's strictures against the metaphor, since his essay attacking it was not published in his lifetime. But it is significant that men of the stature of Williams and Milton attempted to discredit the metaphor, for their efforts attest to its potency in seventeenth-century England.

The point in showing how firmly seventeenth-century Anglicans, Presbyterians and Congregationalists-Independents were wedded to the nursing fathers metaphor is that they were the largest Protestant denominations in Great Britain and sent the largest number of settlers to North America.[39] By carrying the nursing fathers concept with them, members of these denominations established it as the model for church-state relations in most American colonies.

As the eighteenth century dawned in British North America, Anglicans routinely used the nursing father metaphor. Consider the controversy over the behavior of Francis Nicholson, appointed governor of Virginia in 1698. To his enemies among the Virginia planter elite Nicholson was "a monstrous compound of . . . hypocrisy and profaneness."[40] Others admired him, however, for his financial generosity toward the Church of England and acclaimed him a "true son or rather Nursing Father of her in America."[41] At a meeting of Anglican clergymen in Philadelphia in 1704 Nicholson's conduct was strongly endorsed: "we cannot but with a Christian Indignation consider that so good a Nursing Father of our holy Mother, so unparalleled and munificent a promoter of it should be ungratefully traduced."[42] The next year, at least as controversial a figure as

Nicholson, Lord Cornbury, governor of New York, was commended for his financial generosity toward the church: "for his eminent care and protection of us; he is truly our Nursing Father."[43] The most popular Anglican clergymen in eighteenth-century America, though an opponent of the church's hierarchy, was the famous evangelist, George Whitefield, one of the principal promoters of the Great Awakening in the 1740s. Whitefield's partiality to the nursing fathers metaphor was exhibited in a sermon preached before a huge crowd in Philadelphia in 1746 in a recently erected revivalistic arena, the "New Building." George II, Whitefield declared, "deserved that great and glorious title which the Lord promises kings should sustain in the latter days, I mean *a nursing father of the church.*"[44] Whitefield's sermon, immediately published, assured the metaphor the widest possible circulation in America.

Presbyterians did not begin emigrating to the American colonies until the second decade of the eighteenth century and did not become a critical mass in American public life until the 1760s. Their principal spokesman in the revolutionary period was John Witherspoon, who arrived in the colonies from Scotland in 1768. Shortly thereafter, Witherspoon delivered the famous series of lectures to his students at Princeton which were frequently republished as *Lectures on Moral Philosophy.* In this work Scottish Presbyterianism's traditional emphasis on nursing fathers and nursing mothers appeared in the following passage in which civil authorities were compared to a parent in their relations to the church: "many are of opinion, that besides all this, the magistrate ought to make public provision for the worship on God . . . and indeed there seems to be a good deal of reason for it, that so instruction may be provided for the bulk of the common people . . . the magistrates right in this case seems to be something like that of a parent."[45]

Nursing fathers was a central concept of New England Congregationalists. One of their early historians, Edward Johnson, composed an imaginary "proclamation for Volontiers," which Christ himself was depicted as inspiring on the eve of emigration from England in 1628. The Saviour instructed the settlers that once "your feete are safely set on the shores of America" they were to "provoke . . . all that are in authority to caste downe their Crownes at the Feet of Christ, and take them up again at his command under his Standard as nursing Fathers and nursing Mothers to the Churche."[46] Twenty years later, in 1648, New England church leaders adopted the Cambridge Platform, a creed as authoritative among the faithful as the Westminster Confession was among Presbyterians. The

Platform asserted that the "Magistrates are nursing fathers & nursing mothers & stand charged with custody of both Tables."[47] Historians note that the patronage of Increase and Cotton Mather insured that notion of the nursing fathers continued to thrive in New England.[48]

Eighteenth-century sermons teemed with the metaphor. When Jonathan Belcher arrived in 1730 to assume the governorship of Massachusetts, George II was saluted for selecting a man of "Wisdom, Integrity and Piety." "Our King," the colonists declared, "is a nursing Father, and our Queen a nursing Mother, who have express'd their tender Care of, and Concern for us, their poor but dutiful Children, in these distant parts of their Dominion."[49] A few years later in Connecticut Elisha Williams delivered his well-known *A Seasonable Plea for the Liberty of Conscience and the Right of Private Judgment* (1744), in which Williams, the rector of Yale College, 1726-1739, argued that "the civil authority are obliged to take care for the support of religion, or in other words, of schools and the gospel ministry, in order to their approving themselves nursing fathers (as, I suppose, every body will own, and therefore I shall not spend any time in proving it)."[50] In the 1760s preachers of the Connecticut Election sermon featured the nursing fathers metaphor. In 1762, Joseph Bellamy, a stalwart in the "New Divinity" theological movement, described the ideal governor as exhibiting toward the citizens "all the good will and tenderness which are wont to reside in the heart of a nursing father or nursing mother toward an infant child."[51] Three years later the election sermon was preached entirely from the text, Isaiah 49:23. Calling his sermon *The Duty of Civil Rulers, to be nursing Fathers to the Church of Christ,* Edward Dorr listed a variety of ways in which the magistrates were to act as nursing fathers, the principal one being the paying of ministers' salaries from public revenues.[52] In 1771 a Congregational minister in Stonington, Connecticut, Joseph Fish, cited "Isa. 49.23 and kings shall be thy nursing fathers, and queens thy nursing mothers" as an example of God's "precious promise" to support the church. Fish gave the text what by that date had become a reactionary reading by suggesting that it would authorize political authorities to suppress the dissenting zealots who were plaguing his ministry. "As nurses or parents take care of their helpless children," Fish wrote, "carrying them in their arms, treating them with all tenderness and affection, and stretching out their hands for their protection and defence, so shall kings and queens treat the church of Christ."[53]

After the Declaration of Independence the calls for civil authorities to become nursing fathers of the church assumed a sense of anxious urgency in those states where the churches that had enjoyed exclusive state patronage during the colonial period were now under siege by reformers demanding their disestablishment. On September 13, 1783, an article appeared in the *Virginia Gazette, or, The American Advertiser,* which contained, its author claimed, "the sentiments of the judicious Christians in this State." Religion was flagging, the "judicious Christians" declared, and "the friendly aid of the Legislature is wanting." Otherwise, God might inflict "some severe stroke to rouse us to a sense of our duty and interest. Far be it from us to suppose that you [the legislators] conceive it beneath your dignity, to become nursing fathers of the church, and to promote true piety and devotion amongst us . . . and to raise up a numerous body of subjects, who will fear God and honor the Magistrates . . . and will become the best soldiers, the most industrious and wise citizens, that cannot fail to exalt these States to that degree of grandeur and happiness which will . . . raise the admiration of the whole earth." In the same vein the citizens of Amherst County adjured the General Assembly of Virginia on November 27, 1783, not to "think it beneath your Dignity to become Nursing Fathers of the Church" by funding religion in the state.[54]

In revolutionary New England, the nursing fathers metaphor continued to be a coin of the realm. A member of the Massachusetts Constitutional Convention of 1780 asserted that on the convention floor one of the principal arguments used for the continuation of public funding for the state's Congregationalist ministers was the reminder "that the prophet Isaiah, in speaking of gospel times, had declared, that kings should become nursing fathers and queens nursing mothers, to the church; which most certainly implied, that the civil authority would make suitable provision for the support and maintenance of public worship and teachers of religion."[55] Ezra Stiles in his important 1783 sermon, *The United States elevated to Glory and Honor,* vented the postindependence anxiety of the Congregationalist establishment. Stiles worried that "if even the Holy Redeemer himself and his apostles were to reappear among us, while unknown to be such, and importune the public government and magistracy of these states to become nursing fathers to the church, is it not to be feared that some of the states, through timidity and fearfulness of touching religion, would excuse themselves and dismiss these holy messengers . . . ?" "May we not humbly wish," Stiles asked his audience, the members of the Connecticut General Assembly, "that you would not repudiate the idea of being nursing fathers to our spiritual Israel, the church of God within this state? Give us, gentlemen," Stiles continued, "the decided assurance that you are friends of the churches, and that you are friends of the pastors."[56]

It is obvious from the evidence cited that, by 1776, many Americans, especially those with pre-independence religious establishments, were preoccupied with what Calvin and his contemporaries regarded as a distinctly secondary duty of the civil authorities acting as nursing fathers: the use of public funds to provide financial support for the ministry. The reason for this change in focus is simple. The Toleration Act of 1689 and the subsequent commitment of many eighteenth-century lay and clerical leaders to the natural right of freedom of conscience undercut the state's theoretical right to establish the true religion by eradicating the false. Under the new dispensation, what had previously been considered false was permitted to flourish, as the state stood impotently by. Calvin's or James I's or Rutherford's concept of the nursing father, sword in hand, dispatching the heretics became instantly obsolete in 1689 and was succeeded in both England and America by the idea that the nursing father should become the preacher's paymaster.

The idea behind Calvin's concept of the nursing father was clear enough. By establishing the true religion the civil authorities prepared the way for the eternal salvation of its citizens. By what rationale, however, did the state as nursing father confine itself solely to what John Owen called "supportment"? This question became especially pressing after 1776 when many of the new American state governments tried to pass general assessment acts, which laid religious taxes to pay a wide assortment of Protestant preachers. Since every denomination could not be the repository of the one true way to salvation, why should the nursing father pay any of them? The answer given by the intended ecclesiastical beneficiaries and their lay supporters was not, spiritually, a very edifying one; the state was urged to provide financial subventions to the churches as an act of self-interest because the churches were uniquely qualified to help it achieve its secular objectives. This rationale turned on its head Calvin's case for the state as nursing father. To the great reformer the state, in its capacity as facilitator of salvation, acted as the agent of the church; after 1776, the church in many places came to be depicted as the agent of the state.

Most of the post-1776 arguments, stressing the civic contribution of the church, were articulated by Dorr in his 1765 *Nursing Fathers* sermon. According to Dorr, "the civil interests of mankind, the safety of the state requires, that there be some religious establishments." He hammered away at this point: "the practice of religion and virtue, tends, above all other things, to promote those very ends, for which men entered into society"; "the public profession and practice of religion, was a benefit to the state, and absolutely necessary, to the safety and security of civil government"; religion was the "best security mankind can possibly have, of the quiet and peaceable enjoyment of their lives, liberties and properties"; it promotes "the public welfare and happiness of mankind."[57] Postindependence preachers did not improve much on Dorr. Religion was necessary, as Phillips Payson declared in 1778, "to support and preserve order and government in the state":[58] it was the "great foundation of public prosperity and national happiness," as John Witherspoon asserted in 1782;[59] and it was "productive of really great and extensive public good," as Bishop James Madison of Virginia claimed in 1799.[60] During the Founding Period statements such as these became hackneyed observations that tripped from the tongue of every preacher and politician, George Washington included.[61] The problem with the incessant argument for government support of religion on the grounds of its "public Utility"[62] was that it reduced religion to the level of other activities that promoted the secular agenda of the state and resulted, finally, in speakers in the Massachusetts Constitutional Convention of 1820 equating religion with road building programs and the militia,[63] a degrading comparison that, as a style of advocacy, became one of the many factors that produced the disenchantment that led to the disestablishment of religion in the commonwealth in 1833.

Since some of the talk, after 1776, about the obligation of the state, in the interests of social utility, to continue its financial role as the nursing father of the church was obviously special pleading by Anglican and Congregational ministers and their supporters, fearful that their publicly funded salaries would stop, it is a fair question to ask how broad, in fact, was the constituency for the nursing fathers metaphor? Elisha Williams claimed in 1744 that "every body" agreed that civil magistrates should be nursing fathers of the church,[64] but Williams meant "every body" in New England not throughout the colonies. Isaac Backus, the New England Baptist leader, confirmed in 1768 that "many" of his fellow citizens, in justification of his area's entrenched system of religious taxation, "plead in this case that promise to the church, that Kings shall be thy nursing fathers and Queens her nursing mothers."[65] The metaphor continued to be a staple of New England discourse and regularly appeared, after 1776, in the region's political and theological controversies, as the following statement in a 1785 pamphlet by the future chief justice of Massachusetts, Theophilus Parsons, demonstrates: "the

Christian church was formed by christ: she took her name from him, and was so far wedded to state policy as that he made 'kings and queens nursing fathers and mothers.'"[66] In fact, after 1776, to break the monotony of using the term nursing fathers, New Englanders began addressing their magistrates in print as "civil" and "political" fathers.[67] "The people call them fathers," said the preacher of the New Hampshire election sermon in 1791. "We are willing to be their political children, as long as they are good parents."[68] That all the New England states after 1776 laid some form of general religious tax[69] indicates that the majority of legislators and their constituents must have believed that the state as nursing father was obliged to provide financial support to the church.

What was the situation in the Episcopalian (formerly Anglican) colonies from Maryland southward? Here again we have the testimony of a leading Baptist, John Leland, about the power of the nursing fathers metaphor. Reflecting in 1791 on his recently concluded fourteen-year pastorate in Virginia, Leland observed that the "rulers" there, his friends Jefferson and Madison excepted, had been swayed by Episcopal ecclesiastical influence to try to promote the public financing of religion on the grounds that it would be "advantageous to the state" and that "this they often do the more readily when they are flattered by the clergy that if they thus defend the truth they will become nursing fathers of the church and merit something considerable for themselves."[70] That the Virginia and Maryland Assemblies were on the verge of passing a general religious tax in 1785, that the Georgia Assembly actually passed such a measure the same year, and that a similar measure failed by only a handful of votes in South Carolina a few years earlier demonstrates the existence in the South of a strong sentiment in favor of the state assuming the role of the nursing father as paymaster of the church.[71]

General assessment taxes were defeated by the combined opposition of civil libertarians like Jefferson and the Baptists and Presbyterians (some of whose clergy, mindful of Scottish practice, vacillated on the issue of state financial support). Baptists and Presbyterians considered general assessment taxes as a Trojan horse which would lead to the reestablishment of the Church of England in the full plenitude of its pre-1776 power, including the power to persecute "dissenters" which still occurred sporadically after independence. The Baptists and Presbyterians did not, however, repudiate the nursing fathers metaphor, for they valued the spirit of church-state relations that it signified. By redefining the metaphor, they tried to rescue it and make it relevant to the pluralistic religious environment that was emerging in the new American republic.

The Presbyterian act of redefinition was impressive because it involved an alteration in the denomination's creed, the Westminster Confession. In 1729 American Presbyterians adopted the text of the Confession as it had come from the pens of its authors in 1646. The General Assembly held in Philadelphia in 1788, called to align the church with the new American nation, put the spotlight on the nursing fathers metaphor, by elevating it from a footnote reference to Isaiah 49:23 in the 1646 Confession to an exposition in the main body of the text in the section on the Civil Magistrate. According to the 1788 version of the Confession, "as nursing fathers, it is the duty of civil magistrates to protect the Church of our common Lord, without giving the preference to any denomination of Christians above the rest . . . no law of any commonwealth should interfere with, let, or hinder, the due exercise [of religion] among the voluntary members of *any* denomination of Christians."[72] In other words, the state must be fair as well as solicitous, a position strongly supported by the Baptists, whose ministers, after 1776, imitated their Congregationalist counterparts by calling the civil authorities "political fathers."[73] "That promise that kings shall become nursing fathers and queens nursing mothers," Isaac Backus reminded his fellow New Englanders, "carries in its very nature an *impartial care and tenderness for all their children.*"[74] In a memorial to the Massachusetts Provincial Congress, December 2, 1774, the Baptists urged that "civil rulers ought undoubtedly to be nursing fathers to the church, by reproof, exhortation, and their own good and liberal example, as well as to protect and defend her against injustice and oppression."[75]

That there was, by 1788, substantial support for the Presbyterian-Baptist position among members of the old "established" denominations is demonstrated by the Massachusetts election sermon of 1788 in which the Congregationalist preacher, David Parsons, informed Governor John Hancock and the assembled civil and ecclesiastical dignitaries that rulers should "afford protection and encouragement" to all of the state's ministers; "they should be patrons and nursing Fathers to the church of Christ; and use their utmost endeavors to advance his Kingdom. All the which they may do without binding the rights of conscience, or exerting their authority to impose articles of faith, or modes of worship; or enforcing these by penalties. Indeed such an exercise of power in a ruler would be to extend his commission beyond its limits, and to defeat its design, which was to protect and preserve the rights of conscience."[76] Congregationalists in neighboring Connecticut endorsed this position. Possibly fearing that the United States might be infected by the antireligious violence of the French Revolution, the preacher of the 1795 election sermon, Andrew Lee, informed the dignitaries assembled at Hartford that their duty was to protect the state's churches, even as they guaranteed freedom of conscience to all. "It was," said Lee, "incumbent on those who are set to rule for God to be nursing fathers to the cause of God." "Let true religion be defended from external violence," the preacher urged his audience.[77] In 1803 the preacher of the election sermon, Matthias Burnet, captured this shift in emphasis on the rulers' duty by saluting Connecticut's magistrates as the "venerable fathers of your country" who had "become nursing, protecting fathers to the church."[78]

What the Presbyterians and Baptists, with Congregationalist concurrence, were attempting to do was obvious: they wanted to democratize the nursing fathers by redefining their mission from the exertion of coercive authority on behalf of one church, either to vindicate the truth it purported to embody or to pay its ministers, to the exertion of the state's authority to guarantee to all communities of faith the equal protection of the laws. According to the revised conception of the nursing fathers, the state ought to protect all churches within its jurisdiction from malefactors, bigots and bullies; furthermore, it ought to promote Christian worship in a variety of ways, among them by making public facilities—court houses, post offices, federal office buildings—available on a nondiscriminatory basis for church services, by sponsoring the distribution of accurate editions of the Bible, by defending the sanctity of the Sabbath and by providing religious instruction in the public schools.[79]

At the time, say, of Washington's first inauguration, Congregationalists, Episcopalians, Presbyterians and Baptists composed the vast majority of the population of the United States. If the members of these denominations agreed with the positions of their leaders and spokesmen about relations between church and state—and there is no reason to suppose that they did not—a strong case can be made that in 1789 or at any time between 1776 and 1800 a substantial majority of the American people believed that relations between government and religion should be described by the nursing father metaphor. There was, to be sure, disagreement about how far the nursing father could employ coercive authority to support the church, but, at a minimum, all agreed that the state should have warm, paternal feelings for its religious institutions, and that civil authorities, insofar as the law allowed, should be friends, helpers and protectors of the churches, should treat them as any good father would treat his children. Perhaps Isaac Backus expressed the prevailing sentiment best, when he asserted that a "sweet harmony" should exist between church and state.[80]

America's attachment to the nursing father metaphor appeared to many to be threatened by the election of the alleged "atheist," Thomas Jefferson, to the presidency in 1800. During the presidential campaign, John Mitchell Mason, a popular Presbyterian minister in New York City and a founder of Union Theological Seminary, admonished his fellow citizens that "you are commanded *to pray for your rulers:* it is your custom to pray, that they may be men *fearing God and hating covetousness.* You entreat him to fulfill his promise, that kings shall be to his church *nursing-fathers, and queens her nursing-mothers.* With what conscience can you lift up your hands in such a supplication, when you are exerting yourselves to procure a president who does not fear God . . . do you think the church of Christ is to be nurtured by the dragon's milk of infidelity?"[81] While it is certainly true that Jefferson did not, like James I, publicly exult in his role as a nursing father of the church, an argument can be made that, within the space left by his principled aversion to the use of state power to promote religion, he played the part. Jefferson, after all, attempted to give religion his symbolic support by conscientiously attending church services in the House of Representatives and, more to the point, he extended a helping hand to the infant churches in the raw, young city of Washington by permitting them to conduct services in government facilities, specifically, in the Treasury and War Office buildings. In assisting these churches Jefferson was following the practice of public officials in his native Virginia, which was imitated throughout the south and west in the early years of the new republic. Having moved into a new capitol building in the underdeveloped city of Richmond on the heels of the passage of the Virginia Statute for Religious Freedom (1786), the state legislature threw open the capitol to religious groups of all complexions, including Catholics, who conducted in these official precincts everything from masses to vestry meetings.[82]

The nursing fathers metaphor continued to be used in the nineteenth century but its focus became diffuse. In 1826, for example, field representatives of the American Home Missionary Society asked the churches of New York state to redouble their efforts in the "new settlements" in the western United States. How much, they were reminded, "does Isaiah tell us of kings being nursing fathers, and queens nursing mothers, to the church, when he speaks of the wilderness and solitary place budding as the rose."[83] In 1833 the Reverend Jasper Adams, president of the College of Charleston, South Carolina, used the metaphor to explain why the Christian church was "taken under the protection" of the Roman emperor, Constantine, in the fourth century, A.D. "It was the prediction of ancient prophecy," wrote Adams, "that, in the last days, kings should become nursing fathers and queens nursing mothers to the Church;—and what was more natural than to understand this prophecy as meaning a strict and intimate union of the Church, with the civil government of the Empire."[84] A dispute among Virginia churches in 1844-1845 about the wisdom of a seeking from the state legislature a general incorporation act for the state's religious denominations was the occasion for the revival of the metaphor in its more familiar political setting. Opponents of the incorporation act, an innocuous measure similar to those in force throughout the United States, alleged that "a powerful state never grants privileges to the church without requiring, sooner or later, heavy payment. A State, nursing a church, has always been like a she-bear hugging a lamb."[85] The Baptist-Presbyterian attempt to democratize the nursing fathers metaphor had not, obviously, prevented demagogues from employing it to arouse atavistic anxieties about religious oppression.

By the 1850s the metaphor was disappearing from public discourse. The practice which it represented continued, however, until well after the Civil War, most visibly in Congress which did not lose its appetite for helping local religious groups. In 1865, for example, Congregationalists in Washington, attempting to organize a church, approached the leadership of the House, which allowed the petitioners to use its chambers. The result was that by 1868, before the Congregationalists moved into their new church, "nearly 2000 assembled every Sabbath for the regular services in this large hall. This audience was said to be the largest Protestant Sabbath audience then in the United States."[86]

By a curious coincidence in the years immediately after World War II the two principal models of church-state relations in American history crossed paths, heading in opposite directions. In a series of decisions beginning with *Everson v. Board of Education* in 1947, the Supreme Court announced its discovery that religion should be partitioned off from government by a "wall of separation," an enforced estrangement that most Americans in the Founding Period would have found repugnant. At virtually the same time, in 1950 to be specific, the nursing fathers metaphor, having vanished from public discourse, disappeared from the printed page. In 1950 a new, authorized, Catholic, English-language translation of the Bible appeared, *The New American Bible,* followed two years later by a new authoritative Protestant, English-language translation, the *Revised Standard*

Version. In both editions nursing fathers in Isaiah 49:23 was replaced by its earlier competitor, foster fathers. (A new, authoritative Jewish translation of the Old Testament dispensed with fathers altogether, rendering Isaiah 49:23 as "kings shall tend your children.")[87] In the numerous, subsequent reprintings of both the Catholic and Protestant Bibles foster fathers continued to hold its place. Post-war commentaries on Isaiah by distinguished biblical scholars followed the foster fathers trend,[88] as did new scholarly translations of Calvin's *Institutes*.[89] The oblivion into which the nursing fathers metaphor fell is illustrated by a book, published in 1996, by a British scholar, *The Fifth Gospel Isaiah in the History of Christianity*, in which the author surveyed the use of Isaiah by writers from the early Church fathers to modern feminism and found no references to Isaiah 49:23.[90] Another scholar has recently published a volume, arguing that there was an "American revolution against patriarchal authority in the second half of the eighteenth century,"[91] unaware of the inconvenient (for his thesis) prominence of the nursing fathers metaphor during this precise period. Yet another illustration of modern amnesia is a volume published in 1984 by the political scientist, Aaron Wildavsky, entitled *The Nursing Father Moses as a Political Leader*. Wildavsky considered the title, nursing father, a compelling one, even for a modern audience—"what else," he remarked, "is a leader if not a 'nursing father'"—but he found the metaphor's scriptural locus, not in Isaiah, but in Numbers 11:12.[92]

Could the concept of the nursing fathers, as Professor Wildavsky hints, still be serviceable in modern America? This, of course, is a matter of speculation. What is certain, however, is that the nursing fathers metaphor expressed the view of the Founding generation toward the relations between government and religion far more accurately than Jefferson's wall metaphor. In other words, in the early years of the republic, Calvin, whom Jefferson hated with a passion that he reserved for few others, trumped the master of Monticello.

NOTES

1. Massachusetts Provincial Congress, Fast Day Proclamation, April 15, 1775, Broadside Collection, Rare Book and Special Collections Division, Library of Congress, hereinafter cited as RBSCD.

2. The terms "church and state" and "government and religion" are used interchangeably in this chapter. Professor Jon Butler, among others, insists there should be a distinction between the terms, especially in the United States during the Founding Period. In the context of the nursing fathers metaphor an argument could be made that church and state should be used until the passage of the Toleration Act of 1689 on the grounds that before that time the state, in the person of a king or republican civil magistrate, supported one church that was believed to embody the true faith. After 1689 and, especially after 1776 in America, the state often undertook to support several (protestant) denominations, an arrangement that might justify speaking of the state and the *churches,* or, perhaps better, government and religion. Jon Butler, "Why Revolutionary America Wasn't A 'Christian Nation,'" in *Religion and the New Republic,* ed. James H. Hutson (Lanham, Md.: Rowman & Littlefield, 2000), 196.

3. Daniel L. Dreisbach, "Thomas Jefferson, A Mammoth Cheese, and the 'Wall of Separation between Church and State,'" in Hutson, *Religion and the New Republic,* note 2, 89.

4. David C. Steinmetz, "John Calvin on Isaiah 6: A Problem in the History of Exegesis," Richard C. Gamble, ed., *Calvin and Hermeneutics* (New York: Garland Publishers, 1992), 175.

5. Hilton C. Oswald, ed., *Luther's Works* (St. Louis: Concordia Publishing House, 1972), vol. 17, 188.

6. William Pringle, trans., John Calvin, *Commentary on the Book of the Prophet Isaiah* (Edinburgh: Calvin Translation Society, 1850-1853), vol. 1, xvi.

7. Calvin, *Commentary on Isaiah,* vol. 4, 39-40.

8. John Allen, trans., John Calvin, *Institutes of the Christian Religion* (Philadelphia: Presbyterian Board of Christian Education, 1928), vol. 2, 637.

9. Calvin, *Commentary on Isaiah,* xxii, xxiv.

10. Calvin, *Commentary on Isaiah,* xvi.

11. Calvin, *Commentary on Isaiah,* xvii-xviii.

12. Steinmetz, "John Calvin on Isaiah," 177.

13. Basil Hall, "Calvin against the Calvinists," in *John Calvin,* ed. G. E. Duffield (Grand Rapids, Mich.: Eerdmans, 1966), 35.

14. W. M. Southgate, "The Marian Exiles and the Influence of John Calvin," in *The Making of English History,* ed. Robert L. Schuyler and Herman Ausubel (New York: Dryden Press, 1952), 173. Southgate argued that scholars had exaggerated Calvin's influence on the Marian exiles, even though he admitted that "Calvin was probably the strongest single influence upon their thought," 173.

15. For Jewel, see the sketch by Mandell Creighton in Sidney Lee, ed., *Dictionary of National Biography* (London: Smith, Elder & Company, 1908), vol. 10, 815-19.

16. For Hooker's use of the metaphor, see W. Speed Hill, ed., *The Folger Library Edition of the Works of Richard Hooker* (Cambridge, Mass.: Harvard University Press,

1977-1998), vol. 3, 233.

17. John Jewel, *An Apology of the Church of England* , ed. John E. Booty (Ithaca, N. Y.: Cornell University Press, 1963), 115. Jewel wrote the *Apology* in Latin; Booty's text is the 1564 English translation by Lady Ann Bacon, considered the "official English version" of the book, xlv.

18. John Jewel, *A Defense of the Apologie of the Churche of Englande* (London: Henry Wickes, 1570 edit.), preface (unnumbered), RBSCD.

19. Lady Ann Bacon translated Jewel's Latin into the English word, nurse; see note 17.

20. John Calvin, *Commentarii in Isaiam Prophetam* . . . (Geneva: Joannis Crispini, 1551), 486, 495-96; (Geneva, 1559), 426, 436-37; (Geneva, 1570), 426, 436-37; John Calvin, *Institutio Christianae religionis* . . . (Geneva: Robertus Stephanus, 1559), 551. Folger Shakespeare Library, Washington, D.C.

21. D. P. Simpson, *Cassell's New Latin Dictionary* (New York: Funk and Wagnalls Company, 1968), 400.

22. Norton's translation went though seven printings between 1561 and 1599. Cited here is the 1562 edition: [Thomas Norton], tr., John Calvin, *The Institution of the Christian Religion . . . translated into Englishe . . . by T.N.* (London: Richarde Harrison, 1562), 551. Folger Shakespeare Library, Washington, D.C.

23. William Allen, *An Apologie and true declaration of the two English colleges* (Rheims, 1581), cited in *Works of Hooker*, vol. 6, 1029.

24. Bernhard Fabian, ed., *James I: The Workes* (Hildesheim: G. Olms, 1971), 349.

25. Matthias Symson, *The Hanoverian Succession: One of the Blessings of the Restoration* (London, 1729), 8. The British Library. For Charles I's claim, see *The New Encyclopaedia Britannica* (Chicago: Encyclopaedia Britannica, Inc., 15th ed., 1979), vol. 4, 53.

26. For a reminder to Charles II that "to be a *Nursing Father of the Church* is one of the richest jewels in a Kings Crown," see Henry King, *A sermon preached at White-Hall on the 29th of May* (London: Henry Harringman, 1661), 16-17. RBSCD.

27. John James Caesar, *The Glorious Memory of a Faithful Prince* . . . (London: Henry Mortlock, 1702), 6. For Queen Mary as a "Nursing Mother of this Church of England," see Thomas Dawes, *A Sermon preach'd at the Parish Church of St. Chad's in Shrewsbury, March 5. 1694/5 Being the Funeral Day of our Most Gracious Sovereign Queen Mary* (London: Gabriel Rogers, 1695), 28-29. For Queen Anne "as a Nursing Mother to His Church and a Terrour to its Enemies," see Samuel Chandler, *England's great Duty on the Death of their Josiah* . . . (London: T. Parkhurst, 1702), 22. The British Library.

28. For Filmer, see Johann P. Somerville, ed., *Patriacha and Other Writings* (Cambridge: Cambridge University Press, 1991), 238; John Locke, *Two Treatises of Government*, ed. Peter Laslett (London: Cambridge University Press, 2nd ed., 1967), 360.

29. Edmund Burke, "Vindication of Natural Society," in *The Writings and Speeches of Edmund Burke*, ed. T. O. McLoughlin and James T. Boulton (Oxford: Oxford University Press, 1997), vol.1, 140.

30. Williston Walker, ed., *The Creeds and Platforms of Congregationalism* (New York: Pilgrim Press, 1991), 71-72.

31. John Owen, "Righteous Zeal Encouraged by Divine Protection; with a Discourse about Toleration . . . ," in *The Works of John Owen*, ed. William Goold (London: Banner of Truth Trust, 1965-1968), vol. 8, 192.

32. William C. Dickinson, ed., *John Knox's History of the Reformation in Scotland* (London: Thomas Nelson and Sons, 1949), vol. 2,17.

33. *The Confession of Faith* . . . (Edinburgh, 1967), 102. This work is a reprinting, by the Free Presbyterian Church of Scotland, of the 1646 text of the Westminster Confession.

34. Samuel Rutherford, *Lex, Rex: The Law and The Prince* . . . (London: John Field, 1644), 6-7, 111, 141, 191, 430, 431. RBSCD.

35. *The Examiner Examined* (London, 1652), 3. Union Theological Seminary Library.

36. *The Complete Writings of Roger Williams* (New York: Russell and Russell, 1963), vol. 7, 207-13.

37. For Wolleb, see Samuel Jackson, ed., *The New Schaff-Herzog Encyclopedia of Religious Knowledge* (New York: Funk and Wagnalls Company, 1912), vol. 12, 407.

38. John Milton, *Christian Doctrine*, in *Complete Prose Works of John Milton*, ed. Don M. Wolfe (New Haven, Conn.: Yale University Press, 1953-1982), vol. 6, 797-99.

39. New England and the southern colonies were settled, respectively and almost exclusively, by Congregationalists and Anglicans. The overwhelming majority of inhabitants in each region retained its allegiance to its mother church until the eve of the American Revolution, although, beginning in the 1740s, Baptists began to make inroads in both sections. Presbyterians began immigrating to the middle colonies in substantial numbers early in the eighteenth century; by 1776 approximately 275,000 had arrived. James G. Leyburn, "Presbyterian Immigrants and the American Revolution," *Journal of Presbyterian History* 54 (Spring, 1976): 26. Figures on the exact number of members of religious denominations in colonial America are imprecise. In 1740 Congregational churches were the most numerous in the 13 colonies, 423 in number, followed by 246 Anglican churches and 160 Presbyterian. In 1780 Congregationalists still led with 749 churches, followed by Presbyterians, 495, Baptists, 457, and Episcopalians (formerly Anglicans), 406. Edwin S. Gaustad, *Historical Atlas of Religion in America* (New York: Harper & Row, 1976), 4-5.

40. Fouace (?) to the Bishop of London, September 28, 1702, Fulham Palace transcripts, Manuscript Division, Library of Congress.

41. John Talbot to SPG (Society for the Propagation of the Gospel), October 20, 1704, SPG transcripts, Manuscript Division, Library of Congress.

42. Pennsylvania Convention to the Bishop of London, August 31, 1704, in *Historical Collections relating to the American Colonial Church,* ed. William S. Perry (New York: AMS Press, 1969), vol. 2, 506-507.

43. William Urquhart and John Thomas to SPG, November 14, 1705, SPG transcripts, Manuscript Division, Library of Congress.

44. George Whitefield, "Britain's Mercies, and Britain's Duties," in Ellis Sandoz, ed., *Political Sermons of the American Founding Era* (Indianapolis: Liberty Fund, 1991), 125.

45. Jack Scott, ed., *An Annotated Edition of Lectures on Moral Philosophy by John Witherspoon* (Newark: University of Delaware Press, 1982), 161.

46. J. Franklin Jameson, ed., *Johnson's Wonder-Working Providence 1628-1651* (New York: C. Scribner's Sons, 1910), 32.

47. See Walker, *Creeds,* 221.

48. David Hall, *The Faithful Shepherd* (Chapel Hill: University of North Carolina Press, 1972), 227, 240.

49. Ebenezer Gay, *The Duty of People to pray for and praise their Rulers* (Boston: Thomas Fleet, 1730), 33.

50. See Sandoz, *Political Sermons,* 109.

51. *The Works of Joseph Bellamy, D.D.* (New York: Garland Publishers, 1987), vol.1, 584.

52. Edward Dorr, *The Duty of Civil Rulers, to be nursing Fathers to the Church of Christ* (Hartford: Thomas Green, 1765). RBSCD.

53. Joseph Fish, *The Examiner Examined* (New London: Timothy Green, 1771), 57-58. RBSCD.

54. Revolutionary Religious Petitions, Library of Virginia, Richmond, Virginia.

55. A Member of the Convention, *Boston Independent Chronicle,* February 10, 1780.

56. Ezra Stiles, *The United States elevated to Glory and Honor . . .* (New Haven, 1783), in *The Pulpit of the American Revolution,* ed. John W. Thornton (New York: Burt Franklin, 1970), 490, 512.

57. Dorr, *The Duty of Civil Rulers,* 10, 11, 17, 24.

58. *Pulpit of the American Revolution,* 340.

59. John Witherspoon, Thanksgiving Proclamation, October 11, 1782, in *Journals of the Continental Congress 1774-1789,* ed. Worthington C. Ford and Gaillard Hunt (Washington, D.C.: Library of Congress, 1904-1937), vol. 22, 647.

60. Bishop James Madison, *An Address to the Members of the Protestant Episcopal Church, in Virginia* (Richmond: T. Nicholson, 1799), 23.

61. Washington asserted that religion and morality were the "great pillars" of human happiness and public prosperity. Farewell Address, 1796, broadside, RBSCD.

62. The idea of the "public Utility" of religion was everywhere during the revolutionary period. See James H. Hutson, *Religion and the Founding of the American Republic* (Hanover, N.H.: University Press of New England, 6th ed., 2002), 61-65.

63. Heman Lincoln, speech, December, 26, 1820, in *Journal of Debates and Proceedings in the Massachusetts Constitutional Convention 1820-1821* (New York: DaCapo Press, 1970), 423; for the equation of religion and the militia, see "Defence of the Third Article," in *The Christian Examiner and General Review* 13 (January 1833), 353.

64. Sandoz, *Political Sermons*, 109.

65. Isaac Backus, *A Fish Caught in his own Net* (Boston, 1768), in *Isaac Backus on Church, State, and Calvinism Pamphlets 1754-1789*, ed. William McLoughlin (Cambridge, Mass.: Harvard University Press,1968), 238.

66. [Theophilus Parsons], *An Answer to a Piece, entitled, 'An Appeal to the Impartial Public'* . . . (Salem, 1785), 19. RBSCD.

67. See, for example, Samuel Cooke, *A Sermon preached at Cambridge* . . . (Boston, 1770); Phillips Payson, *A Sermon preached before the Honorable Council* . . . (Boston, 1778); Simeon Howard, *A Sermon preached before the Honorable Council* . . . (Boston, 1780); *Pulpit of the American Revolution*, 179, 181, 340, 393; David Tappan, *A Sermon preached before his Excellency John Hancock* . . . (Boston, 1792); Stephen Peabody, *Sermon before the General Court of New Hampshire* (Concord, 1797); Sandoz, *Political Sermons*, 1118, 1121, 1336; Thomas Stone, *A Sermon Preached before his Excellency Samuel Huntington* . . . *May 10, 1792*, 29. Evans microfiche, 24820, Library of Congress. The practice began at least as early as 1730, in which year Ebenezer Gay asserted that "Rulers are political Fathers of their People" and that "they are Fathers of their Countries." Gay, *The Duty of People*, 16, 25.

68. Israel Evans, *A Sermon, Delivered at Concord* . . . *at the Annual Election* (Concord, N.H., 1791), in Sandoz, *Political Sermons*, 1070.

69. Thomas Curry, *The First Freedoms: Church and State in America to the Passage of the First Amendment* (New York: Oxford University Press, 1986), 163-92.

70. John Leland, *The Rights of Conscience Inalienable* (New London, [1791]), in Sandoz, *Political Sermons*, 1091.

71. Curry, *First Freedoms*, 134-58.

72. *The Constitution of the Presbyterian Church of the United States of America* (Philadelphia, 1955), 67.

73. Curry, *First Freedoms*, 190.

74. Isaac Backus, *An Appeal to the Public for Religious Liberty* (Boston, 1773), in McLoughlin, *Isaac Backus*, 323.

75. Memorial to the Massachusetts Provincial Congress, December 2, 1774 , in Alvin Hovey, *A Memoir of the Life and Times of the Rev. Isaac Backus* (New York: DaCapo Press, 1972), 217.

76. David Parsons, *A Sermon preached before His Excellency John Hancock* . . . (Boston: Adams and Nourse, 1788), 12-13. RBSCD.

77. Andrew Lee, *A Sermon, preached before His Excellency Samuel Huntington* (Hartford: Hudson and Goodwin, 1795), 16-17. Evans microfiche, 28957, Library of

Congress.

78. Matthias Burnet, *An Election Sermon, preached at Hartford . . .* (Hartford: Hudson and Goodwin, 1803), 22. Evans microfiche (Shaw-Shoemaker continuation), 3919, Library of Congress.

79. For the Baptists' support of these positions, see Lucy Warfield Wilkinson, "Early Baptists in Washington, D.C.," *Records of the Columbia Historical Society,* 29-30, (Washington, 1928), 215-16; William G. McLoughlin, *Isaac Backus and the American Pietistic Tradition* (Boston: Little, Brown, 1967), 149-50; Curry, *First Freedoms,* 190.

80. McLoughlin, *Isaac Backus,* 191.

81. John Mitchell Mason, *The Voice of Warning, to Christians, on the Ensuing Election of A President of the United States* (New York, 1800); Sandoz, *Political Sermons,* 1471.

82. See James H. Hutson, "Thomas Jefferson's Letter to the Danbury Baptists: A Controversy Rejoined," *William and Mary Quarterly* 56, no. 4 (October 1999): 787.

83. *Constitution of the American Home Missionary Society . . . Held in the City of New-York, May 10, 1826* (New York, 1826), 73.

84. Daniel Dreisbach, ed., *Religion and Politics in the Early Republic* (Lexington: University of Kentucky Press, 1996), 40.

85. Thomas Buckley, "After Disestablishment: Thomas Jefferson's Wall of Separation in Antebellum Virginia," *Journal of Southern History* 61, no. 3 (August 1995): 462.

86. Everett O. Alldredge, *Centennial History of the First Congregational United Church of Christ, Washington, D.C., 1865-1965* (Baltimore, 1965), 10.

87. *Tanakh: The Holy Scriptures: The New JPS Translation* (Philadelphia: The Jewish Publication Society, 1985), 725. Compare to the 1941 JPS edition: "And kings shall be thy foster-fathers, And their queens thy nursing mothers," 539.

88. Walter Brueggemann, *Isaiah 40-66* (Louisville, Ky.: Westminster John Knox Press, 1998), 117–19.

89. John T. McNeill, ed., Ford Lewis Battle, tr., *Institutes of the Christian Religion* (Philadelphia: Westminister Press, 1960), vol. 2, 490.

90. John F. A. Sawyer, *The Fifth Gospel Isaiah in the History of Christianity* (Cambridge: Cambridge University Press, 1996).

91. Jay Fliegelman, *Prodigals and Pilgrims: The American Revolution against Patriarchal Authority 1750-1800* (Cambridge: Cambridge University Press, 1982), 267.

92. Aaron Wildavsky, *The Nursing Father Moses as a Political Leader* (University: University of Alabama Press, 1984), 57-58. Another recent volume that also focuses on political leadership to the exclusion of state-church relations and that displays no curiosity about Isaiah 49:23, its history, or its theological dimensions, is Benjamin L. Price, *Nursing Fathers: American Colonists' Conception of English Protestant Kingship 1688-1776* (Lanham, Md.; Rowman & Littlefield, 1999).

Chapter 3

Rights as Moral Powers: The Founders and the French Connection

In recent decades French social historians—members of the so-called Annales School—have been widely read in the United States. Their influence is evident in many areas of American scholarship, especially in the writing of the history of colonial America.[1] French legal historians, on the other hand, are virtually unknown in this country. Dealing with a legal order radically different from the Anglo-American system, their work is rarely relevant to the problems that interest American scholars.

The one French legal historian who has come to the attention of American writers in recent years is Michel Villey (d.1990).[2] Villey's specialty was Roman law, on which he wrote prolifically during a long academic career at the University of Strasbourg and later at the Sorbonne.[3] His particular interest was the Roman definition of right (*jus*) and the evolution of the concept from the time of Gaius to Grotius, from imperial Rome to seventeenth-century Europe. Villey had only a passing acquaintance with the jurisprudence of the United States and never tried to fit his ideas into an American context. Those ideas are, nevertheless, applicable to issues in American legal history. It is the argument of this chapter that Villey's theories can correct a major misconception about the development of rights in this country and can offer new insights into the meaning of rights as used during the Founding Period.

One theme—complaint might be a better word—runs through Villey's writings: lawyers in their professional capacity are inhospitable to history. The French legal mind, as Villey described it, is ahistorical in the sense that it takes fundamental concepts as it finds them and is not inquisitive about the extent to which they may have changed over time. Rights are approached in this spirit, a point Villey illustrated by citing the eminent law school dean, Gabriel Le Bras, who asserted in 1953 that the definition of a right then current in France was "as old as Adam and Eve."[4] Villey mentioned other French scholars who claimed that the understanding of a right had not changed since "cuneiform" times.[5] French law itself assumed the static character of a right, for Villey pointed to a right called the "proprieté à la Romaine,"[6] whose name presumed that it had existed since the days of Caesar Augustus.

Villey vigorously contested this assumption that the definition of a right was changeless. Although the Romans and their successors used the term *jus* (right) profusely, Villey insisted that a "modern" definition of a right was not articulated in Europe until the fourteenth century and did not obtain a significant following until well into the seventeenth century. As a result, Villey argued that for more than a millennium and a half of the Christian era *jus* (right) meant something far different than it does today. So much, then, for Adam and Eve and the immutability of right.

The attitude of American students of rights is similar to that which Villey encountered among his countrymen. Americans, no less than the French, consider the concept of a right as immutably embedded in their history. They assume that the people who stepped off the *Mayflower* and the *Susan Constant* brought with them the idea of a right and understood the concept much as we do today. In a typical scholarly assessment two constitutional experts claimed in 1987 that "from the beginning, it seems, the language of America has been the language of rights";[7] in 1991 a government commission took the same position, boasting that "America has always been about rights,"[8] rights which another scholar—in the manner of Dean Le Bras—claimed in 1992 to be links in an "indissoluble chain of liberty that stretched back to ancient Greece and continued through the Roman Republic . . . to the thirteen colonies."[9]

In affirming the immutability of rights, American scholars seem to have been influenced by the authority of the leaders of the Revolution who from 1764 onward aggressively asserted that American rights had descended to their countrymen intact from the remote reaches of English history through the first settlers of the colonies. Revolutionary leaders insisted, even when they knew that the early charters mentioned only liberties and privileges, that their ancestors had carried with them documents that put them in "full Possession of the Rights of Englishmen."[10] "By removing themselves hither," a patriot declared in 1768, the first settlers "brought with them every right which they could or ought to have enjoyed had they abided in England."[11] Political parsons went even further and assured their flocks that their rights could be traced back to apostolic times (if not to Adam and Eve), since St. Paul was a "strong advocate for the just rights of manhood."[12] By making these assertions the revolutionary leaders were initiating a well-honed strategy, practiced by English popular leaders from the reign of the Stuarts onward, of enhancing the status of rights—even freshly minted ones—by investing them with great antiquity.[13] In accepting such claims for the immutability of rights, modern American scholars have unwittingly passed off patriot propaganda for historical fact.

A recently published volume of essays, *The Bill of Rights and the States*, is a striking example of the American scholar's penchant for attributing rights to distant generations. The first settlers of South Carolina are said to have received "specific rights" from Charles II's charter of 1663,[14] yet an inspection of that charter reveals that the term rights does not appear. Similarly, North Carolinians are said to have obtained "certain individual rights" from the Fundamental Constitutions of Carolina of 1669,[15] yet, once again, an inspection of that instrument does not disclose the presence of the term rights. A similar claim is made for the Georgia charter of 1732—that it set forth the "general rights" of the colonists[16]—and it is equally without substance. The southern charters are not the only early documents on which rights are boldly superimposed. The preamble to a 1650 Connecticut legal code is called a "Declaration of Rights"; when the said "Declaration" is read, it is found to contain no mention of the term rights.[17]

Uncomfortable, perhaps, with these casual ascriptions of rights to the first generation of Americans, A. E. Dick Howard in an introductory essay to *The Bill of Rights and the States* enclosed the rights of Englishmen in quotation marks, when describing what appeared to be libertarian language in the early colonial charters.[18] Professor Howard's caution seems well advised, for the existence of anything approaching the contemporary concept of a right is difficult to document in early America. Benjamin F. Wright, for example, found rights "very rarely" discussed in the seventeenth century.[19] Lawrence Leder observed that seventeenth-century Americans did not "catalog" their rights.[20] Although John Phillip Reid took issue with Leder's statement, he himself called attention to the "vagueness" of the talk about rights in colonial America.[21]

The current presumption that the idea of a right was an unchanging feature of American society "from the beginning" conflicts with evidence that, at the dawn of American history, a "modern" understanding of rights was absent or, at best, inchoate. Villey found the same situation in tracing the history of rights in Europe. Is this a coincidence or did the French scholar discover a model that may be relevant to the development of rights in America? Further commending Villey's work to the attention of American scholars is the fact that the concept of a right actually current in the first decades of seventeenth-century America was a modified version of the "old" definition of right which, Villey contends, dominated European thought from the Roman Empire to the Age of Discovery.

Villey asserts that Western civilization has known only two conceptions of a right. One was classical natural right (*"droit natural classique"*) which he also called objective right (*"droit objectif"*). Rooted in Aristotle and refined by the lawyers of imperial Rome, classical natural right maintained its ascendancy over the European mind for centuries and began to lose its grip only in the seventeenth century when it was challenged by its modern successor—subjective right (*"droit subjectif"*). According to Villey, subjective right is the "master word" of modern judicial thought, a concept even more fundamental to modern jurisprudence than positivism.[22] Subjective right, Villey contends, is what contemporary writers have in mind when they project the concept of a right back across the centuries to create the illusion of the unchangeable meaning of a right in Western history.

How do classical natural right and subjective right differ? Villey explained that when the Romans and their successors used the term right (*jus*), they meant, in the broad sense, the just—*"la res justa, l'objectum justitiae, l'id quom justum est."*[23] The specific meaning of the term stemmed, Villey asserted, from the classical world's view of what was "natural." The Greeks and Romans believed that civil society itself was "natural" and that man was "naturally social and even political." A right, therefore, was a "social phenomenon," which must be discerned in the complex web of relationships between people.[24] The good society would "give to everyone his right." This phrase, a translation of Ulpian's famous dictum, *suum jus cuique tribuere*, Villey regarded as a key to understanding classical natural right.[25] To give someone his right (*suum jus*) meant in the classical world to give him "what he deserved," "his due."[26] What was due to the individual in society? His just share (*"le part juste," "le bon partage"*).[27] Here, said Villey, was the meaning of classical natural right: a just or fair share for every individual of society's benefits and burdens.

Who, in the classical world, was the arbiter of right? Who decided what each individual's just share was? The task, Villey explained, fell, not to philosophers and "*theoriciens in chambre*," but to the courts, where judges in consultation with lawyers—"*practiciens (ou jurisprudents)*"—reached their decisions on a case-by-case basis.[28] Classical natural right, Villey argued, was fluid, was "*souplesse meme*,"[29] and, therefore, could be ascertained only by the consideration of the various and peculiar facts at issue in each case. Judges could not know the "just solution . . . in advance," for that solution was "mutable, as it ought to be if it results from the nature of changing things."[30]

An unusual feature of classical natural right, as described by Professor Villey, was its association with burdens. The modern mind does not consider rights as imposing burdens on their possessors, but Villey insisted that what he variously called "*charges*" and "*peines*" were important aspects of classical natural right.[31] Villey did not mean to belittle the importance of benefits—for the Romans always the most important feature of right. A plot of land, for example, could confer several different benefits, all of which could be described as rights (*jura*): a right of usage, of passage, of habitation, of drawing water, and so on. But the same piece of property might also be encumbered by the burdensome right of not raising the height of an existing structure (*jus non altius tollendi*).[32] The *jus civitatis* was another burdensome right, for it obliged its possessor to perform military service.[33]

Whether burdensome or beneficial, a right, Villey asserted, was considered by classical jurisprudence as a "*res incorporales*." Rights were "things, institutions, which owed an artificial existence to the invention of jurists."[34] As a "thing, an object," more precisely, a share or "fraction" of a thing or object,[35] a classical right was by definition "objective." It was objective in another sense as well, being a product, Villey explained, of the Aristotelian world view that held that "Nature" or "universal reason" imposed on all animate and inanimate beings a just and harmonious order. Under these circumstances the just share of an individual in a given society was objectively established and the "objective natural right" of each person could be discerned by the human mind.[36] Classical natural right was objective, then, in a double sense: it was a share of an object and a standard fixed by a superintending wisdom.

One of the most controversial aspects of Villey's work was his theory about the sudden appearance ("*eclosion*") in the fourteenth century of subjective right.

Villey asserted that subjective right was invented by the Franciscan monk and philosopher, William of Ockham, who enunciated the concept in his book, *Opus nonaginta dierum* (1332).[37] The occasion for Ockham's foray into jurisprudence was the famous quarrel over Franciscan poverty. St. Francis founded his order on a commitment to poverty, but as its reputation grew, its admirers showered it with gifts of real estate, money, and so on. A sympathetic papacy devised a legal fiction that permitted the Franciscans to retain both their gifts and their vows. According to papal lawyers, the Franciscans merely had the use of the property donated to their order; the "*jus, proprietas* [and] *dominium*" over their goods was vested in the Bishop of Rome.[38] An opponent of the Franciscans, Pope John XXII refused to abide by his predecessors' accommodations with the order and early in the fourteenth century "undertook to generalize the regime of property and to impose it on the Franciscan community";[39] that is, John XXII attempted to compel the order to admit that it had property rights in the goods it administered. The Franciscans took refuge in the old "artifice" that they had the use of, but not the right to, property. Their spokesman, Ockham, gave the formula a new twist, however, by redefining right to show its incompatibility with his order's ideals. A right, Ockham announced, was a power ("*potesta licita*")[40] and power, however defined, was anathema to the Franciscans.

Right as power! Here, according to Villey, was a "Copernican moment" in jurisprudence,[41] the advent of a new way of thinking which eventually carried all before it. The Romans, Villey observed, "naturally knew the idea of powers of the individual, but without giving to these powers a juridical quality, without calling powers rights."[42] By uniting the two concepts Ockham created subjective right. This new species of right was subjective because power, its essence, was part of the individual subject. Villey hammered this point home. Subjective rights were "qualities," "faculties," of the individual, "the forces which radiated through his being."[43] A subjective right was a power "drawn from the being itself of the subject, from his essence, from his nature." A subjective right was an "attribute of the subject," a power that "appertained to his essence, that was inherent in him."[44] The difference between classical or objective natural right and the new subjective right was stark: the former was the share of some external object; the latter was power inherent in an individual.

The source of the individual's power, Ockham assumed as a matter of course (he was, after all, a member of a religious order), was God. For Ockham and thinkers of his era subjective right was "an indication of the absolute power of God which was partially conferred upon man, created in his image."[45] Therefore, subjective right, as understood by its creators, was grounded in religion, although "its dependence . . . on Christian morality" was a fact, Villey ironically noted, that the "majority of our contemporaries had difficulty acknowledging."[46]

Villey considered Ockham the obvious candidate to introduce a new concept of rights because of his prowess as a philosopher. Villey was guided by the principle that the idea of a right was the creation of philosophy and that philosophy inexorably invaded the law. As a product of Aristotelianism, classical natural right flourished as long as its philosophical underpinnings held firm. These crumbled under the onslaught of the *"via moderna,"* the new philosophical system of nominalism which Ockham helped to create. Nominalism rejected the "universal" categories of Aristotelianism and asserted that reality could only be found in individuals.[47] The emphasis on individuals and the power inherent in them led to the new definition of right. Nominalism became, then, "the mother of subjective right."[48] "All philosophy," Villey explained, "is *'tentaculaire'* . . . its spirit obliges [mankind] to see the whole world from its perspective. It was inevitable that modern individualistic philosophy would impose its definition of right, not merely by destroying the old classical concept of right, but by replacing it."[49]

The process of replacement, if sure, was, nevertheless, slow. Ockham's formulations were too recondite for the ordinary jurist and for more than two centuries the new concept of subjective right, like the mystery of an ancient cult, was the intellectual property of a coterie of cognoscenti. From Ockham, Villey traced the new concept to the French nominalists, Pierre d'Ailly and Jean Gerson. He regarded Gerson as a particularly important figure, who not only furnished a definition of subjective right "en forme" in his book, *De Vita Spirituli Animae* (1402)—*"jus est facultas seu potestas propinqua conveniens alicui"*—but also served as a link to the Spanish scholastics of the sixteenth century whose importance in the formation and transmission of the idea of a subjective right could not, in Villey's opinion, be overestimated.[50]

The sixteenth century, Villey reminded us, was the "era of Spanish preponderance,"[51] a period in Europe when the influence of Spain's thinkers matched the power of its kings. The authority of the Spanish scholastics (by whom Villey meant the Dominicans Vitoria, DeSoto, and Banez and the Jesuits Vasquez, Molina, and Suarez) imposed itself with "particular force" in Germany and the Netherlands, where even staunch Calvinists "pillaged" their writings.[52]

According to Villey, the new concept of subjective right became the "doctrine courante" of the Spanish school,[53] and he quoted statements like Vitoria's "*jus est potestas*" to prove his point.[54] Yet the Spaniards continued to use the old vocabulary of classical natural right and integrated the old and new ideas of right so awkwardly that even the works of luminaries like Suarez, who called a right a "moral power,"[55] conveyed the impression of being "an indigested and incoherent mixture, the product of a mediocre eclecticism."[56]

Villey argued that the "honor" of formulating the first thoroughly modern definition of subjective right, stripped of all residues of Roman law, was reserved for Thomas Hobbes whose major works—*Elements of Law, De Cive*, and *Leviathan*—appeared in the mid-seventeenth century. In common with all who, from Ockham forward, had cultivated the concept of subjective right, Hobbes was a philosopher. His "great definitions in form" of subjective right, which were influenced by the Spanish scholastics,[57] appeared in all of his principal writing, as, for example, in *Leviathan*: a right "is the liberty each man hath to use his own power, as he will himself, for the preservation of his nature."[58] Hobbes's lucid, uncompromising definitions "sealed the decisive victory" of subjective right over its venerable rival, classical natural right. "Philosophy had," Villey concluded, "as it ordinarily does, preceded the jurists on the revolutionary path."[59]

Whatever his strengths as an expositor of philosophical ideas, Hobbes was a poor proselytizer for subjective right because his reputed atheism repelled potential readers (this was especially true in America). Whether because of Hobbes' reputation or an innate conservatism, large numbers of "jurists" recoiled at the introduction of the new concept of a right into the law. Villey describes this recalcitrant majority as "technicians of the judicial art," traditionalists, and ordinary members of the bar. "These jurists," he said, "resisted for a long time, being essentially attached to tradition. A good part of the authors of the *Ancien Regime* continued to reproduce and apply Roman law and customs without transforming them."[60] Subjective right gained a foothold in the law only in the seventeenth century through the agency of attorneys "capable of a certain culture," lawyers with intellectual interests operating as "philosophical jurists, publicists, and professors of legal philosophy."[61] Foremost among this group was the Dutch master, Hugo Grotius, saluted by Villey as "one of the most efficacious mediators that history has ever known between a philosophical vision of the world and the science of law."[62]

In his great work, *De Jure Belli ac Pacis* (1625), Grotius offered a definition of subjective right as a moral power, a *"qualitas moralis personae,"* a *"potestas . . . in se"* and a *"potestas . . . in alios."*[63] Yet he also paraphrased Ulpian's classic dictum about right—"the Obligation of rendering what is owing"[64]—and reverted to the old definition of right as the just. Grotius, in fact, employed so many elements of classical natural right in his work that, like Suarez's writings which seem to have influenced him, his treatise was "not exempt from embarrassment and contradictions."[65] Therefore, Grotius could not, in Villey's judgment, be credited with conceiving "subjective right in a perfectly firm manner."[66] Only toward the end of the seventeenth century did Villey discover lawyers who were in "full possession of the idea of subjective right."[67]

Villey's energies seemed to flag as he reached the eighteenth century and he spent little time with familiar subjective rights publicists like Wolff and Burlamaqui. Villey saw subjective right gradually insinuating itself into the minds of the most stiff-necked traditionalists and finally "triumphing towards the end of the eighteenth century."[68] In his view a famous document like the French Declaration of the Rights of Man of 1789 testified to its ascendancy. "The rights of man," Villey claimed, "are precisely subjective rights."[69]

Reflecting on the victory of subjective rights, Villey observed that "the moderns had repudiated Right . . . and substituted the natural Rights of the individual."[70] Villey considered the distinction between *droit* (right) and *droits* (rights) as significant. He held that a speaker or author using the singular, right, meant classical, objective right, while the use of the plural, rights, indicated subjective rights. Although this rule frequently falls afoul of the vagaries of spelling in colonial America—one encounters "Ryght" and "rites" as well as right and rights—it can be a useful diagnostic tool.

Villey's argument for a medieval origin of the modern, subjective definition of a right has been accepted by scholars, although it received some criticism when it first appeared. In 1954, for example, the Italian jurist, Giovanni Pugliese, asserted that the Romans had, in fact, possessed a concept of subjective right,[71] and a few years later the distinguished German Romanist, Helmut Coing, professed to have found the word *jus* in a "subjective sense" in certain Roman legal texts. Nevertheless, Coing endorsed Villey's view that "subjective right played for classical Roman jurisprudence no decisive role."[72] Other critics took issue with Villey for identifying William of Ockham as the inventor of subjective right. Reinhold Schwartz argued that the credit for the first clear formulation of the concept should go to Jean Gerson,[73] whom Villey regarded as no more than a conduit for Ockham's ideas. Brian Tierney, on the other hand, believed that subjective right preceded Ockham and that it could be found as far back as the twelfth century in the writings of canonists like Rufinus and Huguccio.[74]

With the exception of Thomas Hobbes and John Locke (to whom Villey devoted some attention), all of the protagonists of subjective right who appeared in his pages were continental Europeans. So, too, with a few exceptions, are the commentators on and critics of his work. The term subjective right itself was continental, having been coined by the German jurists Windscheid, Puchta, and Savigny in the nineteenth century.[75] How, then, does subjective right relate to Great Britain and, by extension, to America with their systems of common law jurisprudence, so different from the civil law context in which subjective right took root on the continent? A British lawyer, Frederick Lawson, claimed that the term subjective right would be incomprehensible to most practitioners in his country. "An ordinary English jurist," he wrote in 1959, "would not know whereof one spoke if you would use in a conversation with him the technical expressions (*fachausdrucke*) objective right and subjective right. Even if one would explain to him their significance, it would still be very difficult for him to understand why right was designated as objective on the one hand and subjective on the other."[76] Commenting on Lawson's observations, a German specialist, Konrad Zweigert, stressed the "*bewegende Nichtverstehenwollen*" of the common law as compared to the "*luziden Dogmengeschichte*" of subjective right on the continent.[77] The resistance of British legal discourse to the term subjective right does not mean, however, that the idea which it represented was absent in England nor does it mean that Villey's thesis was inapplicable in an English context. Villey's ideas appear, in fact, to "work" as well in England as they do on the continent, as an examination of writings as far back as Bracton will indicate.

In Bracton's great treatise, *On the Laws and Customs of England*, compiled in the middle of the thirteenth century, there is no sign of an acquaintance with a modern, subjective definition of right. No surprise this, since Bracton was a civilian, deeply immersed in Roman law, who introduced "almost five hundred different sections of the Digest and Code" into his opus.[78] For Bracton, right meant justice, the characteristic feature, in Villey's view, of classical natural right. "Right is thus called justice," Bracton wrote, "because all right is included in justice. Right likewise, is derived for justice and it has various significations." One of Bracton's significations, lifted directly from Roman sources, equated right with the process of law; right, he explained, could mean a court ("the place where justice is awarded"), actions at law, or various kinds of law—civil, natural, or praetorian. Bracton quoted Celsus's definition of a right, "*ars boni et aequi*," as well as Ulpian's even more celebrated definition, "*jus suum cuique tribuere.*"[79] By using this phrase Bracton appeared to indicate that he understood right in the way Villey considered to be its purest classical form: an individual's "*juste partage*," his just share.

Bracton's reliance on Roman sources can be misleading, however, for early English lawyers did not appropriate wholesale the classical concept of right; they developed a distinctive understanding of the term which revealed itself in the operation of the *breve de recto*, the writ of right. The writ of right was a "cluster" or "group" of writs—the writ of right patent, the *praecipe in capite*, and the little writ of right.[80] Of "great antiquity"—in use at least two centuries before Bracton wrote—the writ of right served to "originate actions for land in a feudal court."[81] Although a writ of right could relate to all kinds of property, it was associated in the English mind with land to the virtual exclusion of all else. Writs of right were "orders to do justice."[82] They enjoined courts, feudal and royal, to assure that justice was done between rival claimants to land. Typically, each claimant would assert that his right—by which he meant his title—to a piece of land was superior to his adversary's. The writ of right required the court to decide "*quis habeat major jus*" in the disputed land.[83] The successful claimant would obtain ownership and usually, although not always, possession (*seisin*) of the land. A right, then, in medieval England was a title which, if validated by a court, conferred ownership of land.[84]

English right was similar in many ways to classical natural right as formulated on the Continent. In both places courts defined right on a case-by-case basis. In both places right was considered the handmaiden of justice. And in both places right was held to involve incorporeal things—titles to land, according to Holdsworth, being viewed in medieval England as incorporeal.[85] The principal difference between the two concepts was the severe constriction of the meaning of right in England, where it was almost exclusively identified with real property. Right in medieval England can be considered, therefore, as a derivative of classical natural right, differentiated by its real property bias.

Right underwent little change in meaning from Bracton's time to the reign of the Tudors. Examination of the law dictionaries which began to be published in sixteenth-century England illustrates this point. The earliest English law dictionary, if St. Germain's *Doctor and Student* is excluded from consideration, was John Rastell's *Termes de la Ley*, published in law French in 1527. The *Termes de la Ley* enjoyed remarkable popularity, being reprinted with occasional changes in title seven times in the sixteenth century,[86] at least twelve times in the seventeenth century, and appearing in a new edition as late as 1812. Rastell defined right (he used the French word *droit* for more than a century and a half) by reference to the writ of right. Through his 1575 edition, right was described as a writ that "lyethe where a man claymeth any landes or tenements and aledgeth no title but only that one of his auncestoures in olde tyme was seized." Rastell offered a new definition in 1579 modelled on the writ of right *praecipe*, which asserted, as a basis for litigation, that land had been wrongfully taken.[87] Rastell now defined right as the "challenge or claime" of the victim to have the validity of his title upheld. This definition was expanded in 1624 with the addition of language for Coke's *Reports*. It was not altered thereafter.

The next important dictionary, John Cowell's *The Interpreter: or Booke Containing the Signification of Words*, was published in 1607 and, despite being burned at the order of the House of Commons for its alleged absolutist bias, was reissued three times during the seventeenth century. *The Interpreter* followed Rastell in defining right by reference to the writ of right, observing "whereas other writs in real actions, be only to recover the possession of land, or tenements in question . . . this aimeth to recover both the seisin . . . and also the propertie of the thing."[88]

The publication in 1628 of Sir Edward Coke's *Institutes of the Laws of England* had a major influence on the definition of right, not because the great lawyer changed the meaning of the term—he used without apology the traditional definition—but because Coke's treatise established an immediate authority over English lawyers who obediently quoted him when describing a right. Coke offered two definitions of a right. One asserted that a right could be considered not simply as a title to land but as "the estate in esse," a position that Coke's rival, Francis Bacon, had taken in his *Reading on the Statute of Uses* (1600).[89] More popular with legal writers was Coke's second definition: "*jus* or right, in general signification includeth not only a right for which a writ of rights doth lie, but also any title or claime, either by force of a Condition, Mortmaine or the like, for which no action is given by law, but only an entrie."[90] This definition was used with slight alteration by William Sheppard who "published something like an official law dictionary during the Protectorate,"[91] by Thomas Blount in his *Nomo-Lexikon* (1691), and in later editions of Cowell's *Interpreter*. In his *The Compleat Lawyer* (1651), Charles I's attorney general, William Noy, also used Cokean language in differentiating between "naked" and "cloathed" rights, perpetuating in the process the medieval distinction, which was becoming obsolete, between possession (*seisin*) and ownership. A "cloathed" right, Noy explained, combined ownership and possession of land; a "naked" right separated the two.[92] Coke had made the same distinction in his *Institutes*: "there is a *jus proprietatis*, a right of ownership, a *jus possessionis*, a right of *seisin* or possession and *jus proprietatis* and *possessionis*, a right of both propertie and possession: and this is anciently called *jus duplicatum* or *Droit droit*." In a less pedantic passage Coke explained, simply, that "every right is a title . . . and signifieth the means whereby a man commeth to land."[93]

In the hands of the House of Commons this venerable definition of right underwent a remarkable transformation during the reign of James I, so remarkable that it is no exaggeration to say that the parliamentarians confronting the first Stuart king invented "civil" rights just as deliberately as Ockham, in Villey's view, invented subjective right and that they did it in a "tentacular" way by extending the reach of the real property concept of right to enclose in its protective grasp various endangered elements in English public life.

James I ascended the English throne in 1603 with exaggerated ideas of royal power and disdain for the political aspirations of his subjects. In his view, popular freedoms were nothing more than revocable royal favors. As James informed his first Parliament in 1604, the people "derived all matters of privilege from him and by his grant," an opinion the king repeated in 1621, lecturing Parliament in that year that "your privileges were derived from the grace and permission of our ancestors and us."[94] The Stuarts and their spokesmen took this position for as long as they ruled. Charles I's chaplain claimed in 1637 that since kings gave the people their liberties, they could withdraw them at will. Robert Filmer described parliamentary privileges as "liberties of grace from the king" that were "derived from the bounty or indulgence of the monarch."[95] After the Restoration royalist writers, following Filmer, argued that "all the liberties of Englishmen, owed their being to the will of the King [who] might revoke any of them."[96] In James II's reign Robert Brady's historical studies purported to prove that "all the Liberties and Privileges the people can pretend to were the Grants and Concessions of the

King," nothing more than a "pure gift" of the monarch, as one of Brady's cronies argued.[97]

Parliament's response to Stuart efforts to trivialize popular liberties was consistent throughout the seventeenth century. James I's first House of Commons considered it imperative to respond to the new King's denigration of the country's freedoms and staked out the popular position in its famous "Form of Apology and Satisfaction" of June 20, 1604. Parliament's strategy was simple: it denied that the King had any control over popular freedoms and asserted that, on the contrary, Englishmen owned their liberties and privileges by a right or title as incontestably as they owned their lands. "We must truly avouch," the Apology asserted, "that our privileges and liberties are our right and due inheritance, no less than our very lands and goods."[98]   The same sentiments were expressed in subsequent Parliaments. In 1621, for example, in response to James's contention that popular liberties were royal favors, Sir Randolph Crew responded: "We have our privileges of right not of grace. This [James's claim] were to make us from freeholders of inheritance to make us Coppiholders ad placitum, or rather, tenants at will."[99] Extending the idea of titled ownership of land to such incorporeal matters as were at issue between the king and Parliament in 1604—the members' exemption from imprisonment during sessions of Parliament, their liberty to speak freely in Parliament—created a wholly new category of non-property rights involving freedom to conduct civic affairs. It is in this sense that Parliament can be said to have invented civil rights in 1604. Challenged by an aggressive monarch, the members appropriated the most invulnerable tenure conceivable to the seventeenth-century mind—ownership of land by good title—to protect their liberties. James I's confrontational tactics sowed dragons' teeth, for if Parliament could assimilate to land activities as dissimilar as speech and criminal justice there was no limit to what might be considered—to the detriment of monarchical pretensions—as a right. The new understanding of right, strengthened in constant combat with the Stuarts, would in the course of the seventeenth century become known by the familiar term "rights of Englishmen," conveying the idea of the impregnability of rights, owned and possessed, like choice lands, by an unassailable title.

It is necessary to insist on the novelty, the inventiveness, of Parliament's actions of 1604 in extending rights of land ownership to the political and civic arenas. Despite the assertions of the seventeenth-century English popular leaders of the antiquity of the various rights they were claiming, before 1604 the use of the term right seems to have been confined to discussions about and litigation over land. The published proceedings of Elizabeth I's parliaments reveal, for example, the absence of the term right from political discourse.[100] The members repeatedly requested that the queen respect their liberties and privileges, not their rights. Liberty was the traditional English word for popular "freedoms." Liberty, however, had liabilities as a weapon in a forensic contest with arbitrary rulers. In medieval England it had been enjoyed by groups, "organized collectivities" like towns and guilds.[101] Medieval liberties were exclusive and discriminatory. Groups who possessed them, always as a favor from the monarch, used them to collect tolls from their fellow subjects or to monopolize certain trades and industries to the exclusion of other Englishmen. By James I's time liberties were being conceived individualistically,[102] but, as Coke himself admitted, they were still considered as gifts from the monarch.[103] Parliament was sensitive to this fact and, lest it be considered as begging the king for favors when its speaker petitioned the monarch at the beginning of each session for accustomed liberties and privileges, it affirmed in the Apology of 1604 "that our making of request in the entrance of Parliament to enjoy our privilege is an act only of manners, and doth weaken our right no more than our suing the King for our lands by petition."[104]

Liberties and privileges remained well into the seventeenth century the terms of choice for Englishmen discussing their freedoms. The process by which right eventually displaced these words is clear enough. In debates on impositions in 1610, the House of Commons used the phrase "the fundamental right of the liberty of Parliament"[105] to free speech, which in the context of the recent expansion of the term meant Parliament's ownership of the liberty of speech. As the seventeenth century progressed such locutions began to seem tautological, and in the interest of economy of speech, liberty dropped out in favor of the stronger term right, just as over the course of the century possessive adjectives disappeared from phrases like "God his Throne on earth," used by James I in his *Trew Law of Free Monarchies* (1598)[106] and yielded to apostrophes.

Right, it must be emphasized, achieved no easy or immediate ascendancy, as the drafting of the Petition of Right of 1628 demonstrates. Coke and many of his allies who drafted the Petition had been active in the Parliament of 1604 but preferred to use older, more familiar language in making their case against Charles I. According to Conrad Russell, the Parliament of 1628 displayed an "obsessive concentration on issues of liberties," not rights.[107] One contemporary called the Petition of Right "the ancientist . . . way" of dealing with the monarch[108] and claimed that such petitions were at least as old as Magna Carta. The Petition of Right was a demand by Parliament for justice from the king. The Petition recited the laws of England as they related to the issues in dispute between the king and the people (taxation, the administration of criminal justice and quartering), gave examples of royal malfeasance, and demanded that the laws be obeyed. The king's answer, "let right be done as is desired," conveyed his intention to do "justice," as James I promised in reply to a petition of right in 1604.[109] Justice would be done by royal obedience to the law. A government of law would be established (or reestablished) and the benefits conferred by the rule of law would be considered as the people's "rights." By presenting rights as benefits of the rule of law or as the law itself, Parliament gave the Petition of Right a strong classical flavor, for it employed one of the principal Roman definitions of rights: right as law.

The Petition of Right was a temporary accommodation between the king and Parliament which failed to contain the tensions that burst into civil war in the 1640s. The Civil War is considered by scholars to be a boom time for rights;[110] a few even argue that it was the occasion for the introduction into England by the Levellers of the concept of subjective right.[111] It is true that rights as titled ownership—or as the rights of Englishmen, as they were being called by the 1640s—flourished during the Civil War but the role of the Levellers as promoters of subjective right becomes questionable under close scrutiny. The Levellers' objective, as their spokesmen indicated at the Putney Debates in the fall of 1647, was to secure the people's "birthrights." We intend, said Sexby, "to recover our birthright and privileges as Englishmen. There are many thousands of us soldiers that have ventured our lives; we have had little propriety in the kingdom as to our estates, yet we have had a birthright."[112] Birthrights or "native rights," as they were also called during the Civil War, were not subjective rights; rather they were a special kind of title by which land was owned. An Elizabethan case, *Willons v. Berkeley*, had given land acquired by birth or inheritance specific immunity from royal intervention[113] and, therefore, these titles enjoyed a prized status. By emphasizing birthrights, popular leaders during the Civil War were trying to invest their claims to a wider suffrage and to forms of participation in the political process with strength superior to ordinary rights. Also unfavorable to claims that Levellers were innovators in rights was the tendency of leaders like John Lilburne to present his group's demands as claims for liberties, not rights.[114] Richard Tuck has argued, in addition, that the Levellers had an ambivalent attitude toward rights, taking at times the medieval view that rights, like liberties, were "collective."[115]

Tuck has pointed out that Grotius, in Villey's view the principal seventeenth-century conduit for subjective rights, was read by "many of the more important radical theorists" during the Civil War[116] and that these radicals may have given England its first taste of the new theory of rights. Grotius asserted that the individual could exert his subjective right, the power inherent in him, over external objects as well as over his own person. Self-empowerment could manifest itself in the free choice of religion, and it is possible, as a few commentators have asserted, that the claims for the right to religious freedom, made by the Levellers and other dissenting groups, can be considered as expressions of subjective right. This question requires much more study, but what we do know is that, after the Restoration, England was fatigued by what it regarded as the tiresome agitation by fringe groups for religious rights. It was not until the close of the century that Locke, a philosopher and apostle of subjective right, obtained a respectful hearing from a broad audience for the concept, serving thereby as the channel through which subjective right passed in England from the world of philosophy to the world of law and public affairs. Locke's role is consistent with developments on the continent where Villey discerned toward the end of the seventeenth-century subjective right migrating from philosophy to law and acquiring among lawyers champions such as Pufendorf, Feltman, and Thomasius.[117]

The new, modern concept of subjective right was not instantly adopted by English statesmen. Consider, for example, the Bill of Rights of 1689. Save for the "right of the subjects to petition the King" and for Protestants to bear arms, there was little in that famous document concerning the exercise of power by individuals. The Bill of Rights resembled nothing so much as the Petition of Right of 1628; "many members," Lois Schwoerer explained, "intended it to be closely identified with that time honored device."[118] Like the Petition of Right, the Bill of Rights contained a list of illegal royal actions which Parliament enumerated for the purpose of "vindicating and asserting their ancient rights and liberties." On February 13, 1689, the Bill (at this time the Declaration) of Rights was presented to William and Mary along with the offer of the English crown. In accepting the crown, William declared, less explicitly than Charles I had done sixty years earlier but in words whose meaning could not be mistaken, that he "would preserve the nation's rights."[119] Since rights had been presented to the king as a list of violations of the law, preserving rights meant to William and his Parliament the observing of the law. In 1689, as in 1628, on important occasions rights could still be defined, without arousing objections, in the classical sense as benefits of the rule of law or as the law itself.

The Englishmen who settled North America during the first decades of the seventeenth century brought with them the mother country's understanding of right. They obviously had no acquaintance with the "modern" conception of subjective right, which appeared in England toward the end of the century. What is surprising is the minimal penetration in the colonies of the idea of right that appeared at the beginning of the century, the expanded notion of titled ownership. America lagged behind the mother country in acquiring the new rights vocabulary and, as a result, libertarian language in the colonies had an antiquated, even medieval quality.

This fact has been obscured by historians of the individual colonies who, in company with other twentieth-century historians, attribute to the first settlers modern concepts of rights. Historians of Virginia have been conspicuous offenders in this respect, motivated by a desire to establish a genealogy of rights that will connect settlers at Jamestown to Jefferson's generation. Thomas J. Wertenbaker contended that the first Virginia Company charter of 1606 was a beacon which Virginians followed "throughout the entire colonial period [as] they contended for all the rights of native Englishmen." Wertenbaker assailed Gates' Law of 1610 as being "in open violation of the rights guaranteed to the settlers in their charters" of 1606 and 1609.[120] Alexander Brown, who believed that "Give me liberty or give me death was the inspiration of our foundation as well as the battle cry of our Revolution" extolled the charter of 1609 for granting "liberal charter rights."[121] In fact, neither the charters of 1606 or 1609 mentioned the rights of the settlers of Virginia. The charters conferred upon the colonists merely "Liberties, Franchises, and Immunities,"[122] boilerplate language, borrowed from the numerous trading company charters issued by the English government in the late sixteenth and early seventeenth centuries. James I certainly did not consider that, in issuing charters to Englishmen departing for the New World, he was creating rights, for the "plain truth is," he informed his advisers, "we cannot with patience endure our subjects to use such anti-monarchical words to us concerning their liberties."[123] Just how fragile Virginia's freedoms were became apparent in James's policy toward the lottery which he gave the settlers the "Liberty and License" to establish in 1612. Nine years later the king arbitrarily abolished the lottery, demonstrating that in Virginia liberties were nothing more than revocable royal favors.[124]

A standard work, Richard Morton's *Colonial Virginia*, published in 1960, followed the lead of Brown and Wertenbaker. Morton described the "Great Charter of 1619," which authorized a representative assembly in Virginia, as conferring "all the rights of Englishmen,"[125] when, in fact, rights were not mentioned in the document; the members of the first assembly, July 31, 1619, thanked authorities in England, not for granting rights, but for extending "privileges and favours."[126] Morton then called attention to laws passed by the newly constituted Assembly, 1623-24, "to protect their [the peoples'] rights."[127] Rights were not mentioned in any of these statutes.

The term rights, it should be understood, was not absent from public discourse during the Virginia Company's tenure, 1607-1624. The third Virginia charter of 1612 stipulated that certain new investors should enjoy full benefits of membership in the Virginia Company and included "Right" in a list of "Interests . . . Profits and Commodities."[128] In the same spirit the first Massachusetts charter, issued a few years later, listed "Rightes" among an array of shareholders' benefits that included "Landes and Groundes, Soyles, Woods and Wood Grounds."[129] Here right was obviously being used in its old, narrow sense as a title to land. Virginia Company officials certainly understood the term in this way.[130] In 1617 Captain Samuel Argall pledged to support the inhabitants of Bermuda Hundred in a land dispute, assuring them that he would "not Infringe their rights."[131] On July 20, 1619, Governor George Yeardly wrote to a friend, expressing the hope that "I may not be wronged in that which is my deu and Ryght, I mean my Land of Weyonock."[132] And on April 6, 1626, the governor and Council of Virginia sent an address to the English Privy Council, thanking Charles I's government for recognizing the validity of the land titles which the settlers had purchased in good faith from the defunct Virginia Company, whose charter had been revoked two years earlier. Virginians rejoiced, the local authorities asserted, at "his majesties gratious assurance that every man should have his particular right preserved."[133]

From 1624 until the advent of the Civil War in England Virginia records reveal little, if any, use of the term rights. A sudden and modern sounding claim for rights appeared in a "Declaration" of April 5, 1647, in which the governor, Council, and House of Burgesses protested against rumors that Parliament intended to exclude Dutch merchants from Virginia and denounced proponents of the anti-Dutch laws as "Oppugners of our undoubted rights."[134] Edmund S.

Morgan's belief that Governor William Berkeley wrote this manifesto is plausible since Berkeley had been in England in the 1640s and would have been exposed to the rights talk that emerged during the Civil War.[135] An autocratic royalist, Berkeley was certainly no tribune of the people—the beneficiaries of the rights he was claiming would have been a coterie of big planters—and, when Virginia capitulated to parliamentary forces in 1652, he negotiated a settlement which granted the citizenry only "freedomes and priviledges."[136] Rights of the extended sort which Parliament began claiming in 1604 are encountered in 1653 in the acknowledgment by an acting governor of the "right of Assemblies in the free choice of a speaker."[137] The ancient real property definition of right appears in 1674 when a court ordered one Anthony Vauson to assign "all his rights" in an escheated estate to a certain Peter Starke.[138]

However defined, rights were infrequently asserted in Virginia before Bacon's Rebellion of 1676. That upheaval demonstrated how shallow the roots of rights were in the Old Dominion a century before the American Revolution. Bacon claimed to be seeking to establish the colony's "liberties,"[139] not rights, and in none of the literature generated by his followers is rights mentioned. Bacon's Rebellion, as Professor Morgan observed, produced "no revolutionary manifesto, not even any revolutionary slogans."[140] More striking still are the reports of the royal commissioners sent to Virginia in the wake of Bacon's Rebellion to investigate the causes and consequences of the turmoil. The commissioners visited all the counties in the colony and collected reports on the popular mood based on interviews with local officials. The citizens related numerous grievances, but in none of the reports is there any mention that rights had been violated.[141] It was as if the concept of rights had not yet entered popular consciousness.

Rights did not play a significantly greater role in seventeenth-century New England than they did in Virginia. New England was a network of towns in which a communitarian ethic based on shared religious beliefs prevailed. A society organized on these principles was inhospitable to the aggressive individualism of a rights-based culture. Rights, to be sure, were occasionally mentioned in the first decades of New England, especially in a celebrated legal code, the "Body of Liberties," written in 1641 by Nathaniel Ward. The Body of Liberties, or, to give it its correct name, "Coppie of the Liberties of the Massachusetts Collonie in New England," is exactly what it purports to be, a list of the liberties—the term is used repeatedly—of the citizens of Massachusetts to do everything from appealing a court decision to electing deputies to the legislature. A long instrument, consisting of ninety-eight sections, some with sub-sections of twelve articles, the "Coppie of Liberties" uses "Rites" just four times and explicitly subordinates rights to the more familiar term liberty; in the words of section 96, "the above specified rites, freedomes, Immunities, Authorities and priveledges, both Civil and Ecclesiastical are expressed only under the name and title of Liberties."[142]

New England's coolness to rights surfaced in the conflict with Dr. Robert Child in 1645. A Presbyterian, Child claimed that the Congregational establishment in Massachusetts was persecuting him because of a difference of opinion over religion. Like Governor Berkeley, Child borrowed from the Mother Country the Civil War rhetoric of rights to argue his case, claiming that "natural rights, as freeborne subjects of the English nation" were being violated by the intolerant Puritans."[143] The authorities in Boston rebuffed Child and drove him from the colony. Massachusetts then steeled itself in a policy of "doctrinaire intolerance."[144] The author of the Body of Liberties cheered the colony's officials on. Ward detested "polypiety" and railed against the "Toleration of divers Religions, or of one Religion in Segregant Shapes."[145] In the 1650s and 1660s Massachusetts displayed her contempt for the rights of minorities by hanging Quakers in the name of religious uniformity.

Arguments for rights occasionally cropped up in the political arena after the restoration of Charles II. On June 10, 1661, a committee of the Massachusetts General Court, responding to reports that the new king meant to alter its government, used right in the old sense of the rule of law; the charter of 1629, claimed the assembly, granted in good faith by Charles I and still in force, guaranteed them immunity from the new king's innovations. "We conceive," declared the committee, "any imposition prejudicial to the country contrary to any just lawe of ours . . . to be an infringement of our right."[146] Four years later, the town of Northampton submitted what a recent scholar has called a "commonwealth petition" to the General Court, urging it to oppose the machinations of royal commissioners sent to the colony in 1664, and "to maintain our former and ancient rights, liberties and priveleges, both in church and commonwealth."[147] Rights in this context, although undifferentiated from liberties and privileges, had a modern sound but the Bay Colony's response twenty years later to the Dominion of New England showed that in Massachusetts, as in Virginia, right was not yet the term of choice for most participants in political and legal controversies.

The Dominion was a shotgun wedding, a union imposed on the New England colonies by the government of James II. A military man, Sir Edmund Andros, was appointed governor in 1686 and ruled without a representative assembly. Andros's regime proceeded to tax New England, raising precisely the issue that helped precipitate the American Revolution: the taking of property without consent. Although a few New Englanders protested Andros's actions "as a violation of the Common Rights, which all Englishmen justly count themselves born unto,"[148] many more, including the most notable dissidents, John Wise and his Ipswich followers, did not invoke the language of rights at all. At an Ipswich Town Meeting, August 23, 1687, Wise "made a Speech . . . and said we had a good God, and a good King, and should do well to stand for our Privileges." The Ipswich selectmen then voted that "it was against the common Privileges of English Subjects to have money raised without their consent in an Assembly or Parliament." Imprisoned for their defiance, Wise and his compatriots were denied a writ of habeas corpus and were tried under irregular circumstances in Boston. At the trial the prisoners once again asserted "the privilege of Englishmen not to be taxed without their consent" and also claimed the "privileges of English law."[149] The absence of the term rights in protesting taxation without representation indicates that the concept of rights was as unfamiliar in Ipswich as it was to a committee of Bostonians who, seeking to describe a written guarantee of rights allegedly promised to Increase Mather by James II, could find no better term than "a certain Magna Charta" to designate a document that later generations would have automatically called a bill of rights.[150]

If dealings about land are excepted, a right was an exotic concept in the 1680s in both New England and Virginia. It was scarcely less so in the other colonies, with the possible exception of Pennsylvania, where ambiguities abounded even though the colony was often considered to be on the cutting edge of rights discourse because Quakers were a despised religious minority who in England had defiantly asserted rights to protect their beliefs. In a pamphlet published in 1687 William Penn used rights in the subjective sense as inherent power; "each man," Penn wrote, had a "fixed Fundamental Right born with him."[151] But Penn's Charter of Liberty and Frame of Government, both issued to the settlers of Pennsylvania in 1683, treat rights as the Virginia Company charters did seventy years earlier. Penn granted his colonists not rights but "liberties, franchises and properties." A right appeared only once in these famous instruments—in its ancient sense as a title to land. In Article 21 of the Frame of Government, Penn permitted the heirs of an unnaturalized alien "who is, or shall be a purchaser," to inherit "his right and interests."[152]

Rights became a major component of political and legal discourse in eighteenth-century America. What catalyst raised rights consciousness in the colonies from its dim seventeenth-century level? Beyond doubt it was the Glorious Revolution and its enduring testament, the Bill of Rights of 1689. Americans regarded the Bill of Rights as a talisman that patriots had wielded to save England from "Popery and Arbitrary Power"[153] and perceived that they, no less than citizens of the metroplolis, could use rights to defeat autocrats in their midst. What increased America's interest in rights was the appealing way—the integration of rights with religion—in which the concept was presented by Locke and his continental contemporaries such as Samuel Pufendorf. Pufendorf's impact on colonial American thought is just beginning to be appreciated. Recently, a scholar has observed that Grotius and Pufendorf were "omnipresent in the eighteenth century" and that Pufendorf was "required reading in . . . many English dissenting academics and American colleges."[154] When John Wise wrote his *Vindication of the Government of New England Churches* in 1717, it was Pufendorf rather than Locke upon whom he relied for his discussion of "the civil being of man." "I shall," Wise advised his readers, "principally take baron Pufendorff for my chief guide and spokesman."[155]

Both Locke and Pufendorf defined a right as a power—"the several kinds of Power have . . . a particular Name . . . we have thought it convenient to give it the name Right."[156] They also insisted, in opposition to Hobbes, but in conformity to writers stretching back to Occam, that a right was a moral power. The iconoclast as usual, Hobbes had argued that a right was "absolute," "unlimited" power, restrained by no considerations of justice, religion, or morality.[157] In his view men had a "Right to everything, even to one another's body."[158] This "aberration" was corrected in short order by Locke, Pufendorf, and others "who restored the moral content" of right.[159] Pufendorf was "preoccupied with . . . moral power conceived as right"[160] and so was Locke. John Dunn, who has stressed that Locke's concept of rights must be understood in the "context of his religious belief," has asserted that "for Locke all the rights humans have . . . derive from, depend upon and are rigidly constrained by a framework of objective duty: God's requirement for human agents."[161] Villey explained that in deriving rights from duties, Locke was following Grotius. Paraphrasing Grotius's and Locke's argument, Villey wrote: "had God not given to each man by the natural law (confirmed in the Holy Scriptures) a duty to preserve himself, to increase and multiply? Man therefore must have received the means to increase and prosper, that is, the rights indispensable to the exercise of these duties."[162] For Grotius, Pufendorf, and Locke, rights were the means, the powers, God granted men to perform the duties He imposed upon them. As powers inherent in individuals, these natural rights were, of course, subjective.

A religious society, as eighteenth-century America was, opened its arms to natural/subjective right, presented as moral power inherent to individuals. Ministers of the gospel, as Edmund S. Morgan has shown, were enthusiastic proponents of subjective rights[163] and lawyers displayed none of the aversion to the new concept that Villey discovered among their eighteenth-century European brethren. Subjective right did not, however, instantly sweep the field of rival theories of rights. In fact, during the first decades of the eighteenth century many American political leaders continued to speak in the language of Coke and his contemporaries. In 1711, for example, the New Jersey Assembly presented an address to Governor Robert Hunter, complaining about the arbitrary conduct of his predecessor, Lord Cornbury, who was accused of taking "Daring and Violent Measures, to subvert the Liberties of this Country." Cornbury was repeatedly assailed for undermining the colony's "liberties." The Assembly used the term right, but only in its ancient sense as a title to land, as when it censured Cornbury for invading the "Rights" of the former proprietors of the colony, those "Rights" being their "Title to their Lands and Rents, violently and Arbitrarily forced from them."[164]

By the 1730s natural/subjective rights had found their way into the public discourse. Commenting on the Zenger trial in 1737, James Alexander warned opponents of freedom of speech and of the press that "whoever attempts to suppress either of those our natural rights, ought to be regarded as enemies to liberty and to the constitution."[165] The Great Awakening of the 1740s promoted the use of subjective rights because the "New Lights," dissenters from the established order, adopted the customary tactics of English religious minorities in claiming the "inaliable Right" to practice religion as they saw fit. Some New Lights insisted that the "inherent natural Rights of Englishmen" be applied in the political as well as in the religious sphere.[166] During the French and Indian War, 1755-1763, natural/subjective rights were often invoked to protest the British military's practices of impressment and quartering.[167]

That Americans had become comfortable with the concept of subjective rights by the 1750s was owing to a growing familiarity with the writings of Grotius, Locke, and Pufendorf, produced by a large number of popularizers who recycled and amplified their ideas. These writers, who belonged to what a recent scholar has called the "natural law-based moral philosophy" school,[168] found a wide audience in America from mid-century onward. The best known among them were Jean Jacques Burlamaqui, Emer de Vattel, Christian Wolff, and the members of the Scottish Enlightenment among whom Francis Hutcheson had the widest following in America. From their works a reader would learn that rights were "moral qualities" (Hutcheson).[169] Burlamaqui emphasized that "a right is a moral power," not to be confounded with a "simple power," and explained that rights were bestowed by God and "have a natural connection to our duties and are given to man only as a means to perform them."[170]

By the end of the French and Indian War subjective right had taken its place among an array of overlapping and often incompatible libertarian concepts which Americans had not until then been obliged to sort out: rights as titles to land; rights as expanded titled ownership (the rights of Englishmen); rights as the benefits of the rule of law; liberties, privileges, and other miscellaneous notions such as franchises and immunities. Compounding the confusion was the lack of clarity with which some of these concepts had been presented. Grotius, according to Villey, commingled classical natural right and subjective rights.[171] Pufendorf explicated subjective rights in the "antique vocabulary" of Roman law.[172] Hutcheson and the eighteenth-century moral philosophers taxed their readers with a technical vocabulary that dilated on "adventitious rights [which] are either real or personal" and "natural rights which are of the imperfect sort."[173] By stressing, in imitation of British libertarians, the antiquity and the timelessness of rights, American leaders created the impression that rights were not fully intelligible because their origins were beyond the reach of human memory. The process that had begun early in the seventeenth century of extending land rights to the political sphere had proven to be irresistible; in Revolutionary America no popular desire or bias (including restricting public office to Protestants)[174] appeared to be too trivial or ignoble to be claimed as a right, with the result that the term appeared to lack boundaries and thus to defy definition. Finally, by the 1760s, there seemed to be a recognition that liberty and privilege were incompatible with the newer, stronger term right, yet the older terms continued to be employed indiscriminately as synonyms for a right. The result of this bewildering jumble of usages was that, on the threshold of the conflict with Britain, many Americans—and not merely those of "inferior condition" and education—found the concept of a right to be incoherent and even incomprehensible.

Consider the case of Massachusetts's agent to London, William Bollan. "A learned man of indefatigable research," Bollan in 1762 proposed to write a book "establishing . . . the native equal and permanent rights of the colonists against all Opponents," but found that "the facts and arguments necessary on this occasion . . . are so numerous and various, and many of them so difficult in their nature, that the completion of a work of this kind" was beyond his capacity.[175] Bollan might have been consoled by experts like Francis Hutcheson, who admitted in 1755 that "our notion of right is a complex conception,"[176] or by public officials like Thomas Hutchinson, who testified to the abundant confusion about rights among practicing politicians. As a young member of the Massachusetts Assembly in the 1740s and 1750s, Hutchinson affected "to catechize . . . about English rights," but subsequently admitted that "no precise idea seems to have been affixed" to the term "natural rights of an English man."[177] In 1765 John Adams attributed the problem of understanding to his countrymen's intellectual diffidence, to their "reluctance to examine into the grounds of our priveleges."[178] Years later Adams conceded that rights might not, after all, be "definable."[179] Recent scholars have commented on the Americans' perplexity over rights. John Phillip Reid noted a "vagueness" in their discussion of the subject, an absence of a "precision of definitions."[180] Knud Haakonssen concluded that in discussing rights few Americans "understood exactly what they were talking about,"[181] a judgment that echoed James Wilson's contention in 1787 that "there are very few who understand the whole of these rights."[182]

The dispute with Britain, beginning with the Sugar Act of 1764, improved, if it did not perfect, America's understanding of rights. Americans, declared the First Continental Congress in 1774, "were animated by a just love of our invaded rights."[183] Making rights the principal issue in the contest with Britain compelled the colonists to strive for a common definition of a right and to differentiate rights from superficially similar concepts. Leading patriots investigated rights with the "utmost precision," a postwar writer boasted.[184] As early as 1765 James Otis warned his countrymen against confounding "the terms rights, liberties, and priveleges, which in legal as well as vulgar acceptation denote very different ideas."[185] The General Assembly of New York anticipated Otis's admonition in 1764 when it informed Parliament that a British legislature in which Americans were unrepresented could not compel them to pay taxes. "The People of this Colony," the Assembly declared, "nobly disdain the thought of claiming that Exemption as a Privilege. They found it on a Basis more honourable, solid and stable; they challenge it and glory in it as their Right."[186] In 1766 Governor Stephen Hopkins of Rhode Island made the distinction Otis demanded: "Americans," said Hopkins, "do not hold those rights as priveleges granted them, but possess them as inherent and indefeasible."[187] As independence approached, fewer and fewer Americans confused rights with liberties and privileges. In 1778, to be sure, one finds political leaders stringing together, as though they were equivalents, "Rights Franchises, Immunities, and Liberties,"[188] but as time passed such locutions began to disappear.

The decade of conflict ignited by the Sugar Act saw a steady increase in the use of a right in its modern, subjective sense, culminating in the "Bill of Rights," drafted by the First Continental Congress in 1774, which gave natural/subjective rights priority over all others.[189] Studying Thomas Jefferson's composition of the Declaration of Independence in 1776, Morton White concluded that Jefferson and his fellow citizens understood rights in a subjective sense, as a "moral species of power" and attributed this view to the influence of Burlamaqui,[190] whose authority along with that of other philosophers of natural/subjective rights, continued to expand in America from the middle of the eighteenth century onward.[191]

Striking testimony to the significance of these writers was contained in a report sent to James Madison in 1774 about the debates in the First Continental Congress: "Vattel, Burlemaqui, Locke, and Montesquieu seem to be the standard to which they refer when settling the rights of the colonies," Madison was told.[192] The next year in his *The Farmer Refuted* Alexander Hamilton recommended "Grotius, Pufendorf, Locke, Montesquieu and Burlemaqui" to the perusal of his opponent.[193] Ten years later Elbridge Gerry, while serving in the Confederation Congress, asked a friend to send him "Vattel's Law of Nations, Burlemaqui's principles of natural and political law, Burlemaqui's Law of Nations if the Reputation of it is equal to his other Works" and a translation of "Grotius on War and peace."[194] Surveying experts on rights, James Wilson in 1787 observed that "all political writers, from Grotius and Puffendorf down to Vattel, have treated on this subject."[195] The next year John Adams offered the following advice to his son, John Quincy, a fledgling lawyer: "To Vattel and Burlamaqui, whom you say you have read, you must add Grotius and Puffendorf."[196] In the nineteenth century legal commentators with views as diverse as St. George Tucker and Joseph Story cited these writers with approval.[197] Their influence, together with that of the Scottish moral philosophers and other lesser figures who shared their views, produced by 1776 the ascendancy of morality-based, subjective right and created the intellectual climate in which Thomas Paine, writing in a Pennsylvania newspaper in 1777, could offer this quintessentially subjective definition of a right: "a natural right is an animal right, and the power to act it, is supposed, either fully or in part, to be mechanically contained within ourselves as individuals."[198]

After independence, as modern, subjective right flourished in the new nation, it absorbed one of the distinguishing features of its rival concept, the rights of Englishmen. As a reminder of the British yoke, this phrase became suspect in the young republic for chauvinistic reasons; nevertheless, the idea that it represented, ownership by title, persisted. Subjective right also conveyed the idea of ownership, since power, its essence, when exercised over things or the individual himself, produced possession. Although no intellectual impressario orchestrated a merger between rights of Englishmen and subjective right in the postwar years, the fundamental idea of the rights of Englishmen—ownership—lived on in the possessive sense of subjective right. A right, therefore, in the new United States meant, in its fullest sense, power inherent in and owned by an individual to act in a way consistent with Christian morality. In the words of the authoritative Vattel, a right was "nothing more than the power of doing what is morally possible."[199] That rights were grounded in Christianity was for the Founding generation axiomatic. Commenting on Rousseau, John Adams dismissed the philosopher's claim that Americans had invented the "science of rights." No, retorted Adams; they "found it in their religion."[200]

Having so masterfully traced the evolution of the meaning of a right in Europe, Professor Villey would not have been surprised that in the United States the meaning of the term has changed since the Founding Period. Nor would he have been surprised—he, in fact, would have expected—that the agents of change would have been philosophers like John Rawls or lawyers specializing in moral philosophy like Ronald Dworkin. What, perhaps, would have surprised Villey is abruptness of the change—it has occurred since World War II—and its radical nature. Christian morality has been detached from the definition of a right, shed like an obsolete, restrictive skin. A right, its current advocates claim, must now be understood as a raw power to gratify a sweeping range of appetites in the name of vindicating individual equality and autonomy. If proponents of the Founding Era understanding of a right as a power grounded in Christian morality have not ceded the field to this new definition, they are, at least, retreating in disarray before its *tentaculaire* advance.

NOTES

1.See, for example, James A. Henretta, "Social History as Lived and Written," *American Historical Review* 84, no.4 (October, 1979): 1293-1322.

2. See Brian Tierney, "Villey, Ockham and the Origin of Individual Rights," in *The Weightier Matters of the Law,* ed. John Witte, Jr. and Frank Alexander (Atlanta: Georgia Scholars Press, 1988), 1-31.

3. Most relevant for this chapter were Villey's *Leçons d'Histoire de la Philosophie du Droit* (Paris: Dalloz, 1957); *La Formation de la Pensée Juridique Moderne* (Paris: Montchrestien, 1968); *Seize Essais de Philosophie du Droit* (Paris: Dalloz, 1969); *Philosophie du Droit* (Paris: Dalloz, 1978).

4. *La Formation,* 226.

5. "Droit Subjectif, I," in *Seize Essais,* 147.

6. *La Formation,* 231-32; "Droit Subjectif, I," 150.

7. Philip B. Kurland and Ralph Lerner, *The Founders' Constitution* (Chicago: University of Chicago Press,1987), vol. 1, 424.

8. United States Constitution Bicentennial Commission, *The Bill of Rights and Beyond 1791-1991* (Washington, D.C.: Government Printing Office, 1991), foreword.

9. John Kominski, "Liberty versus Authority: The Eternal Conflict in Government," *Southern Illinois University Law Journal* 16 (1992): 214.

10. Stephen Hopkins, "Rights of Colonies Examined," in *American Political Writing during the Founding Era, 1760-1805,* ed. Charles Hyneman and Donald Lutz (Indianapolis: Liberty Press, 1983), 1, 46.

11. Silas Downer, "A Discourse Delivered in Providence . . . at the Dedication of the Tree of Liberty," *Political Writing during the Founding Era,* 98.

12. Samuel West, "Election Sermon," *Political Writing during the Founding Era,* 427.

13. On this point see, among others, G. R. Elton, *The Parliament of England, 1559-1581* (New York: Cambridge University Press,1986), 337-38; J. H. Hexter, "Parliament, Liberty, and Freedom of Elections," in *Parliament and Liberty from the Reign of Elizabeth to the English Civil War,* ed. J. H. Hexter (Stanford, Calif.: Stanford University Press, 1992), 43; and Lois G. Schwoerer, *The Declaration of Rights* (Baltimore: Johns Hopkins University Press, 1981), 283.

14. Michael E. Stevens, "Their Liberties, Properties and Privileges: Civil Liberties in South Carolina," in *The Bill of Rights and the States: The Colonial and Revolutionary*

Origins of American Liberties, ed. Patrick T. Conley and John J. Kominski (Madison, Wisc.: Madison House, 1992), 400.

15. William S. Price, "There Ought to Be a Bill of Rights: North Carolina Enters a New Nation," *Bill of Rights and the States,* 426.

16. Kenneth Coleman, "Frontier Haven: Georgia and the Bill of Rights," *Bill of Rights and the States,* 444.

17. Christopher Collier, "Liberty, Justice, and No Bill of Rights: Protecting Natural Rights in a Common-Law Commonwealth," *Bill of Rights and the States,* 101.

18. A. E. Dick Howard, "Rights in Passage: English Liberties in Early America," *Bill of Rights and the States,* 4-5.

19. Benjamin F. Wright, Jr., *American Interpretations of Natural Law* (New York: Russell & Russell, 1962), 7.

20. Lawrence Leder, *Liberty and Authority: Early American Political Ideology* (Chicago: Quadrangle Books, 1968), 7.

21. John Phillip Reid, *Constitutional History of the American Revolution: The Authority of Rights* (Madison: University of Wisconsin Press, 1986), 4, 10-11, 93.

22. *La Formation,* 225, 262.

23. "La Nature des Choses," in *Seize Essais,* 24.

24. "Droit Subjectif, II," *Seize Essais,* 182; *Philosophie du Droit,* 74.

25. "Droit Subjectif, I," in *Seize Essais,* 148, 152-53; "Droit Subjectif, II," *Seize Essais,* 182-83; "Le Origines de la Notion de Droit Subjectif," in *Leçons d'Histoire,* 262; *La Formation,* 229, 234, 236, 546.

26. *La Formation,*365; Thomas Sandars, ed., *The Institutes of Justinian* (London: Longman, Greene and Company, 1888), 6.

27. *La Formation,* 381, 650; "Le Humanisme et le Droit," in *Seize Essais,* 69; *Philosophie de Droit,* 150.

28. "La Nature des Choses," in *Seize Essais,* 150.

29. "Une Definition du Droit," in *Seize Essais,* 27.

30. "La Nature des Choses," in *Seize Essais,* 51.

31. *Philosophie du Droit,* 77, 115, 144.

32. "Les Origines de la Notion de Droit Subjectif," in *Leçons d'Histoire,* 261.

33. *Philosophie du Droit,* 150.

34. "Les Origines de la Notion de Droit Subjectif," in *Leçons d'Histoire,* 261.

35. "Droit Subjectif, I," in *Seize Essais,* 153.

36. "Les Origines de la Notion de Droit Subjectif," in *Leçons d'Histoire,* 256, 276.

37. "Droit Subjectif, I," in *Seize Essais,* 158, 168.

38. *Seize Essais,* 159.

39. *Seize Essais,* 161.

40. *Seize Essais,* 166.

41. *La Formation,* 261.

42. *La Formation*, 232.

43. *La Formation*, 230.

44. "Droit Subjectif, I," in *Seize Essais*, 144-45.

45. *La Formation*, 653.

46. *Philosophie du Droit*, 116.

47. *Philosophie du Droit*, 137-39; *La Formation*, 209-10, 652; "Droit Subjectif, II," in *Seize Essais*, 184-85.

48. *La Formation*, 253.

49. *Philosophie du Droit*, 143.

50. "Les Origines de la Notion de Droit Subjectif," in *Leçons d'Histoire*, 272; *La Formation*, 365, 381.

51. *La Formation*, 341.

52. *La Formation*, 351.

53. "Les Origines de la Notion de Droit Subjectif," in *Leçons d'Histoire*, 273.

54. *La Formation*, 364.

55. Quoted in Morton White, *The Philosophy of the American Revolution* (New York: Oxford University Press, 1978), 145.

56. *La Formation*, 393.

57. *La Formation*, 654.

58. "Droit Subjectif, II," in *Seize Essais*, 188.

59. *La Formation*, 650; "Les Origines de la Notion de Droit Subjectif," in *Leçons d'Histoire*, 272.

60. "La Pensée Moderne et le Systeme Juridique Actual," in *Leçons d'Histoire* , 66.

61. *Leçons d'Histoire*, 66.

62. *La Formation de la Pensée Juridique Moderne*, 598.

63. "Les Origines de la Notion de Droit Subjectif," in *Leçons d'Histoire*, 249.

64. Richard Tuck, *Natural Rights Theories: Their Origin and Development* (Cambridge: Cambridge University Press, 1979), 74.

65. *La Formation*, 654.

66. "Les Origines de la Notion de Droit Subjectif," in *Leçons d'Histoire*, 250.

67. "Les Origines de la Notion de Droit Subjectif," 274-76.

68. "La Pensée Moderne et le Systeme Juridique Actual," in *Leçons d'Histoire*, 66.

69. *Philosophie du Droit*, 69.

70. "Les Origines de la Notion de Droit Subjectif," in *Leçons d'Histoire*, 277.

71. "Villey, Ockham and the Origin of Individual Rights," in *The Weightier Matters of the Law*, 1-31.

72. Helmut Coing, "Zur Geschichte des Begriffs 'subjektives Recht,'" in *Das subjektive Recht und der Rechtsschutz der Personlichkeit*, ed. Konrad Zweigert (Frankfurt: M.A. Metzner, 1959), 11.

73. Brian Tierney, "Origins of Natural Rights Language: Texts and Contexts, 1150-1250," *History of Political Thought* 10 (1989): 624.

74. Tierney, "Origins," 630-37.

75. "Droit Subjectif," in *Seize Essais,* 144.

76. Frederick Lawson, "Das subjektive Recht im englishen Deliksrecht (law of torts)," in *Das subjektive Recht und der Rechtsschutz der Personlichkeit,* 24.

77. Konrad Zwigert, "Vorwort," *Das subjektive Recht,* 5.

78. Samuel E. Thorne, ed., *Bracton on the Laws and Customs of England* (Cambridge, Mass.: Harvard University Press, 1968), xxxvi.

79. Thorne, *Bracton,* 24; Sir Travers Twiss, *Henrici de Bracton de Legibus et Consuetudinibus Angliae* (Buffalo: W.S. Hein, 1990), 16-18.

80. F. W. Maitland, "History of the Register of Original Writs," in *The Collected Papers of Frederic William Maitland,* ed. H. A. L. Fisher (Cambridge: Cambridge University Press, 1911), 139; William S. Holdsworth, *A History of English Law* (London: Methuen and Company, 1923), 5-6.

81. R. C. Van Carnegem, *Royal Writs in England from the Conquest to Glanvill, Publications of the Selden Society* (1959), 212.

82. *Royal Writs,* 195.

83. *Royal Writs,* 313-15.

84. At the least it conferred a "sort of ownership." S. F. C. Milsom, *Historical Foundations of the Common Law* (London: Butterworths, 1981), 120.

85. *A History of English Law,* 3.

86. The title of the 1567 edition changed to *Exposisions of the terms of the laws of England* and until 1624 the several editions were published with slight variations upon this title. In 1624 *Les Termes de la Ley* was resurrected as the title and used throughout the remainder of the volume's publishing history. Early editions contain no pagination; until the 1667 edition, the definition of a right must be sought under *droit.* All editions consulted are in the Rare Book Section, Law Library, Library of Congress.

87. For an explanation of the writ of right praecipe, see *Royal Writs in England from the Conquest to Glanvill, Publications of the Selden Society,* 234-38.

88. John Cowell, *The Interpreter; or the Booke Containing the Significations of Words* (1607); no pagination; see under "Right Rectum." For a modern reprint, see Cowell, *The Interpreter* (Union, N.J: Lawbook Exchange, 2002).

89. Francis Hargrave and Charles Butler, eds., *The First Part of the Institutes of the Laws of England* (London: E. & R. Brooke, 1794), bk. 3, ch. 11, sect. 650; Bacon asserted that "there are but two rights. The one is an estate, which is Jus in re." James Spedding, ed., *The Works of Francis Bacon* (Boston: Brown & Taggart, 1861), 287.

90. *The First Part of the Institutes of the Laws of England,* bk. 3, ch. 8, sect. 445.

91. William Sheppard, *An Epitome of All the Common and Statute Laws of this Nation, Now in Force . . .* (London: W. Lee, 1656), 466-67.

92. William Noy, *The Compleat Lawyer: or, A Treatise Concerning Tenures and Estates* (London: D. Pakeman, 1651), 82-83.

93. *The First Part of the Institutes of the Laws of England*, bk. 3, ch. 8, sect. 447; bk. 3, ch. 11, sect. 650.

94. J. R. Tanner, ed., *Constitutional Documents of the Reign of James I A.D. 1603-1625 with an Historical Commentary* (Cambridge: Cambridge University Press, 1930), 204, 286.

95. Johann P. Sommerville, "Parliament, Privilege, and the Liberties of the Subject," in *Parliament and Liberty*, 81.

96. J. G. A. Pocock, *The Ancient Constitution and the Feudal Law* (New York: Cambridge University Press, 1987), 213.

97. *The Ancient Constitution*, 218.

98. *Constitutional Documents of the Reign of James I*, 94.

99. Wallace Notestein, et al., eds., *Commons Debates in 1621* (New Haven, Conn.: Yale University Press, 1935), 334-35.

100. See T. E. Hartley, *Proceedings in the Parliaments of Elizabeth I, 1558-1581* (Wilmington, Del.: M. Glazier, 3 vols., 1981).

101. David Harris Sacks, "Parliament, Liberty, and the Commonweal," in *Parliament and Liberty*, 93.

102. *Parliament and Liberty*, 94.

103. Edward Coke, *The Second Part of the Institutes of the Laws of England* (1669), ch. 29 (on Magna Charta), 47.

104. *Constitutional Documents of the Reign of James I* , 221.

105. *Constitutional Documents of the Reign of James I*, 246.

106. Paul Christianson, "Royal and Parliamentary Voices on the Ancient Constitution, 1604-1621," in *The Mental World of the Jacobean Court*, ed. Linda Levy Peck (Cambridge: Cambridge University Press, 1991), 73.

107. Conrad Russell, *Parliaments and English Politics 1621-1629* (Oxford: Clarendon Press, 1979), 359.

108. Elizabeth Read Foster, "Petitions and the Petition of Right," *Journal of British Studies* 14 (1974): 24.

109. "Petitions and the Petition of Right," 34.

110. See J. P. Sommerville, "James I and the Divine Right of Kings: English Politics and Continental Theory," *The Mental World of the Jacobean Court*, 63.

111. *History of Political Thought*, 623.

112. A. S. P. Woodhouse, ed., *Puritanism and Liberty Being the Army Debates (1647-49) from the Clarke Manuscripts* (London: Dent, 1986), 69, 445.

113. Clive Holmes, "Parliament, Liberty, Taxation, and Property," *Parliament and Liberty*, 139.

114. See C. B. Macpherson, *The Political Theory of Possessive Individualism Hobbes to Locke* (Oxford: Clarendon Press, 1989), 137.

115. *Natural Rights Theories*, 149.

116. *Natural Rights Theories,* 144.

117. "Les Origines de la Notion de Droit Subjectif," in *Leçons d'Histoire,* 274-76.

118. *The Declaration of Rights,* 16.

119. *The Declaration of Rights,* 258-60.

120. Thomas J. Wertenbaker, *Virginia under the Stuarts, 1607-1688* (New York: Russell & Russell, 1959), 34, 23.

121. Alexander Brown, *English Politics in Early Virginia History* (New York: Russell & Russell, 1968), 13.

122. Willam F. Swindler, ed., *Sources and Documents of United States Constitutions* (Dobbs Ferry, N.Y.: Oceana Publications, 1979), vol. 10, 22, 34.

123. *Constitutional Documents of the Reign of James I,* 287.

124. Susan M. Kingsbury, ed., *The Records of the Virginia Company of London* (Washington, D.C.: Government Printing Office, 1906-1935), vol. 3, 434.

125. Richard Morton, *Colonial Virginia* (Chapel Hill: University of North Carolina Press, 1960), vol. 1, 58.

126. *The Records of the Virginia Company of London,* Vol. 3, 161.

127. *Colonial Virginia,* Vol. 1, 104.

128. *Sources and Documents of United States Constitutions,* vol. 10, 40.

129. *Sources and Documents of United States Constitutions,* vol. 5, 34.

130. The gadfly, Captain John Bargrave, occasionally invoked the term, as when he charged in 1621 that "all the rights privileges and liberties together with the government of law is laid aside" by the Company's monopoly of trade, but it is doubtful that Bargrave understood right in a modern subjective sense, since on another occasion he defined right by reference to Aristotle. *The Records of the Virginia Company of London,* vol. 3, 519; vol 4, 410.

131. *The Records of the Virginia Company,* vol. 3, 76.

132. *The Records of the Virginia Company,* vol. 3, 152.

133. *The Records of the Virginia Company,* vol. 3, 571.

134. "Declaration Concerning the Dutch Trade," *Virginia Magazine of History and Biography* 23 (1915): 247.

135. Edmund S. Morgan, *American Slavery American Freedom 1606-1689* (New York: Norton, 1975), 147n.

136. Warren Billings, ed., *The Old Dominion in the Seventeenth Century: A Documentary History of Virginia* (Chapel Hill: University of North Carolina Press, 1975), 241.

137. Billings, *Old Dominion,* 65.

138. Billings, *Old Dominion,* 59.

139. Stephen S. Webb, *1676: The End of American Independence* (New York: Knopf, 1984), 67.

140. *American Slavery American Freedom,* 269.

141. P.R.O., C.O. 1/39, 244 ff. Library of Congress microfilm copies.

142. *Sources and Documents of United States Constitutions*, vol. 5, 46, 66.

143. Perry Miller, *The New England Mind from Colony to Province* (Cambridge, Mass.: Harvard University Press, 1953), 121.

144. *The New England Mind*, 122.

145. Dumas Malone, ed., *Dictionary of American Biography* (New York: Charles Scribner's Sons, 1936), 19, 434.

146. *The Glorious Revolution in America*, Michael G. Hall, Lawrence H. Leder, Michael G. Kammen, eds. (Chapel Hill: University of North Carolina Press, 1964), 13.

147. Robert Bliss, *Revolution and Empire* (Manchester: Manchester University Press, 1990), 156.

148. W. H. Whitemore, ed., *The Andros Tracts* (Boston: The Prince Society, 1868), vol. 3, 194.

149. *Andros Tracts*, vol. 1, 82, 85; vol. 2, 6.

150. *Andros Tracts*, vol. 1, 17.

151. *The Founders' Constitution*, vol. 1, 432.

152. *Sources and Documents of United States Constitutions*, vol. 8, 263, 266.

153. *Andros Tracts*, vol. 1, 75.

154. Knud Haakonssen, "From Natural Law to the Rights of Man," unpublished paper, 5; the published version of this essay may be found in *A Culture of Rights: The Bill of Rights in Philosophy, Politics, and Law 1791 and 1991*, ed. Knud Haakonssen and Michael J. Lacey (New York: Cambridge University Press, 1991), 19-61.

155. John Wise, *Vindication of the Government of New England Churches* (Boston: John Boyles, 1772), 23.

156. Samuel Pufendorf, *The Law of Nature and Nations* (London: J. & J. Bonwicke, 1749), 11-12.

157. *La Formation*, 230, 660-61.

158. Richard Tuck, ed., *Leviathan* (Cambridge: Cambridge University Press, 1991), 91.

159. "Origins of Natural Rights Language: Texts and Contexts, 1150-1250," 622.

160. *The Philosophy of the American Revolution*, 188.

161. James Kloppenberg, "The Virtues of Liberalism: Christianity, Republicanism, and Ethics in Early American Political Discourse," *Journal of American History* 74, no.1 (June 1987): 16n.

162. *Philosophie du Droit*, 155.

163. In the sense that they dispensed Locke's ideas, see Edmund S. Morgan, "The American Revolution Considered as an Intellectual Movement," in *Causes and Consequences of the American Revolution*, ed. Esmond Wright (Chicago: Quadrangle Books, 1966), 176.

164. Eugene Sheridan, ed., *The Papers of Lewis Morris* (Newark: New Jersey Historical Society, 1991), 1, 115, 116, 125, 130.

165. James Alexander, *A Brief Narrative of the Case and Trial of John Peter Zenger,* ed. Stanley N. Katz (Cambridge, Mass.: Harvard University Press, 1963), 190.

166. Patricia Bonomi, *Under the Cope of Heaven* (New York: Oxford University Press, 1986), 156.

167. Alan Rogers, *Empire and Liberty: American Resistance to British Authority 1755-1763* (Berkeley: University of California Press, 1974), 84-85.

168. *A Culture of Rights,* 43.

169. "From Natural Law to the Rights of Man," 35.

170. *The Philosophy of the American Revolution,* 140, 189-90.

171. *La Formation,* 654.

172. "La Pensee Moderne et le Systeme Juridique Actuel," in *Leçons d'Histoire,* 73.

173. Francis Hutcheson, *A System of Moral Philosophy* (London: A. Millar, 1755), vol. 1, 303, 340.

174. Andover Town Meeting, May 1, 1780, in *The Popular Sources of Political Authority: Documents on the Massachusetts Constitution of 1780,* ed. Oscar and Mary Handlin (Cambridge, Mass.: Harvard University Press, 1966), 904.

175. Charles G. Washburn, ed., *Jasper Maduit, Agent in London for the Province of the Massachusetts Bay 1762-1765* (Boston: Massachusetts Historical Society [*Collections*], 1918), 28-29.

176. *A System of Moral Philosophy,* vol. 1, 258.

177. *Empire and Liberty: American Resistance to British Authority, 1755-1763,* 84-85; Thomas Hutchinson to Thomas Pownall, March 8, 1766, in *Prologue to Revolution: Sources and Documents on the Stamp Act Crisis, 1764-1766,* ed. Edmund S. Morgan (Chapel Hill: University of North Carolina Press, 1959), 123.

178. John Adams, *Dissertation on the Canon and Feudal Law* (1765), in *Papers of John Adams,* ed. Robert Taylor et al. (Cambridge, Mass.: Harvard University Press, 1977), 123.

179. John Adams to Thomas Boylston Adams, March 18, 1794, in the Adams Papers (microfilm ed.), reel 377, Library of Congress.

180. *Constitutional History of the American Revolution: The Authority of Rights,* 10, 11, 93.

181. *A Culture of Rights: The Bill of Rights in Philosophy, Politics, and Law 1791 and 1991,* 61.

182. James Wilson, speech, Pennsylvania Ratifying Convention, December 4, 1787, in *Documentary History of the Ratification of the Constitution,* ed. Merrill Jensen (Madison: State Historical Society of Wisconsin, 1976), vol. 2, 470. John J. Kaminski and Gaspare J. Saladino are now editors of this series.

183. "A Letter to the Inhabitants of the Province of Quebec," October 26, 1774, in *A Decent Respect to the Opinions of Mankind: Congressional State Papers 1774-76*, ed. James H. Hutson (Washington, D.C.: Government Printing Office, 1975), 66-67.

184. "Republicus," *Kentucky Gazette*, February 16, 1788, in *Documentary History of the Ratification of the Constitution*, vol. 8, 375.

185. James Otis, *A Vindication of the British Colonies* (1765), in *Pamphlets of the American Revolution*, ed. Bernard Bailyn (Cambridge, Mass.: Harvard University Press,1965), 558.

186. Petition to the House of Commons, October 18, 1764, *Prologue to Revolution: Sources and Documents on the Stamp Act Crisis*, 10.

187. *Constitutional History of the American Revolution: The Authority of Rights*, 108.

188. Berkshire County (Mass.) Representatives, statement, November 17, 1778, in *American Political Writing during the Founding Era, 1760-1805*, vol. 1, 457.

189. For the Bill of Rights and List of Grievances, see *A Decent Respect to the Opinions of Mankind: Congressional State Papers 1774-1776*, 50-57.

190. *The Philosophy of the American Revolution*, 192, 195.

191. Burlamaqui also exerted a major influence on Blackstone who defined right in the conventional subjective sense as "a power of acting as one thinks fit, without any restraint or control, unless by the law of nature." *The Philosophy of the American Revolution*, 225; William Blackstone, *Commentaries on the Laws of England*, ed. Stanley N. Katz (Chicago: University of Chicago Press, 1979), vol. 1, 121.

192. William Bradford to James Madison, October 17, 1774, in *The Papers of James Madison*, ed. William Hutchinson and William M. E. Rachel (Chicago: University of Chicago Press,1962), vol. 1, 126.

193. *The Papers of Alexander Hamilton*, H. C. Syrett, ed. (New York: Columbia University Press, 1961), vol. 1, 86.

194. Gerry to Timothy Pickering, October 15, 1785, Gerry Papers, Library of Congress.

195. Wilson, Speech of December 4, 1787, *Documentary History of the Ratification of the Constitution*, vol. 2, 470.

196. John Adams to John Quincy Adams, January 23, 1788, The Adams Papers (microfilm edition), reel 371, Library of Congress.

197. St. George Tucker, *Blackstone's Commentaries* (Philadelphia: William Young Birch and Abraham Small, 1803), appendix to vol. 1, pt. 1, 64-73, 332, 382, passim; Joseph Story, *Commentaries on the Constitution of the United States* (Boston: Hilliard, Gray and Company,1833), vol. 3, 538, 722.

198. "Ludlow," *Pennsylvania Journal*, June 4, 1777.

199. Emer de Vattel, *The Law of Nations, or, Principles of the Law of Nations* (London: W. Clarke and Sons, 1811), x.

200. John Adams to Thomas Boylston Adams, March 18, 1794, Adams Papers (microfilm edition), reel 377, Library of Congress. An earlier version of the present chapter was published in *The American Journal of Jurisprudence* (1994).

Chapter 4

The Christian Nation Question

Within the past decade well-credentialed scholars have asserted that the United States during the Founding Period was not a Christian nation, a claim that, on first impression, seems as absurd as a declaration that grass is not green. The white population of the United States in 1790 has been estimated at 3,173,000.[1] Of this number a thousand or so were Jews who lived in cities along the Atlantic seaboard. Muslims, Hindus and Buddhists could be counted on the fingers of one hand.[2] Since virtually everybody else would have described themselves as Christians, how can sober scholars claim that the new American republic was not a Christian nation?

They can cite statistics which have been bandied about for some time in scholarly circles which purport to show that the vast majority of Americans at the time of the Founding were "unchurched," i.e., were not members of any Christian church. The "churched" remnant is estimated at around 10 percent. Since so few Americans were "real," practicing Christians, there is nothing bizarre about denying that the United States during the Founding Period was a Christian nation. Fidelity to the evidence seems, in fact, to require such a judgment.

According to a distinguished historian of American religion, the thesis that an overwhelming percentage of eighteenth-century Americans were "unchurched" was introduced into the scholarly literature in 1935 by William Warren Sweet in an article, "The American Colonial Environment and Religious Liberty."[3] In a brief, impressionistic section of this article, Sweet ventured to assert, without supplying evidence, that in 1760 only one in seven New Englanders was a church member; for the Middle Colonies his estimate was one member per "fifteen or eighteen"; for Virginia the proportion was "one in twenty; in the Carolinas still less."[4] The idea that church membership in early America was minimal caught on with later historians of American religion; Sydney Ahlstrom, for example, in his magisterial *A Religious History of the American People* (1972) asserted that by the 1790s "church membership had dropped both relatively and absolutely, so that not more than one person in twenty or possibly one in ten seems to have been affiliated."[5]

The assumption that religion during the Founding Period was in the doldrums was not, of course, invented by twentieth-century professional historians. Nineteenth-century denominational historians had called attention to what they believed was the sad state of religion during the Founding. The cause of faith endured a "very wintry season" then, wrote the Baptist historian Robert Semple.[6] According to the Congregationalist Increase Tarbox, the Founding Era "must be regarded as a period peculiarly unfavorable to religious growth and prosperity in New England."[7] The nineteenth-century writers did not consider the religious drought that they discerned as evidence of a nation suddenly become de-Christianized; rather they regarded it as a low point in one of those periodic cycles, so familiar in Christian history, that inevitably rotated into renewal, as, in fact, happened with the advent of the Second Great Awakening at the beginning of the nineteenth century. Nor did Sweet think that the supposed legions of the unchurched were in any way unchristian. They were, in his estimation, "good people who . . . still believe in religion; they believe in all the churches, but no one of them holds their especial loyalty."[8]

In recent years some scholars have suddenly converted the Founding Period's putative mass of unchurched Americans into a godless host whose existence demonstrates that the new republic was not a Christian nation. This radical revision of accepted wisdom has been motivated by a desire to cripple a political campaign mounted by the so-called religious right which is accused of using the notion of a "Christian nation" as a weapon to roll back political gains by advocates of abortion, homosexual rights, and secularized public education. Reactionaries on the right are depicted as scheming to stamp out such initiatives by branding them as illegitimate on the grounds that they are incompatible with the Christian principles on which the nation was founded. Their scholarly opponents have mobilized to thwart such tactics by demonstrating that the United States during the Founding Era was not a Christian nation and that the history to which the right is appealing is wrong.

Those making the case against the Christian nation candidly acknowledge that they are employing scholarship for partisan purposes. Isaac Kramnick and R. Laurence Moore, for example, in a chapter, "Is America a Christian Nation?" in their book, *The Godless Constitution* (1996), concede that they are writing a "polemic" against "the party of religious correctness," i.e., the Christian Coalition and its allies.[9] This concession, they evidently assume, absolves them of the obligation to respect historical evidence, for in the space of three pages they incorrectly identify one delegate to the Federal Constitutional Convention (Charles Pinckney) as a state governor, misquote Alexander Hamilton and assert that the *Federalist* papers "fail to mention God anywhere," a striking statement since in *Federalist* 2 John Jay refers in three successive paragraphs to the workings of "Providence" on America's behalf.[10] This error pales, however, before the authors' failure to mention that in *Federalist* 37 Madison ascribed the success of the Philadelphia Convention to the power of God. That the Convention agreed upon a constitution with a "unanimity almost as unprecedented as it must have been unexpected" made it "impossible," Madison wrote, "for the man of pious reflection not to perceive in it a finger of that Almighty hand which has been so frequently and signally extended to our relief in the critical stages of the revolution."[11] Well might Professors Kramnick and Moore have ignored this statement, for it exposes a breathtaking paradox in their thesis: in *Federalist* 37 Madison, the Father of the Constitution, acknowledges God's assistance in creating a godless constitution.

Why, in the opinion of Kramnick and Moore, is the Constitution, as drafted in 1787, "godless" and proof, therefore, that the United States was not established as a Christian nation? The Constitution, they claim, is a "godless document" because it does not mention God. It displays "utter silence with respect to God and to the United States as a Christian nation."[12]   Professors Kramnick and Moore must have read the Constitution with as little attention as they did the *Federalist*. Did they not notice the word "Lord" in Article 7? Do they doubt that it is a synonym for God? Article 1, section 7, poses an even greater problem for the authors' credibility than their treatment of *Federalist* 37. It states: "If any Bill shall not be returned by the President within ten Days (Sundays excepted) after it shall have been presented to him, the Same shall be a Law, in like Manner, as if he had signed it, unless the Congress by their Adjournment prevent its Return, in which Case it shall not be a Law." This language does nothing less than write the Christian Sabbath into the Constitution by presuming that the president will not work on Sunday. Does this section make the United States a Christian nation? Many Americans in the early nineteenth century would have argued that it did, for they thought that the recognition of the sanctity of the Sabbath in official documents "furnished one of the strongest proofs that the United States was truly a Christian nation."[13]

How do Professors Kramnick and Moore explain the emergence of a godless constitution in the summer of 1787? They view it as the progeny of an essentially godless nation, which they document with two kinds of evidence. One is the favorite proof text of those arguing for the torpor of American religion during the Founding Period: the claim in Crèvecoeur's *Letters from an American Farmer* (1782) that "religious indifference is imperceptibly disseminated from one end of the continent to the other."[14] In fact, there were numerous complaints about American religious "indifference" during the second half of the eighteenth century: in 1760, for example, Lutheran ministers in Pennsylvania were alarmed about the "dangerous indifferentism" among their flocks;[15] in 1773 Nicholas Collin, a Swedish pastor in New Jersey, was distressed that his people were "indifferent and scattered";[16] in 1797, the Presbyterian president of Dickinson College, Charles Nisbet, deplored the "Indifference of Religious Opinions" that he encountered in central Pennsylvania.[17]

Consider the sources from which these complaints came: from Crèvecoeur, a Frenchman; from a group of German pastors, many freshly arrived in America; from Collin, a Swede late of Stockholm; and from Nisbet, for many years the pastor of a church at Montrose, Scotland. In rebuking American indifference, these recent immigrants were reacting to an ecumenicism in the new republic that had progressed beyond the passionate, Old World denominationalism to which they were accustomed and which they evidently cherished. Too many Americans, Nisbet discovered, tended to be "Anythingarians who hold all Religions equally good."[18] The European-style complaints about "indifferentism" in no way bespoke a lack of religious ardor or Christian commitment among Americans. Crèvecoeur, for example, mentioned "religious indifference" in one sentence and in the next described bustling religious activity: "when any considerable number of a particular sect happen to dwell contiguous to each other, they immediately erect a temple and there worship the Divinity agreeably to their own peculiar ideas."[19] Similarly, Collin described how some of his "indifferent" parishioners were "drawn to the Moravian sect, and together with other English and German members built a meeting-house about half a mile from the Raccoon church [his own] to which they have belonged ever since."[20] Collin's parishioners may have been indifferent to his ministrations; they certainly did not lack a religious vision and the energy to implement it. Indifference, as used during the Founding Period, was a shibboleth of newcomers, which described an absence of denominational partisanship not a stultifying religious apathy, as Moore, Kramnick and others would have us believe. Indeed, to argue that indifference in its European sense of weak denominational allegiance proved that the new American republic was unchristian would be equivalent to assuming that because George Whitefield, the eighteenth century's greatest evangelist, was scornful of denominational barriers, he was a secular humanist.

The second kind of evidence which Kramnick and Moore used to prove that Americans during the Founding Period were not "securely Christian" or "strongly anything else relating to a religious persuasion" was the statistic, mentioned earlier, that "only about 10-15 percent of the population [were] church members."[21] The authors could only make this statement by ignoring the important article, published in 1982 by Patricia Bonomi and Peter Eisenstadt, that demonstrated that the church adherence of Americans in 1776 was between 71 and 77.5 percent, a figure fatal to any claim about an unchristian nation.[22] Kramnick and Moore appear to have obtained their percentages from an article published in 1988 by two sociologists, Rodney Stark and Roger Finke, which has obtained some currency among scholars.[23]

Stark and Finke appropriately censure earlier historians like Sweet and Ahlstrom who asserted a "church membership rate for colonial America without deigning to offer any basis for it at all."[24] They presented what purported to be a rigorous statistical analysis of church membership rates and concluded that the guesswork of earlier historians that no more than 10 percent of the population in 1776 belonged to churches was correct after all. Although Stark and Finke were not concerned with the Christian nation question, their findings were grist for the mill of the skeptics.

Confidence in Stark and Finke is shaken by their casual regard for facts. They misstate, for example, Ezra Stiles's estimate of the population of New England in 1760 by 58,000.[25] The major problem with their work, however, is their methodology. They present what appears to be a simple scheme for estimating the percentage of church membership at the Founding. They multiply the number of American churches in 1776—3,228—by an average number of members—75; the product—242,100—they then divide by the population of the new nation—2,524,296; the quotient—9.6 percent—is the percentage of church membership in the country.

One problem with this scheme is that Stark and Finke skew their figures to produce a low percentage for church membership. Their estimate of the population for the United States in 1776 is 300,000 higher than the calculations of the best American demographic historians.[26] More damaging to their credibility, however, is their figure for average church membership—75—in American congregations in 1776. They must have expended considerable energy in finding sources which would support such a low number. They managed to uncover three, but one, for Presbyterians, is startling, for it is derived from an estimate of Presbyterian congregational size—70— in 1826. What relevance this figure has to *1776* is a mystery that the authors do not explain. That the number is embarrassingly low is demonstrated by the fact that even in 1761, on the western Pennsylvania frontier, a Presbyterian congregation reported 260 communicants.[27] The other two estimates used by the authors are for the sizes of Baptist and Methodist congregations. They use a single Baptist estimate of 74.5 members per congregation in 1784 but this number dates from an even later period, 1841, than the Presbyterian estimate. The Methodist membership count for 1776, 75.7, seems more reliable,[28] but to use it in connection with only two other estimates, dating from 1826 and 1841, as the sole evidence for church membership in 1776 guarantees an artificially low national membership number.

Stark and Finke correctly state that in 1776 many of the nation's sixty-odd Methodist churches had "existed for only a year or two,"[29] an observation that would apply to many of the Baptist churches as well. The focus of the activity of both of these denominations, moreover, was on the frontier or in other sparsely populated areas. The result is that the membership in their fledgling, recently formed churches in thinly populated areas was far lower than in those churches in older, thickly populated sections of the country. Consider the following: in the 1740s Gilbert Tennent's Presbyterian church in Philadelphia had 332 communicants; twenty years later a sister Presbyterian church in New York City had a membership of "12 or 1400 souls." Five Congregational churches in Boston in 1760 had an average membership of 216 families, which, if multiplied by 1.5 to include half as many husbands as wives, would yield a figure of at least 324 members per congregation; during the same period 200 families belonged to the Quaker meeting in Newport, Rhode Island. In Virginia figures for eleven churches in the earliest settled, eastern part of the state revealed 420 members per church.[30] Had Stark and Finke derived average membership numbers from churches in the oldest, most populous parts of the United States, they would have been compelled to increase their estimate of the percentage of Americans belonging to churches in 1776 by a multiple of between three and five. They would, in other words, have been obliged to conclude that 30 to 50 percent of the American population in 1776 was "churched."

There is strong reason to suppose, however, that had Stark and Finke's methodology been sounder their system would have yielded an even higher percentage of "churched" Americans in 1776. Their major problem is that they posit an average membership figure for congregations across the country without offering a definition of what church membership in America meant. Qualifications for membership differed from denomination to denomination and, often, from congregation to congregation within denominations. Devising a one-size-fits-all definition of church membership is so difficult that Bonomi and Eisenstadt, whose article Stark and Finke ignored for obvious reasons, renounced the attempt and used the term adherence as an inclusive word that comprehended the "ministers' interchangeable use of the terms *member, adherent, parishioner and auditor.*"[31]

What can be safely said about church membership during the Founding Period is that in most denominations (the Baptists being a conspicuous exception) it consisted of what might be described as a two-tier system. The most conspicuous example was the Congregational churches of New England, where since 1662 there was a distinction between "half way" members—those who only enjoyed the privilege of baptism—and full members—those who had undergone a regenerative spiritual experience and who could therefore take communion. As time passed, the boundaries between these two kinds of membership disappeared in some churches but were reemphasized in others. Bonomi and Eisenstadt explain, however, that in many New England churches measures were instituted that permitted all who wanted to be baptized to receive the sacrament with the result that most New England Congregationalists and their children were, at a minimum, halfway members or, as Stark and Finke frequently write, were "churched."

Sociologists appear to have an affinity for the term "churched." In 1994 three of Stark and Finke's colleagues offered the following definition of the term: "to be categorized as churched, a person must (1) be a member of a religious body now, and (2) have attended a religious service at least six times during the past year."[32] This definition would fit Congregationalist full and halfway members, including children, all of whom would be considered members by virtue of their baptism and all of whom would certainly have gone—or, as children, been taken—to church six times a year in an area where attendance was legally required and enforced by civil authorities. According to Ezra Stiles, who should have known, the average Congregational church in New England in 1760 contained 160 families.[33] Demographers assume that the average family in colonial America contained 5.7 to 6.0 persons.[34] Using the number five to compensate for the fact that not every family member would have been a church member would yield 800 members per Congregational church or in the sociological parlance 800 "churched" persons per congregation. According to Stark and Finke's formula, the percentage of the "churched" relative to population can be obtained by multiplying the 800 "churched" per congregation by the 661 New England Congregational churches in existence in 1776;[35] the product is 528,800 church members. The best estimate of the population of New England in 1776 is that presented in 1985 by McCusker and Menard: 645,000.[36] Dividing this sum into the number of Congregational church members, 528,800, produces the percentage of "churched" in New England in 1776 as 82, a figure not far from Ezra Stiles's estimate of 87 percent in 1760.[37]

Similar results can be obtained for others colonies. In eighteenth-century Virginia Anglicans dominated, although Presbyterians emerged in force at mid-century, followed a few decades later by Methodists and Baptists. Like their Congregationalist neighbors to the north, Anglicans, Presbyterians and Methodists all had a two-tier system of church membership. All three practiced infant baptism which conferred church membership. The Church of England considered the "act of Baptism [as] the true reception into the Church,"[38] although confirmation and communion, usually administered in the teenage years, were required to perfect membership. Presbyterian authorities explicitly ruled that all "children of those who profess faith in Christ and obedience to his commands are to be considered to be members of the church."[39] Presbyterians recognized a "State of Adult Church membership" which required not only confirmation but also, in many places, the experience of a "work of grace in their souls,"[40] which was similar to the requirement for "full" membership in the Congregational Church. Virginia Anglicans and Presbyterians who had not progressed to full membership would, of course, meet the sociological definition of being "churched" by virtue of their baptism and attendance at church, which in Virginia, as in New England, was customary as well as a legal obligation enforced by civil authorities.

According to the premier authority on the Anglican Church in eighteenth-century Virginia, George Maclaren Brydon, the average congregation contained 150 families.[41] Assuming 5 church members per family, as above, yields 750 "churched" per congregation. Although the average size of Presbyterian congregations in Virginia is difficult to ascertain, Samuel Davies' statement in 1753 that he pastored "between 500 and 600" (whether families or individuals is not clear) might be used for computational purposes.[42] The best set of figures available for the number of congregations in Virginia in the mid-eighteenth century is the list for the year 1750, presented in Edwin Gaustad and Philip Barlow's *New Historical Atlas of Religion in America* (2001): 96 Anglican; 17 Presbyterian; 5 Lutheran; 5 German Reformed; and 3 Baptist.[43] Multiplying the 96 Anglican churches by 750 members and the 17 Presbyterian by 500 and using the same membership figure for each of the 10 German churches, which adhered to membership policies similar to the Anglicans and Presbyterians, yields 85,500 "churched" Virginians in 1750. The best estimate of the white population in Virginia in 1750 is that provided in 1985 by McCusker and Menard: about 142,000.[44] Using this number as the divisor for the 85,500 "churched" in Virginia in 1750 produces a "churched" population of about 60 percent of Virginians.

If the 60 percent figure for Virginia in 1750 is combined with the 82 percent figure for New England in 1760 (derived from a higher sample population, to be sure) the percentage of "churched" people in these two major areas on the eve of the revolutionary agitation would be at least 71 percent, the figure that Bonomi and Eisenstadt obtained in 1982 using different methods. It would be rash to assert that this figure is precise, but it is based on better data and methodology than the irresponsible guesswork of Sweet and the faulty techniques of Stark and Finke which yielded the impossibly low figure of 10 percent churched which Kramnick and Moore used to deny that the United States was a Christian nation. The various processes employed to reach the 10 percent figure resemble, in fact, what might be called Enron-in-reverse research in which numbers are grotesquely deflated to serve the interests of select groups.

Another scholar who has recently entered the lists over the Christian nation question is Professor Jon Butler of Yale, one of the nation's premier authorities on religion in early America. Butler stated his case in an essay, published in 2000, entitled "Why Revolutionary America Wasn't a 'Christian Nation.'"[45] Unlike Kramnick and Moore's broadside, Butler's essay was not a sensationalized, ad hoc polemic. His conclusions about the Christian nation problem flow directly from two decades of stimulating scholarship about eighteenth-century religion and deserve, therefore, the most respectful attention

The thrust of Butler's work has been to restore a comparative dimension to American religious history. He has argued that the recent popularity of social history with its obsessive concentration on local communities has introduced into American religious history a myopia that must be cured by casting the eye on Europe, as earlier scholars did. "A transatlantic focus is a sine qua non," Butler argues, if the religious landscape in eighteenth-century America is to be properly appreciated.[46] Butler analyzes the nature of Christian practice in seventeenth- and eighteenth-century Europe with particular attention to "lay religion" in the Old World. What he finds is a "fragile adherence to Christianity" among "an indifferent and lethargic laypeople." "The crisis of popular and public faith," "the persistent, even deepening, lay indifference to institutional Christianity" afflicted Britain as well as continental Europe. Butler argues that Europeans carried their "incomplete and erratic" adherence to Christianity to America with the result that there was "a remarkable . . . indifference" to religion among the mass of ordinary eighteenth-century Americans, so widespread that the United States in 1776 could not be considered as a nation of committed Christians.[47]

That Butler in his various writings stresses the "*indifference* to Christian practice" in eighteenth-century America is no accident, for he repeatedly cites with approval Crèvecoeur's misleading application of this term to the citizens of the new republic.[48] Butler also cites the unreliable figures of Stark and Finke as confirmation of his conclusion that church membership in America was in the 10 to 20 percent range.[49] Had Butler done nothing more than graft this discredited data onto his theory about the transference of tenuous religious practice from Europe to America, his thesis about a non-Christian America could be regarded as no better than the other recent entrants into the field. But Butler used independent source material to document his claim. When examined, however, it does not support his conclusions.

One of the strengths of Butler's work is his insistence that Puritanism and New England Congregationalism must be deemphasized as the explanatory motifs of American religious history. Accordingly, Butler turned to other denominations, especially to the Church of England, for his documentation. What Butler sought in Anglican and other records was evidence of "strong" religious commitment,[50] characteristic of those who in this chapter have been called the higher tier of colonial Christians, that is, the true believers, those who had experienced the "new birth" or whose faith permitted them to make the solemn affirmations necessary to enjoy "full" membership in their respective churches which permitted participation in the sacrament of communion. "I stress communication figures," Butler asserted.[51] Establishing the percentage of communicants enabled Butler to estimate the number of lower tier members in the churches, the presumably spiritually disengaged, who, in his view, comprised that large mass of "partially Christian people"[52] whose "indifference" belied claims that the new American republic was a genuinely Christian nation.

When Butler found records of communion practice that were appealing, he tended to recycle them. A particular favorite, which he used in at least four of his writings, was a 1724 survey of Anglican church practice commissioned by the bishop of London.[53] According to Butler, responses to this survey indicated that only 10 to 20 percent of American Anglicans took communion. An examination of this survey, which was reprinted by Bonomi and Eisenstadt, reveals that Butler's computations were extraordinarily selective. Many churches, in fact, reported communion rates of between 30 and 50 percent.[54]

Butler also analyzed the reports sent to London by missionaries of the Society for the Propagation of the Gospel in Foreign Parts. Missionaries were obliged to complete a biannual questionnaire, called the *notitia parochialis,* which required them to state, inter alia, the population of the territory they served, the number of those "who profess themselves of the Church of England" and the "number of actual communicants." Butler made multiple use of two series of reports from locations in Delaware. One from Newcastle showed that "Anglican communicants actually declined from 15 to 20 percent of those eligible to 8 or 12 percent between 1744 and 1776."[55] The 8 percent figure must have been particularly appealing to Butler because it matched an 8.7 communication rate reported in a visitation of Yorkshire in 1743,[56] thus supporting his claim that Old World religious indifference was equally pervasive in the New. Inspection of the Newcastle reports reveals that the parish was small and stable: between 1766 and 1775 membership stayed between 130 and 135 and communicants between 15 and 16.[57] But it was not spiritually indifferent, for despite the small percentage of communicants, the resident priest, Aeneas Ross, repeatedly informed his London superiors that "all seem vary desirous to hear the Word read and preached," that "all seem rejoiced to hear Gods Word read and preached."[58]

The second set of figures favored by Butler is from Apoquiniminck, Delaware. Butler's use of these figures is at least as casual as Stark and Finke's; his errors are all the more curious since they work against his thesis. Butler asserts that clergymen at Apoquiniminck "reported that between 1743 and 1752 communicants accounted for no more than 10 to 15 percent of the area's eligible English speaking residents."[59] Between 1743 and 1752 Apoquiniminck was served by two Anglican priests: John Pugh and Philip Reading. Pugh's replies to the *notitia* were so erratic—between 1742 and 1743 they showed without explanation the population of the town falling by more than 50 percent, church membership by 67 percent—that one strongly suspects bureaucratic errors at the SPG home office. Pugh's most plausible figure, recorded in 1742, showed a communion rate of 9.5 percent.[60]

Pugh died in August 1745 and was replaced the next summer by Philip Reading, who served the parish for the next thirty years. Reading's *notitia* numbers are much more consistent and much higher than Pugh's. Between 1747 and 1752 he reported a slightly fluctuating local population of between 2,529 and 2,386. Church membership averaged 763 per year, but on average only 44 per year took communion,[61] which meant that during these years only 5.7 percent of the church members took communion, a far lower figure than Butler presented and one that, using his assumptions, would indicate an even more massive indifference to Christianity in Apoquiniminck parish than he posited. Were pastors Pugh and Reading in despair about the apparent spiritual poverty of their parish? Far from it. In 1742 Pugh wrote SPG authorities that the behavior of his congregation was "very good . . . they attend the publick worship very duly and behave very seriously and devoutly."[62] On September 30, 1747, Reading informed the authorities that the "Churches within my Mission flourish to the highest of my expectations," adding on March 26, 1748, that "the Congregations under my immediate care continue their usual zeal and wonted attendance, firm and constant to the service of the church."[63]

Lest these statements be considered puffery to conceal the true condition of the parish, Reading's later correspondence with the SPG provides concrete evidence that he was not exaggerating the commitment of his parishioners. Reading's correspondence and *notitia* are lost from 1752 to 1761, after which a steady stream of communication is preserved until American independence. Despite little improvement in the average number or percentage of communicants, Reading continued to praise the devotion of his congregation: "the ordinances of religion are in great esteem among them" and the church "continues in as good a state as can be expected" (1760); the church is "flourishing" (1765); conditions are "laudable" (1771); the church is "truly and emphatically militant" (1772).[64] As proof that Reading was not exaggerating, in 1764 his members launched a building campaign, which they sustained for eight years with the result that in 1772 "a commodious, substantial brick church" which would do credit to "a populous city" was dedicated.[65] If we listen to pastors like Reading and Pugh, to the men on the ground two hundred years ago, it is apparent that the degree of communion participation was not a gauge of Christian commitment, as Butler assumes.

There was a profound gravity about communion in the eighteenth century that could create obstacles to a good Christian's receiving the sacrament. It was a doctrine of the Church of England, for example, that confirmation, which must be conducted by a bishop, was a prerequisite for communion. Since there were no bishops in America, confirmation and communion were theoretically impossible, yet many colonial priests apparently waived the requirements, inviting criticism of sanctioning "an abuse of a thing so very sacred."[66] Doubtless many scrupulous Anglicans rejected the sacrament rather than flout church dogma. Among them must have been the members of a parish in the vicinity of Newcastle, Delaware. When Aeneas Ross, the resident at Newcastle, visited the congregation in 1775, he served communion. Only 13 people came forward. The rest of the congregation? It was, Ross reported to London, "large" and "very devout and attentive."[67]

Communion rates tell only half the story of sacramental participation in American Anglican congregations. While rates of communication may have been low and static at Apoquiniminck, baptism, the second great sacrament of the church, flourished there. There were often more than 100 baptisms per year; in 1769 there were 161.[68] Anglican priests noted their congregations' partiality to baptism. Samuel Magaw, the missionary at Dover, Pennsylvania, wrote the SPG in 1773 that his members were "decent, well behaved and regular in their attendance." They were also "very careful to have Baptism administered to their children, but very remiss in the observation of the other sacrament."[69] To assume that people who insisted on sealing their children in Christ's covenant by baptism, which required a profession of faith from the sponsors and a promise to provide Christian nurture, but who may have had scruples about taking communion, were indifferent to Christianity is profoundly misguided and demonstrates the futility of using communion participation as a measure of Christian commitment.

Many dedicated Presbyterians rejected communion for reasons peculiar to that denomination. During the colonial period Presbyterian congregations conducted, once a year, marathon "communion seasons," lasting from three to five days, which often resembled religious revivals and became, in fact, the model for western camp meetings. Days of preaching and fasting culminated in the Sunday communion service, a striking feature of which was a practice called "fencing the table." The presiding minister fenced the table by discouraging—in some cases by intimidating—the unworthy who might be tempted to participate in the sacrament. Some ministers made fencing a "grim and shuddering ordeal," by dwelling on an interminable list of sins that would disqualify a prospective communicant. The apostle Paul's chilling admonition in 1 Corinthians 11:29-30 was regularly read: "For he that eateth and drinketh unworthily, eateth and drinketh damnation to himself." Preachers often described "Plagues spiritual and temporall" that befell the abuser of the sacrament.[70]

Understandably, fencing the table enveloped the Presbyterian communion in anxiety. Many reported approaching the table with "great tremblings."[71] The scrupulous who were doubtful about their spiritual condition were deterred from participating. Figures are fragmentary but it appears that in Scotland and in the colonies as few as 1 in 10 Presbyterians took communion.[72] But it is an affront to common sense to consider as indifferent to Christianity those who "flocked to hear the word expounded"[73] at the communion seasons, who fasted and prayed for days there, but who, anxious about the purity of their Christian profession, refused to commune lest they drink and eat damnation to themselves, as their preachers warned them that they were in danger of doing.

New England's Congregationalists also experienced low communion rates during the colonial period as a result of the same scrupulousness that was at work in other denominations. In a recent publication David Hall cites figures showing that in some New England churches only 10 to 25 percent of the "half way," lower tier church members took communion in the eighteenth century. In New England communion was tinctured with "judgment and danger." Churchgoers there were as familiar as the Presbyterians with Paul's warning about the unworthy communicant's drinking and eating his own damnation. Before participating in the sacrament, therefore, they wanted "to know they shall be sure they believe, that they love God, that they are in the right way." Nothing could be farther from religious indifference than this kind of scrupulous introspection that restrained many serious Christians from taking the cup.[74]

Among colonial Lutherans the awesomeness of communion also dissuaded many from participating in the sacrament. Collin, the Swedish Lutheran minister in New Jersey, reported that at a service in 1783 only two people came forward for communion. One, a man of 60, stopped short of the altar and said that "the sacredness of the action frightened him and that he was perfectly powerless" to proceed.[75] Martin Luther had a similar experience at the feast of Corpus Christi in Eisleben in 1515.[76] Butler's theory would require that Luther be considered as indifferent to religion; such are the pitfalls of using communion participation as a measure of Christian commitment.

Butler has offered a respectable challenge to the Christian nation consensus but his own evidence does not support his theory. Inferences drawn from low communion rates in Europe do not apply to America. The "standoffishness," in many cases literally, toward communion here was a result of anxiety and scrupulosity—in itself an homage to religion; it was, as colonial ministers themselves reported, in no way inconsistent with "devout," even "militant" lay Christianity. The other evidence produced over the past two decades to discredit the Christian nation is little more than a couple of misinterpreted statements of newly arrived Europeans about American religious behavior mixed with a few specious statistics. The recent argument against the Christian nation proves, in short, to be a brief burst of static that can be eliminated with a slight adjustment of the scholarly dial. What then emerges is a message that, until the last few years, has never known interference: the United States during the Founding Period was a Christian nation.

Addendum

Select reasons why the United States during the Founding Period was a Christian nation:

1. Although precise numbers are unobtainable, most Americans in 1776 were members/adherents of a Christian church. Something in the neighborhood of a 70 percent church adherence rate in 1776, the figure proposed by Bonomi and Eisenstadt, is altogether plausible. The greater the reliance on the recent sociological definition of "churched," the higher the percentage of adherence becomes. Of course, not all of the "churched" experienced the new birth in Christ or some other kind of transforming religious experience. But most of them were, according to their own lights, conscientious Christians, striving to be a credit to their faith. Even if they had not attained communicant status, many were, according to their ministers, "devout" and "militant" Christians.

2. Those "unchurched" by distances and inaccessible locations in the American backcountry were not quasi-pagans or votaries of magic and occultism, as Butler sometimes hints. When ministers from settled areas caught up with them, they often found them organized into makeshift Christian congregations; they always found them "hungry after the Word."[77]

3. Far from being prostrated by a religious depression, Christianity in America flourished after 1776. The war of the American Revolution was, to be sure, disruptive for churches along the Atlantic seaboard. Sanctuaries were destroyed; ministers left their congregations for military service. But a new order, foreshadowing the religious landscape of nineteenth-century America, was taking shape along an arc extending from northern New England to the southern Piedmont. During and after the war this area boiled with evangelical energy. Methodists, Baptists and Presbyterians conducted what seemed to be a series of nonstop revivals. Observers reported that they had "seen nothing equal to it for extensive spread, power, and spiritual glory, since the years '40 and '41," i.e., since the Great Awakening.[78] One scholar who has studied the exponential growth of Baptists, Methodists and Presbyterians in the period after independence asserts "that it is more accurate to characterize the years from 1775 to 1790 as a Revolutionary revival" than as a spiritual stupor.[79]

4. After 1776, no fewer than six states, by Leonard Levy's count, established Christianity as the official religion in their respective jurisdictions.[80] South Carolina was the most explicit, proclaiming in its 1778 constitution the establishment of the "Christian Protestant religion." No one, however, could have mistaken the intention of the other states to establish Christianity, even if they used the generic term religion in their constitutions. Commenting on the meaning of the term religion in the Massachusetts Constitution of 1780, a critic observed: "here we have a body of men who call themselves Christians, engaged to make provision for the public worship of God, meaning the worship of Christians (for certainly they did not mean Jewish or Pagan worship.)"[81] In the state documents of the Founding Era religion invariably meant Christianity.

5. In all but two of the original thirteen states the law restricted public office holding to Christians, in many states specifically to Protestants.[82] All but one of the thirteen states had laws against blasphemy. According to Professor Levy, "a blasphemy law protects and favors Christianity over other religions."[83] These laws together with those officially establishing Christianity indicate an intention to constitute a Christian polity in the new states.

6. During and after the Revolutionary War public officials on both the national and state levels saturated the land with religious proclamations, enjoining fasts and thanksgiving. Most savored of Christian doctrine and some used explicitly Christian language: Congress on May 17, 1776, petitioned God that national sins might be forgiven "through the merits and mediation of Jesus Christ"; John Adams on March 23, 1798, implored "the Redeemer of the World freely to remit all our offenses."[84]

7. After 1776 state governments sanctioned Christianity by permitting Christian congregations to make habitual use of their facilities for their religious activities. As soon as the government of Virginia moved into its new capitol in 1788 the "Hall of the House of Delegates was put into regular and constant use as a place of worship." Presbyterians and Episcopalians conducted services on alternating Sundays in the Hall which the Episcopalians also used for vestry meetings. Methodists and Quakers worshiped in the capitol and in 1791 Abbe Jean Dubois celebrated mass in the "court room of the Capitol . . . on the opposite of the Hall

to that in which his Episcopal and Presbyterian brethren officiated."[85] Other states were equally hospitable to Christian congregations.

8. State practice was imitated on the national level as soon as the federal government moved into the new capital in Washington in 1800. Jefferson offered his symbolic support to religion by regularly attending Christian services in the House of Representatives, frequently hearing evangelical ministers declare that "Christ's Body was the Bread of Life and His Blood the drink of the righteous."[86]

9. In addition, Jefferson permitted Christian congregations to use executive office buildings, especially the Treasury and War Office, for church services, including four-hour communion services. Not to be outdone, Chief Justice John Marshall welcomed Christian services in the Supreme Court chambers.[87] On Sundays in Washington the state literally became the Christian church.

10. Why should we be surprised that on Sundays in Jefferson's Washington services of Christian worship proceeded simultaneously in all three branches of government? What else would one expect in a Christian nation?

NOTES

1. Henry Gemery, "The White Population of the Colonial United States," in *A Population History of North America*, ed. Michael R. Haines and Richard H. Steckel (New York: Cambridge University Press, 2000), 150.

2. An unknown number of African slaves may have been Muslims. See Allan Austin, *African Muslims in Antebellum America: A Sourcebook* (New York: Garland Publishers, 1984).

3. Patricia Bonomi, book review of Jon Butler, *Awash in a Sea of Faith Christianizing the American People* (Cambridge, Mass.: Harvard University Press, 1990) in *William and Mary Quarterly* 48, no. 1 (January 1991): 118.

4. Sweet did, in fact, cite one piece of evidence for New England. For the remainder of the colonies he provided nothing. William Warren Sweet, "The American Colonial Environment and Religious Liberty," *Church History* 4 (March 1935): 52-53.

5. Sydney Ahlstrom, *A Religious History of the American People* (New Haven, Conn.: Yale University Press, 1972), 365.

6. J. Franklin Jameson, *The American Revolution Considered as a Social Movement* (Princeton, N.J.: Princeton University Press, 1926), 94.

7. Justin Winsor, *The Memorial History of Boston* (Boston: J.R. Osgood and Company, 1881-1883), vol. 3, 403.

8. William Warren Sweet, *Religion in Colonial America* (New York: Scribner, 1965), 336.

9. Isaac Kramnick and R. Laurence Moore, *The Godless Constitution: The Case against Religious Correctness* (New York: W.W. Norton & Company, 1996), 12-13.

10. Kramnick and Moore, *Godless Constitution*, 29, 31. Edward Earle, ed., *The Federalist* (New York: Random House, Inc., 1941), 9.

11. *Federalist*, 231.

12. Kramnick and Moore, *Godless Constitution*, 27, 28.

13. Daniel L. Dreisbach, ed., *Religion and Politics in the Early Republic: Jasper Adams and the Church-State Debate* (Lexington: University Press of Kentucky, 1996), 7.

14. Kramnick and Moore, *Godless Constitution*, 17.

15. Patricia Bonomi and Peter R. Eisenstadt, "Church Adherence in the Eighteenth-Century British American Colonies," *William and Mary Quarterly* 39, no. 2 (April 1982): 247.

16. Amandus Johnson, ed., *The Journal and Biography of Nicholas Collin 1746-1831* (Philadelphia: The New Jersey Society of Pennsylvania, 1936), 218.

17. James H. Smylie, "Protestant Clergy, the First Amendment and Beginnings of a Constitutional Debate, 1781-1791," *The Religion of the Republic* (Philadelphia: Fortress Press, 1971), 149.

18. Smylie, "Protestant Clergy," 149.

19. Albert E. Stone, ed., *Letters from an American Farmer and Sketches of Eighteenth-Century America* (New York: Penguin Books, 1986), 73.

20. Johnson, *Nicholas Collin*, 218.

21. Kramnick and Moore, *Godless Constitution*, 16-17.

22. Bonomi and Eisenstadt, "Church Adherence," 274 n.

23. Rodney Stark and Roger Finke, "American Religion in 1776: A Statistical Portrait," *Sociological Analysis* 49 (1988): 39-51.

24. Stark and Finke, "American Religion," 40.

25. Stark and Finke assert (44) that Stiles claimed that the population of New England in 1760 was 449,634; Stiles's actual figure was 507,000. Franklin B. Dexter, ed., *Extracts from the Itineraries and Other Miscellanies of Ezra Stiles* (New Haven, Conn.: Yale University Press, 1916), 93.

26. Stark and Finke calculate the population for the United States in 1776 by multiplying the number of congregations, 3,228, by 782 Americans per congregation (42); the source of this ratio, 782 to 1, is not revealed. In 1975 Robert Wells estimated the

population of the United States in 1775 at 2,204,500. Robert V. Wells, *The Population of the British Colonies in America before 1776* (Princeton, N.J.: Princeton University Press, 1975), 284. In 1985 John McCusker and Russell Menard estimated the population at around 2.1 million in 1770. John McCusker and Russell Menard, *The Economy of British America, 1607-1789* (Chapel Hill: University of North Carolina Press, 1985), 103, 136, 172, 203. Henry Gemery, "White Population," 150, relies on their figures.

27. Stark and Finke, "American Religion," 42. William B. Bynum, "'The Genuine Presbyterian Whine:' Presbyterian Worship in the Eighteenth Century," *American Presbyterians The Journal of Presbyterian History* 74, no. 3 (Fall 1996): 168.

28. Stark and Finke, "American Religion," 42.

29. Stark and Finke, "American Religion," 41.

30. Leigh Eric Schmidt, *Holy Fairs Scottish Communions and American Revivals in the Early Modern Period* (Princeton, N.J.: Princeton University Press, 1989), 105; Bonomi and Eisenstadt, "Church Adherence," 257-58 (note that Bonomi and Eisenstadt equate Anglican auditors with members), 270, 273.

31. Bonomi and Eisenstadt, "Church Adherence," 253.

32. Dean Hoge, Benton Johnson, Donald A. Luidens, *Vanishing Boundaries: The Religion of Mainline Protestant Baby Boomers* (Louisville, Ky.: Westminster/John Knox Press, 1994), 67.

33. Bonomi and Eisenstadt, "Church Adherence," 270.

34. Gemery, "White Population," 145; see also Jim Potter, "Demographic Development and Family Structure," in *Colonial British America: Essays in the New History of the Modern Era*, ed., Jack P. Greene and J. R. Pole (Baltimore: Johns Hopkins University Press, 1984), 146.

35. Stark and Finke identify 668 Congregational churches in the United States in 1776; their figures seem to indicate that 7 of these churches were outside of New England. Stark and Finke, "American Religion," 47,49.

36. McCusker and Menard, *Economy of British America*, 103.

37. Stiles's percentage is obtained by dividing his estimate of the population of New England in 1760, 507,000, into his estimate of membership in the Congregational Church, 445,000. Stiles, *Extracts from the Itineraries*, 93.

38. John H. Blunt, *The Annotated Book of Common Prayer* (New York: E. P. Dutton & Co., 1888), 447-48.

39. Richard R. Osmer, *Confirmation Presbyterian Practice in Ecumenical Perspective* (Louisville, Ky.: Geneva Press, 1996), 132.

40. Schmidt, *Holy Fairs*, 71, 84.

41. Bonomi and Eisenstadt, "Church Adherence," 274.

42. George Pilcher, *Samuel Davies; Apostle of Dissent in Colonial Virginia* (Knoxville: University of Tennessee Press, 1971), 88.

43. Edwin Gaustad and Philip Barlow with the special assistance of Richard W. Dishno, *New Historical Atlas of Religion in America* (New York: Oxford University Press, 2001), 399.

44. McCusker and Menard, *Economy of British America*, 136. In 1750 McCusker and Menard estimate the slave population of the Chesapeake colonies at 40 percent, which must be deducted from their estimate of Virginia's total population in 1750— 236,700.

45. James H. Hutson, ed., *Religion and the New Republic*, (Lanham, Md., Rowman & Littlefield, 2000), 187-202.

46. Jon Butler, *Awash in a Sea of Faith Christianizing the American People* (Cambridge, Mass.: Harvard University Press, 1990), 5.

47. Butler, *Awash in a Sea*, 18, 31, 32, 34, 36, 38, 193.

48. Hutson, *Religion and the New Republic*, 187, 191; Butler, *Awash in a Sea*, 192-93; Jon Butler, "Coercion, Miracle, Reason: Rethinking the American Religious Experience in the Revolutionary Age," in *Religion in a Revolutionary Age*, ed. Ronald Hoffman and Peter J. Albert (Charlottesville: University Press of Virginia), 20.

49. Hutson, *Religion and the New Republic*, 199, note 6.

50. Hutson, *Religion and the New Republic*, 191.

51. Butler, "Coercion, Miracle," 19 n.

52. Hutson, *Religion and the New Republic*, 198.

53. Hutson, *Religion and the New Republic*, 191; Butler, *Awash in a Sea*, 191; Butler, "Coercion, Miracle," 19; Butler, "Church Membership Less Than God-Fearing," in *Mapping America's Past: A Historical Atlas*, ed. Mark C. Carnes and John A. Garraty with Patrick Williams (New York: Henry Holt and Company, 1996), 50.

54. Bonomi and Eisenstadt, "Church Adherence," 277-86.

55. Butler, "Coercion, Miracle," 19.

56. Butler, *Awash in a Sea*, 36.

57. Society for the Propagation of the Gospel transcripts, series B, vol. 21, part II, Manuscript Division, Library of Congress.

58. Aeneas Ross, *notitia parochialis*, October 8, 1761; April 10, 1771; SPG transcripts, Library of Congress; hereinafter cited as LC..

59. Butler, "Coercion, Miracle," 19.

60. For Pugh's replies to the *notitia*, 1742-1745, see SPG transcripts, series B, vols. 10-12, LC..

61. For Reading's replies, see SPG transcripts, series B, vols. 15-20, LC.

62. Pugh to Philip Bearcroft, n.d., but noted as received, March 14, 1742, SPG transcripts, series B, vol. 10, LC.

63. Reading to Bearcroft, September 30, 1747, March 26, 1748, SPG transcripts, series B, vol.16, LC.

64. Reading to Daniel Burton, June 25, 1765, October 2, 1771, October 3, 1772, March 1775 (copies letter of May 1760), SPG transcripts, series B, volume 21, II, LC.

65. Reading to Burton, March 22, 1772, SPG transcripts, series B, volume 21, II, LC.

66. Hugh Jones, *The Present State of Virginia*, ed. Richard Morton (Chapel Hill: The University of North Carolina Press, 1956), 119.

67. Aeneas Ross to Daniel Burton, October 10, 1775, SPG transcripts, series B, volume 21, II, LC.

68. Reading to Daniel Burton, March 31, November 11, 1769, SPG transcripts, series B, volume 21, II, LC.

69. Samuel Magaw to Daniel Burton, November 16, 1773, SPG transcripts, series B, volume 21, II, LC..

70. Bynum, "'Genuine Whine,'" 166-67; Schmidt, *Holy Fairs,* 159-60.

71. Schmidt, *Holy Fairs,* 160.

72. Bynum, "'Genuine Whine,'" 166.

73. Schmidt, *Holy Fairs,* 42.

74. David D. Hall, ed., *Jonathan Edwards Ecclesiastical Writings* (New Haven, Conn.: Yale University Press, 1994), 36-37.

75. Johnson, ed., *Journal of Collin,* 273.

76. Martin Brecht, *Martin Luther Sein Weg zur Reformation 1483-1521* (Stuttgart: Calwer Verlag, 1981), 81.

77. James H. Hutson, *Religion and the Founding of the American Republic* (Hanover, N.H.: University Press of New England, 6th ed., 2002), 22; Bonomi and Eisenstadt, "Church Adherence," 267.

78. Schmidt, *Holy Fairs,* 62.

79. Stephen A. Marini, "Religion, Politics and Ratification," in *Religion in a Revolutionary Age,* ed. Ronald Hoffman and Peter J. Albert (Charlottesville: University Press of Virginia, 1994), 193-99.

80. Leonard Levy, *The Establishment Clause Religion and the First Amendment* (New York: Macmillan, 1986), 25-62. The states were, according to Levy's broad definition of establishment, Georgia, South Carolina, Maryland, Connecticut, Massachusetts and New Hampshire.

81. Philanthropos, *Continental Journal* (Boston), March 23, 1780.

82. Kramnick and Moore, *Godless Constitution,* 30.

83. Leonard Levy, *Blasphemy: Verbal Offense against the Sacred, from Moses to Salman Rushdie* (New York: Alfred Knopf Publishers, 1993), 267.

84. Hutson, *Religion and the Founding,* 54, 82.

85. Hutson, "Thomas Jefferson's Letter to the Danbury Baptists: A Controversy Rejoined," *William and Mary Quarterly* 56, no. 4 (October 1999): 787.

86. Hutson, *Religion and the Founding,* 84-89.

87. Hutson, *Religion and the Founding,* 89-91.

Chapter 5

William Penn and the American Tradition of Religious Liberty

William Penn's Charter of Privileges of 1701 is a landmark of religious liberty which deserves to be commemorated. The topic assigned to me, Religious Liberty from William Penn to the Declaration,[1] assumes that there is a relationship between Penn's Charter of Privileges and Jefferson's Declaration of Independence and seems to invite the inference that by promulgating the Charter, William Penn became, posthumously, a Founding Father of the United States. I have not, I must report, discovered any evidence of a direct connection between the Charter and the Declaration. There is, nevertheless, sufficient evidence to secure Penn a place in the Revolutionary pantheon, for knowledge of his accomplishments helped to shape the debates about freedom of conscience which developed in the new states after 1776, debates which informed the statesmen, who, in 1789, wrote religious liberty into the First Amendment to the Constitution.

It is not widely recognized by present-day Americans that today's rationale for religious liberty has changed little since 1776. In one respect this is a tribute to William Penn, since virtually every claim on behalf of freedom of conscience in the Founding Period can be found in his writings a century earlier. In another sense this is a source of concern, for it means that the arguments currently available for freedom of conscience are, essentially, an ossified legacy of the Christian world of the seventeenth century. In an environment more secular and more religiously pluralistic than Penn or the Founding Fathers could have imagined, these arguments may no longer be adequate to defend religious freedom.

The issuing of the charter of 1701 was emphatically no cause of celebration for William Penn. It represented a capitulation to the cantankerous Quakers of Pennsylvania in a political dispute that had poisoned mutual relations for twenty years and had caused Penn, in assessing the progress of the colony, to observe, as early as 1686, that he had heard "nothing but good said of the place and little thats good said of the people."[2] The Quaker settlers had adamantly insisted against Penn's equally adamant opposition on expanding the power of the assembly at the expense of the council, the apple of Penn's eye. In the fall of 1701, Penn threw in the towel and agreed to issue a new charter that stripped the council of power and created a unicameral assembly with wide authority. "I acquiesced," he complained to a supporter, "having first shewed my Dislike" at the people's demand for a new charter "which their children, as I told them, will have perhaps cause sufficient to repent of their folly therein."[3]

At issue in 1701 was the distribution of political power, not religion, with whose status in the province everyone was satisfied. Penn, nevertheless, in promulgating the Charter of 1701 reiterated the religious principles on which the province had been founded. To emphasize their priority he made them the first article. They cannot be read too often:

> Because noe people can be truly happy though under the Greatest Enjoyments of Civil Liberties if Abridged of the Freedom of theire Consciences as to theire Religious Profession and Worship. And Almighty God being the only Lord of Conscience Father of Lights and Spirits and the Author as well as the Object of all divine knowledge Faith and Worship who only can Enlighten the mind and perswade and Convince the understandings of people. I doe hereby Grant and Declare that noe person or persons Inhabiting in this Province or Territories who shall Confesse and Acknowledge one Almighty God the Creator upholder and Ruler of the world and professe him or themselves Obliged to live quietly under the Civill Governement shall be in any case molested or prejudiced in his or theire person or Estate because of his or theire Conscientious perswasion or practice nor be compelled to frequent or mentaine any Religious Worship

place or Ministry contrary to his or theire mind or Suffer any other act or thing contrary to theire Religious perswasion.[4]

The 1701 Charter also permitted anyone believing in "Jesus Christ the Saviour of the world" to hold office in Pennsylvania, a provision that conferred on Catholics political equality with their fellow citizens. By prohibiting the civil incapacitation of Catholics, Penn seized higher ground than other advanced thinkers of his time. In his *Letter Concerning Toleration* (1689) his friend John Locke argued against any toleration whatsoever for Catholics. Roger Williams would have disarmed them and required them to wear distinctive clothing as a condition for worshiping freely.[5]

To emphasize the surpassing value of liberty of conscience Penn concluded his charter by attempting, benevolently but imperiously, to bind his successors to keep it sacred: "I Doe hereby Solemnly Declare Promise and Grant for me my heires and Assignes that the first Article of this Charter Relateing to Liberty of Conscience . . . shall be kept and remaine without any Alteration Inviolably for ever."[6] This distinctive clause anticipates a later, even more celebrated attempt to bind future public officials to treat liberty of conscience as irrevocable: Thomas Jefferson's Bill for Establishing Religious Freedom, whose passage by the Virginia Legislature in 1786 he commemorated on his tombstone. In the concluding passage of this famous statute Jefferson put future lawmakers on notice that liberty of conscience was a natural right which must not be profaned.[7]

As important as the charter of 1701 is as a milestone on the road to religious freedom, it was not in any sense an innovation. The language in the charter was, in fact, a reiteration with slight modifications of article 35 of the Laws Agreed Upon in England in 1682,[8] which Penn had promulgated to establish religious guidelines for his province on the eve of settlement. An equally expansive offer of liberty of conscience was contained in the West New Jersey Concessions of 1676, which Penn may have assisted in writing.[9] Other colonial charters issued after the restoration of Charles II in 1660 also promised to respect the religious convictions of prospective settlers, all on the pragmatic grounds that, as Penn himself expressed it, "an unpeopled Country can never be planted if there be not due encouragement given to Sober people of all sorts," for who would risk emigrating to America, if the "Sweet of their browes may be made the forfeit of their Conscience?"[10]

In 1661 Charles II's ministers drafted a proclamation for the king's signature offering as an "encouragement" for the settlement of Jamaica, at that time little more than a nest of pirates, religious "freedom for all Protestants willing to live peaceably."[11] In 1669 a group of aristocratic proprietors promulgated the "Fundamental Constitutions of Carolina" in which they offered prospective settlers at least as much religious liberty as Penn did and possibly more, since they permitted Jews and God-fearing "heathens" to form churches and ordered that "no person whatsoever shall disturb, molest, or persecute another for his speculative opinions in Religion."[12] Penn, who studied the earlier charters, was familiar with the language of the Carolina Constitutions but he used as his model for defining liberty of conscience the Rhode Island Charter of 1663. From that charter Penn incorporated into his first charter of 1681 the following words verbatim: "all and everye person and persons may, from tyme to tyme, and at all times hereafter, freelye and fullye have and enjoye his and theire own judgments and consciences, in matters of religious concernments."[13] That these words were struck from the 1681 charter by a royal bureaucrat does not lessen their importance for they connect William Penn to that other towering seventeenth-century apostle of religious liberty, Roger Williams.

Although the careers of Penn and Williams were similar—both persecuted for conscience sake (the one jailed, the other exiled) and both founders of provinces grounded in religious liberty—their theological convictions were different, so different that Williams "hated" everything the Quakers represented and publicly vilified them,[14] receiving in return from the Friends an equal measure of vitriol. In his diatribe against one of the luminaries of Quakerism, *George Fox Digg'd Out of His Burrowes* (1676), Williams flayed the Friends as "greedy Wolves, devouring the souls of the . . . innocent lambs and sheep of Christ."[15] Elsewhere he called them heretics, "poor filthy dreamers as . . . Monstrous, and Blasphemous as the Papists," fanatics possessed of the "spirit of Sathan."[16] The Quakers countered by denouncing Williams as a "filthy" individual, who spread "impudent lyes and slanders" about them.[17] In the summer of 1677 Penn hosted a three-week conclave of Quaker leaders at his summer home in Sussex at which a reply to Williams's polemic was hammered out. Published in 1678 as *A New-England Fire-Brand Quenched,* this screed accused Williams of writing his "scurrilous book" for the benefit of "priests" and "bad magistrates, that licked up his vomit." Williams, the Quakers continued, "hath transgressed for a piece of bread. And so all are joined with the Red Dragon to pour out their flood against the Man-Child."[18] This mudslinging revealed another similarity between Penn and Williams for both endorsed "spiritual warfare" as an alternative to the exercise of the civil police power and, as a result, both were committed to the unrestrained expression of religious sentiments, however obnoxious.

Penn and Williams are also similar in the treatment they have received from historians, who in the post–World War II years have appeared to be on a mission to deflate their reputations. Williams has taken the most damaging blows, especially from the dean of the historians of religion in colonial America, Perry Miller, who declared that although Williams "is celebrated as the prophet of religious freedom, he actually exerted little or no influence on institutional developments in America; only after the conception of liberty for all denominations had triumphed on wholly other grounds did Americans look back on Williams and invest him with his ill-fitting halo."[19] The notion that Penn's ideas had enduring influence in American history has also been challenged recently. In a debunking paper delivered in Philadelphia in 1976 to celebrate the Bicentennial of American Independence the distinguished Bryn Mawr College historian, Caroline Robbins, minimized Penn's legacy. He was, according to Professor Robbins, "seldom cited during the discussions of the last quarter of the eighteenth century. Allusions to him are almost non-existant. Even Quakers, arrested in 1777, and suspected of Tory sympathies, quoted in their own defense, not Penn, but Charles Secondat, Baron de Montesquieu."[20]

Penn does not deserve this disparagement. He has not failed posterity; rather historians have failed to do the necessary research to appreciate his influence during the Founding Period. For reasons that will presently appear, Penn can be shown to have had considerable influence in the southern states in the years after 1776, especially in Virginia during the crucial debates on the relationship between church and state that culminated with the passage of Jefferson's Religious Freedom statute in 1786. Penn was enlisted in the cause of religious liberty in revolutionary South Carolina and was featured in a depiction of a pantheon of heroes of religious freedom in a print produced in Maryland in 1793. Jefferson himself extravagantly saluted Penn in 1825 when Philadelphians invited the ex-president to join a Society for the Commemoration of the Landing of William Penn on the American Shore. "He learns with sincere pleasure," Jefferson wrote the organizers of the event, "that a day will at length be annually set aside for rendering the honors so justly due to the greatest law-giver the world has produced, the first, in either antient or modern times, who has laid the foundation of government in the pure and unadulterated principles of peace, of reason and right."[21]

This effusion suggests that Jefferson may have misunderstood some aspects of William Penn's career. Jefferson owned two of Penn's religious works in which the Quaker leader attacked one of the president's theological bêtes noires, the orthodox concept of the Trinity. Jefferson may, therefore, have assumed that Penn was a rationalist, a Bolingbroke in a broad-brimmed hat. Penn, of course, was nothing of the sort and defended liberty of conscience on grounds different from those employed by the deists of his day. His favorite argument for liberty of conscience was based on the Bible, specifically, on the New Testament, properly interpreted.

Penn was absolutely certain that employing "external force in matters of faith and worship is no less than the overthrow of the whole Christian religion."[22] He was always ready with a long list of New Testament passages to prove his point. His favorite verse, which runs like a leitmotiv through his writings, was John 18:36 in which Christ declared: "My kingdom is not of this world, for then would my servants fight for me." In a characteristic gloss Penn explained that "because the kingdoms of this world are evidently set up by and maintained by worldly force, and that he will have no worldly force used in the business of his kingdom, that therefore it is not of this world. Consequently, those that attempt to set up his kingdom by worldly force, or make that their pretence to use it, are none of his servants."[23] The "gross Apprehension of the nature of Christ's Kingdom," Penn informed the Prince of Orange, accounted for the mistakes "about the means of promoting it, else were it not Credible, that men should think, Clubs, Prisons & Banishments the proper Mediums of inlightening the Understanding."[24] In 1686 Penn summarized his understanding of the teaching of the New Testament: "Christ forbad fire, though from heaven itself, to punish dissenters, and commanded that the tares should grow with the wheat till harvest. In fine, that we should love enemies themselves: and, to exclude worldly strife for religion, that his kingdom is not of this world. This was the doctrine of the blessed Saviour of the world."[25]

Penn's scriptural arguments were not new. In his *Bloudy Tenent, of Persecution, for cause of Conscience* (1644) Roger Williams used many of the same texts and reached the same conclusion as Penn had, that Christ had placed conscience beyond the reach of the magistrate by making the civil and spiritual spheres of "different natures and Considerations," separated in their missions "as far as the Heavens are from the Earth." Penn's conclusions were, in fact, barely distinguishable from those of Martin Luther a century and a half earlier, who had affirmed that the "Lawes of the Civill magistrates government extends no further than over the body or goods, and to that which is externall: for over the soule God will not suffer any man to rule: only he himself will rule there."[26]

Penn's second major argument for liberty of conscience, the pragmatic or what he called the "prudential"one,[27] was also familiar, although few religious figures of his time emphasized it as much as he did. Penn moved on a larger stage than other religious leaders. He was a courtier and entrepreneur, a friend of kings, of leading politicians and investors, and a lobbyist, who patrolled the corridors of power in London. He knew that those who composed this audience would only listen to practical arguments that proved that persecution did not work and that it damaged the concrete interests of the state.

Persecution, Penn tirelessly insisted, was a waste of the state's time and energy. The dearest convictions of men could not be changed by force. "External coercive power," he said, "could not convince the understanding of the poorest ideot."[28] As a sometime prisoner of conscience, Penn could personally testify to the futility of force. "The Tower [of London], he wrote, was the worst argument in the world to convince me, for whoever was in the wrong, those who used force for religion never could be in the right."[29] Persecution, Penn contended, was counter-productive, for its harvest was a "hypocritical conformist, than whom nothing is more detestable to God."[30] The "very sufferings," moreover, of its victims "beget that compassion in the multitude, which rarely misses of making many friends, and proves often a preparation for not a few proselytes. So much more revered is suffering than making men suffer for religion."[31]

Penn was particularly eager to call the attention of the nation's elite to the social damage that persecution inflicted on the country. Contrary to claims of the proponents of religious uniformity, Penn asserted that the dissenters had not been "the true cause of that perplexed disturbance" which had embroiled England throughout the seventeenth century. Crushing dissent would not produce social peace, as they alleged; rather it would merely increase the supply of inflammatory material in the body politic, for "Raped consciences Treasure up Revenge."[32] The only way to procure domestic tranquility was to permit a "hearty toleration, " for if "men enjoy their property, and their conscience . . . without molestation, what should they object against, or plot for?"[33] "On this ground empire stands safe; on the other, it seems more uncertain."[34]

That the nation's economic prosperity depended on liberty of conscience was Penn's strongest prudential argument and he pressed it unremittingly. "Experience tells us," he claimed, that "where it [toleration] is in any degree admitted, the King's affairs prosper most: people, wealth, and strength being sure to follow such indulgence." Look at Holland, he urged his country's political leaders. "That bog of the world, neither sea nor dry land, now rival of the tallest monarchs . . . by her own superlative clemency and industry; for the one was the effect of the other; she cherished her people, whatsoever were their opinions, as the reasonable stock of the country, the heads and hands of her trade and wealth; and making them easy in the main point, their conscience, she became great by them: this made her fill with people, and they filled her with riches and strength."[35] Count the costs of persecution, Penn counseled Charles II. "Can it be to the interest of the Kingdome to have many of all thes sorts of usefull people in the Land Wasted and Distroyed . . . If [this] soe be the polecey of Govermentt which way shall Manufactores goe one? Rents be paid to the Land lord and takses to the King?"[36] Penn also applied the lessons of colonizing the New World to England itself, asserting that persecution "must be a great discouragement to strangers from coming in, and in settling themselves amongst us,"[37] thereby invigorating the kingdom with fresh infusions of human and financial capital. Penn's message was as clear as it was recurrent: liberty of conscience paved the way for "peace and plenty," even "opulency."[38]

The third major ingredient in Penn's argument for liberty of conscience, rights, was a newcomer in the decades-old discourse on religious freedom. Penn's confident and repeated assertion that individuals had an "incommunicable right of government over conscience"[39] was a species of language absent from treatises of Roger Williams and other earlier advocates of religious freedom. Penn, of course, did not invent rights. The last decades of the seventeenth century teemed with "rights talk," generated by seminal thinkers like Penn's friend, John Locke. In introducing rights into the argument for liberty of conscience, Penn was using a concept that had just come on the market in his nation's intellectual emporiums. Penn acknowledged his debt to others by citing, in his powerful pamphlet, *The Great Case of Liberty of Conscience,* "the saying of a person . . . too great to be named now, 'That liberty of conscience is every man's natural right.'" Penn's conviction that the right to liberty of conscience was "the inspiration of the Almighty" and the "gift of God"[40] provides, if not a link, at least a similarity to the

Declaration of Independence whose author also asserted that rights were the gift of the Creator.

For Penn the deprivation of the Quakers' right to liberty of conscience by the king's officials, bad enough in itself, led to an intolerable train of assaults on purely "civil rights" not "forfeitable for religious nonconformity."[41] Under the Conventicle Acts of 1664 and 1670 Quakers could be tried by two justices of the peace who were empowered to confiscate their property without a jury trial. According to Penn, these procedures violated "ancient and undoubted rights of Englishmen"[42] against which he passionately protested, regaling his readers and listeners with legal arguments that he had learned as a student at Lincoln's Inn in the mid-1660s. Some of Penn's most celebrated pamphlets, his *England's Present Interest Considered*, for example, were legal briefs on behalf of rights, serving up large dollops of Sir Edward Coke, explicating the ancient Saxon constitution, and stringing together quotations from Magna Carta, the Petition of Right, and famous law cases with a facility equal to his ability to arrange passages from Scripture. Penn never doubted that, if the king's officials would guarantee "an inviolable and impartial maintenance of English rights,"[43] the Quakers' problems would disappear.

In 1944 the eminent historian of religion, Henry Cadbury, wrote, concerning liberty of conscience, that "nearly everything worth saying on this subject had been said even before William Penn became a Quaker."[44] This is, in general, true, yet Penn's three-pronged argument for religious freedom was powerful because scarcely anyone before had translated such diverse personal experiences into so comprehensive a case for liberty of conscience. As a religious leader, Penn offered Scripture as a foundation for soul liberty; as a politician and businessman, prudence; as a student of the law, rights.

A warm admirer of Penn, Cadbury, nevertheless, anticipated Professor Robbins's approach by warning that it was "very hard to appraise" the influence of Penn's multilayered case for liberty of conscience. Penn often wrote anonymously, fearing, Cadbury speculated, that his identity as a member of a despised sect would prejudice readers against his arguments.[45] Penn's writings were, moreover, not widely available in America, Philadelphia and its environs excepted. Finally, the case for liberty of conscience, as Penn himself conceded in 1675, "hath been so often and excellently done by men of wit, learning and conscience"[46] that, like coins of the realm, the various components of his message were in wide circulation and reached America through multiple channels. As a result, eighteenth-century American spokesmen for liberty of conscience can be found who used the same arguments Penn had employed, without ascribing them to him or even knowing that he had used them.

Grounding freedom of conscience in rights is a good example of how one of Penn's principal arguments was transmitted to America by one of his paragons of "wit, learning and conscience": John Locke. In 1689 and 1690 three of Locke's principal works issued from the presses in England: *A Letter Concerning Toleration, Two Treatises of Government,* and *An Essay Concerning Human Understanding.* Each of these works profoundly influenced Anglo-American thought. Common to the first two was the assertion that men possessed fundamental rights which should be protected by governments. In *A Letter Concerning Toleration,* Locke, for example, declared that "liberty of conscience is every man's natural right, equally belonging to dissenters as to themselves; and that nobody ought to be compelled in matters of religion either by law or force."[47] Locke's ideas were quickly assimilated by America's leading intellectuals, who at the beginning of the eighteenth century were clergymen, as Edmund S. Morgan has pointed out. These divines liberally "dispensed" Locke's doctrines.[48] In 1716 tutors at Yale introduced Locke "as fast as they could."[49] By the 1740s clergymen, especially in New England, were expertly armed with the Lockean doctrine of natural rights and were prepared to use it to repel assaults against conscience.

After the passage of the Toleration Act of 1689 the religious landscape in New England became relatively placid. The Act was received with good grace by local political and religious leaders and in a testimony to the degree to which rights language had penetrated New England it was assumed to have granted rights of conscience, even though it did nothing more than suspend the statutory penalties for dissent from the Church of England and permit dissenting ministers to hold meetings, if they obtained licenses from the authorities. No less a bulwark of the Congregationalist elite than Cotton Mather asserted in 1690 that "for every man to worship God according to his Conviction, is an essential Right of Humane nature."[50] A few years later Mather boasted that "New England has Renounced whatever laws are against a Just Liberty of Conscience" and in 1718 he signaled the coming of the new era in Massachusetts by participating in the ordination of a Baptist minister. In 1727 the Massachusetts establishment sealed the accommodation with its erstwhile ecclesiastical adversaries by exempting Episcopalians, Quakers and Baptists from taxes laid to support the Congregational Church.

A decade later religious conflict was reignited by the Great Awakening, a volcanic religious revival that convulsed the colonies. The Awakening produced new religious groups, whose beliefs and behavior (like the Quakers' a century earlier) scandalized members of the existing churches. Called New Lights in New England and the New Side from the Middle Colonies southward, these new groups were boisterous beneficiaries of the "new birth," interpreted as a dynamic operation of the Holy Spirit which produced often extravagant emotional displays that opponents attributed to operations of Satan.

The New Lights put to the test the professions of toleration that were so profuse in New England after 1689. Their mainline opponents acquitted themselves well enough, refraining from the kind of blanket persecution that might have been initiated in the seventeenth century. In theory they agreed, often grudgingly, to be sure, that the New Lights ought to enjoy freedom of conscience. Problems arose with the manner in which the New Lights wanted to put their convictions into practice. The New Lights insisted on preaching the Gospel anywhere, anytime. Settled ministers resented the intrusion into their parishes of roving evangelists with the result that in Connecticut they persuaded the state legislature to pass legislation prohibiting "itineracy," which provoked an outcry that the state had violated its citizens' liberty of conscience. Locke's influence was unmistakable in the writings of those New Light sympathizers who protested against alleged persecution by Connecticut's legislators. Solomon Paine, for example, cited every believer's "inalienable Right in matters of the worship of God to judge for himself as his conscience receives the Rule from God."[51]

The most comprehensive and closely argued case for liberty of conscience in Connecticut was made in 1744 by a former president of Yale, Elisha Williams. His *Essential Rights and Liberties of Protestants* groaned with New Testament quotations, making the familiar point, which must have seemed hackneyed by the mid-eighteenth century, that the civil and spiritual realms, being totally incompatible, could not partake of each other: "If Christ be the Lord of the conscience, the sole King in his own kingdom; then it will follow, that all such as in any manner or degree assume the power of directing and governing the consciences of men, are justly chargeable with invading his rightful dominion." Williams supplemented the scriptural argument by offering substantial paraphrases of Locke, not apologizing for giving a "sketch of what the celebrated Mr. Locke in his *Treatise of Government* has largely demonstrated; and in which it is justly to be presumed all are agreed who understand the natural rights of mankind." From Locke Williams understood and repeatedly reminded his readers, so that they would understand that every individual possessed a "right of private judgment" in religion and that "this right of private judgment and worshipping GOD, according to their consciences, being the natural and unalienable right of everyman what men by entering into civil society neither did, nor could give up into the hands of the community; it is but a just consequence, that they are to be protected in the enjoyment of this right."[52]

Scriptural and Lockean arguments were also used in New England by the second major offspring of the Great Awakening: the Separate Baptists, most of whom had originally been New Lights. They fell afoul of authorities over ecclesiastical taxation, an exemption from which they refused to accept in the manner authorized by the state. Unable to support their ministry in an uncompromisingly voluntary way, they accused Massachusetts of religious persecution. Their principal spokesman, Isaac Backus, tirelessly lobbied for liberty of conscience by citing familiar scriptural passages like John 18:36 (Christ's kingdom is not of this world) and by quoting Locke's *Letter Concerning Toleration.*[53]

The Great Awakening also roiled the religious status quo in the South. Beginning in the 1740s New Side Presbyterians and Separate Baptists began invading Virginia, arousing official resentment that resulted in persecution. The issue in Virginia was the enforcement of the Toleration Act of 1689. Unlike officials in New England, authorities in the Old Dominion required dissenting ministers to obtain preaching licenses from unsympathetic local authorities often under the guidance of clergymen from the established Church of England. Presbyterians were willing to seek licenses but Separate Baptists, asserting that their commission came from God not man, refused to obtain them and suffered accordingly. The level and frequency of violence they experienced from local officials and Anglican vigilantes far exceeded anything inflicted in other colonies and aroused the sympathy of substantial numbers of their fellow citizens.

A variety of Virginians actively rallied to the support of Baptists and other victims of religious persecution. Foremost among these advocates of liberty of conscience were Thomas Jefferson and James Madison. From 1776 to 1786 these two statesmen, assisted by secular and evangelical allies, fought to emancipate Virginia from the grip of the Church of England and from any potential successor who would oppress conscience. In June 1776 Madison wrote a guarantee of religious freedom into the Virginia Declaration of Rights and in the fall of that year Jefferson set the commonwealth on the road to disestablishing the Anglican Church by revoking its right to collect taxes from dissenters. From 1776 until 1786 both men fought to prevent the state from passing general assessment laws, which would have taxed the citizens for the support of the church of their choice, on the grounds that such a program would inexorably lead to a reestablishment of religion which would extinguish the liberty of conscience so recently secured.

Both Jefferson and Madison grounded their case for liberty of conscience on natural rights. Jefferson was a fervent admirer of Locke, whom he enrolled with Newton and Bacon in his trinity of intellectual heroes. He made extensive notes on Locke's *Letter Concerning Toleration* in preparation for debates in the Virginia General Assembly and concluded that "it was a great thing to go so far" as Locke had done in that seminal book but resolved that "where he stopped short, we may go on."[54] What Jefferson meant was that he would interpret the right to liberty of conscience to comprehend Locke's pariahs—Catholics, "Mahometans" and even atheists. Locke's influence is also evident in Madison's approach to liberty of conscience, for the very first article in his famous Memorial and Remonstrance of 1785 was a painstaking explication of the Lockean theory that religion "is the right of every man to exercise it as [conviction and conscience] dictate. This right is in its nature an unalienable right."[55] The dozens of petitions that Virginia's Baptists submitted to the Assembly in the decade after 1776 on behalf of liberty of conscience also referred to rights but stressed the scriptural justification for "soul liberty." "Matters of Religion," they said, echoing their brethren in other states, "are not the Objects of Civil Government" since "Christ the Head of the Church has left plain Directions concerning Religion" which foreclosed the intervention of the civil magistrate.[56]

Arguments from rights and from Scripture were more or less the same in Virginia and New England. But the Virginians and their neighbors to the south added another string to conscience' bow which they borrowed from Pennsylvania, a virtual terra incognita to parochial New Englanders. Virginians knew Pennsylvania. Philadelphia was an entrepôt through which they received European goods as well as newspapers and information. Many Virginia planters went to Philadelphia on business. Others had studied in Philadelphia or had passed through it on the way to and from the College of New Jersey at Princeton. Madison was one of the latter and was deeply impressed by the tangible effects of freedom of conscience in the Quaker state in contrast to what he regarded as the benighted condition of the Old Dominion. Pennsylvanians, he wrote a Philadelphia college friend in April 1774, have "long felt the good effects of their religious as well as Civil Liberty. Foreigners have been encouraged to settle among you. Industry and Virtue have been promoted . . . Commerce and arts have flourished and I can not help attributing those continual exertions of Genius which appear among you to the inspiration of Liberty."[57]

After independence the material and intellectual prosperity of Pennsylvania became an argument in the southern states for liberty of conscience. No one made the case more eloquently than Jefferson in his *Notes on the State of Virginia,* written in 1781. "Our sister states of Pennsylvania and New Jersey," asserted the future president, "have long subsisted without any establishment at all. The experiment was new and doubtful when they made it. It has answered beyond conception. They flourish infinitely. Religion is well supported; of various kinds, indeed, but all good enough. All sufficient to preserve peace and order . . . their harmony is unparalleled . . . they have made the happy discovery, that the way to silence religious disputes is to take no notice of them. Let us too give this experiment fair play."[58]

In a petition to the Virginia General Assembly, October 24, 1776, the Hanover Presbytery asserted that "Religious Establishments are highly injurious to the temporal interests of any community . . . such establishments greatly retard population and consequently the progress of Arts, Sciences and Manufactures; witness the growth of the Northern Provinces compared to this." Virginia, continued the Presbyterians, "might have now been the Capitol of America, and a match for British arms, without depending on others for the necessities of War" had it imitated Pennsylvania and adopted liberty of conscience.[59] In the profusion of petitions for liberty of conscience which the Baptists submitted to the Virginia Assembly, they constantly cited the success of Penn's "Holy Experiment." "Witness Pennsylvania," they urged their representatives, "wherein no such establishment hath taken place; their government stands firm; and which of the neighbouring States has better members, of brighter Morals, and more upright Characters?"[60] Madison touted Pennsylvania. In notes for a speech to the Virginia Assembly in December 1784 he reminded himself that the "Case of Pa." must be "explained" to demonstrate to his audience the advantages of liberty of conscience.[61] In his Memorial and Remonstrance Madison argued for the economic advantages of religious liberty in precisely the manner Penn had done a century earlier. "Offering an Asylum to the persecuted and oppressed of every Nation and Religion," Madison observed, "promised a lustre to our country and an accession to the number of citizens." Conversely, restrictions on conscience would drive useful citizens away and "would be the same species of folly which has dishonoured and depopulated flourishing kingdoms."[62]

Farther to the south, William Tennent delivered a speech to the South Carolina General Assembly, January 11, 1777, pleading for religious freedom, in which he explicitly saluted William Penn. Like Madison, Tennent knew Pennsylvania well, for he was a Presbyterian minister, born in New Jersey and educated at Princeton, who had crisscrossed the Quaker state. Liberty of conscience, he informed his fellow legislators, was one of those issues on which "the claims of good policy join those of common and confessed justice. Religious establishments discourage the opulence and cramp the growth of a free state. Every fetter, whether religious or civil, deters people from settling in a new country . . . an entire equality has made Pennsylvania the emporeum of America to the immortal honour of its wise legislator; what good effects may not be expected from the same spirit of laws in this state? That state in America which adopts the freest and most liberal plan will be the most opulent and powerful and will well deserve it."[63]

There is no indication that Tennent or the Virginia statesmen were familiar with those of Penn's writings in which he had predicted that freedom of conscience would bring prosperity. But they had something better–first hand knowledge that the experiment in statecraft that Penn had launched was a spectacular success. Government intervention in religion, they knew from personal observation, was not necessary to produce the "peace and plenty" that Penn had promised a century earlier. The revolutionary generation in America was instructed not by what Penn had written but by what he created on the ground. To adopt an aphorism from one of Jefferson's intellectual mentors, Lord Bolingbroke, Pennsylvania was Penn's philosophy teaching by example. Those scholars who belittle Penn's influence in the United States have looked in the wrong places. Employing a bibliographic approach, they have concluded that because they could not find Penn quoted by any notable revolutionary writer, he was a cipher. Had they looked at the business of living in Pennsylvania and the response to it by revolutionary leaders, especially those in the southern United States, they would have perceived that the society Penn created made a major contribution to the case for liberty of conscience in the United States.

The pragmatic case for liberty of conscience entered the mix of arguments on its behalf which by the time of the writing of the Constitution in 1787 consisted of a threefold rationale: the teachings of the New Testament, natural rights, and practical success. Religion was little discussed at the Constitutional Convention and there was no systematic discussion of the case for liberty of conscience during the drafting of the Bill of Rights in 1789. The First Amendment, unlike religion clauses in some of the revolutionary state bills of right, does not assert liberty of conscience as a positive entitlement for each individual citizen but, rather in the manner of the English Toleration Act of 1689, leaves it to be inferred from the obligation of the Congress not to establish religion or interfere with its free exercise. The principle of freedom of conscience, even if indirectly asserted, has become over time sacred to the American public and, as a result, is taken as much for granted as the air American citizens breathe. The rationale for liberty of conscience is rarely articulated because the fundamental concept is rarely challenged. If problems arise, it is sufficient to say that freedom of conscience is guaranteed by the Constitution, an assertion that usually forecloses further discussion. Freedom of religion is, as Oliver Wendell Holmes remarked in another context, one of those "ideas that become encysted in phrases, and thereafter for a long time cease to provoke further analysis."[64]

Aside from citing by rote the phrases of the First Amendment, very few present-day Americans are adept at explaining *why* liberty of conscience should prevail. One of the few fresh arguments proposed on its behalf since 1789 was most cogently offered by John Stuart Mill in his *On Liberty* (1859). Anticipated by David Hume and other eighteenth-century thinkers, Mill argued that liberty of conscience was necessary because genuine religious truth had yet to be discovered; it was still "out there" and, as a result, the free mind might discover a "better truth" than any dispensed by current religious organizations.[65] Most Americans, however, have never been receptive to Mill-style scepticism. Another notable effort to articulate a rationale for religious liberty was mounted after World War II by American Catholic clergymen whose efforts bore fruit in the Second Vatican Council's 1965 Declaration on Religious Freedom.[66] According to a recent student of the Council, the Declaration's authors were beholden to arguments developed during the American Founding by Madison and his associates.[67] There can be no dispute that the Declaration (drawing, to be sure, on non-American sources as well) contains precisely those justifications for religious liberty that had crystallized in the United States between 1776 and 1789, Penn's distinctive, prudential argument excepted. The Declaration averred that "the human person has a right to religious freedom" and that religious freedom is founded on the

"Light of Revelation" as recorded in the New Testament. It cites, in fact, one of William Penn's favorite scriptural passages, i.e., John 18:36, in defense of religious liberty.[68] Penn and the American Founders would, in fact, have found nothing new in the 1965 Declaration, as pathbreaking as it was for the Roman Catholic Church. It remains true, therefore, that the basic rationale for liberty of conscience in modern America is at least three hundred years old.

How do these venerable arguments hold up today? In a diverse population with increasing numbers of non-Christians and substantial numbers of the secularly inclined, arguments from the Christian New Testament are likely to be rejected by many as lacking binding authority. The pragmatic case for liberty of conscience, the claim that it is good for business, is unlikely to impress proponents of secular and religious utopias who are contemptuous of bourgeois values. The argument from natural rights appears at first glance to be stronger, even though natural rights have been denounced from both the right and left. The inability of the drafters of the United Nations Declaration of Human Rights to agree, in 1948, on any definition of rights is well-known.[69] And the uproar over natural rights at recent hearings for certain Supreme Court justices revealed anew their controversial nature.

Still, the right to religious liberty may be less problematic than others. One of the leading modern rights theorists, Ronald Dworkin, asserts that if an individual has a right "in the strong sense . . . we imply that it would be wrong to interfere" with his doing something, even if by exercising his right the individual brings himself into harm's way.[70] Penn and his contemporaries, who advocated liberty of conscience, understood a right in this "modern" sense; they would forbid any interference in acts of individual conscience, even if those acts brought the irreparable harm of eternal perdition for misguided belief. But other kinds of "harm" Penn and his contemporaries were not prepared to countenance in the name of exercising rights. From Penn through Jefferson men held that rights were derived from God—an endowment of the Creator, as the Declaration of Independence expressed it— and that they were, therefore, "moral qualities," "the power of doing what is morally possible," as was repeatedly said at the time of the American Revolution.[71] For Penn and succeeding generations, rights, therefore, were confined within the boundaries of Christian morality. Penn was exceedingly anxious lest Pennsylvanians let liberty of conscience spin out of control into immoral activities, that they "useth not this Christian Liberty to Licentiousness."[72] If they did, he had no doubt that "the wrath of god is very nigh to be revealed, and many and dreadfull are those Judgments thatt are att the Doore. Ready to break in upon us."[73] Therefore, in his Laws Agreed upon in England, Penn criminalized a wide variety of what he considered harmful conduct including gambling, fornication, sodomy, drinking toasts, attending plays, and playing cards, on the grounds that indulgence in these actions exposed the civil state to the peril of being devastated by divine retribution. Rights understood in the traditional sense as manifestations of Christian morality are incompatible with current theories that consider them to be expressions of individual autonomy that permit precisely those kinds of conduct that Penn proscribed. These conflicting conceptions of rights make anchoring liberty of conscience in them a formidable challenge, indeed.

What, after all, is the urgency about bringing the case for liberty of conscience up to date by reconceptualizing it? To suggest that the First Amendment protection for conscience is in danger may appear to be a chimera. Complacency, it seems, ought to be the order of the day. And perhaps William Penn would agree that we should celebrate the anniversary of his great Charter with contentment and gratitude. But at this moment I am reminded of one of Penn's famous pamphlets, *The Sandy Foundation Shaken*, in which he exposed the fragility of certain "generally believed and applauded [religious] Doctrines" of his own day.[74] If the intellectual foundations of freedom of conscience have, in fact, become sandy, might we not better celebrate this anniversary by considering ways to shore them up?

NOTES

1. An earlier version of the present chapter was delivered at the Spirit of Liberty Symposium at the University of Pennsylvania, November 13, 2001.

2. Gary Nash, *Quakers and Politics, Pennsylvania, 1681-1726* (Princeton, N.J.: Princeton University Press, 1968), 175.

3. Mary M. Dunn and Richard S. Dunn, eds., *The Papers of William Penn* (Philadelphia: University of Pennsylvania Press, 1981-1987), vol. 4, 105; hereinafter cited as *PWP*.

4. *PWP*, vol. 4, 106.

5. John Locke, *A Letter Concerning Toleration* (Chicago: Encyclopaedia Britannica, Inc., 1952), 17-18; Edmund S. Morgan, *Roger Williams: The Church and State* (New York: Harcourt, Brace & World, 1967), 137.

6. *PWP*, vol. 4, 108.

7. Julian P. Boyd, ed., *The Papers of Thomas Jefferson* (Princeton, N.J.: Princeton University Press, 33 vols. to date, 1950—), vol. 2, 547.

8. *PWP*, vol. 2, 225.

9. *PWP*, vol. 1, 396-97.

10. *PWP*, vol. 12, 143.

11. Agnes M. Whitsun, *The Constitutional Development of Jamaica, 1660-1729* (Manchester: University of Manchester Press, 1929), 19.

12. Mattie Parker, *North Carolina Charters and Constitutions 1578-1698* (Raleigh: Carolina Charter Tercentenary Commission, 1963), 148-50.

13. *PWP*, vol. 2, 76.

14. Morgan, *Roger Williams*, 57.

15. Glenn LaFantasie, ed., *The Correspondence of Roger Williams* (Brown University Press/University Press of New England: Hanover, N.H: 1988), vol. 2, 682.

16. *Correspondence of Roger Williams*, vol. 2, 648, 652; Morgan, *Roger Williams*, 60-61.

17. *Correspondence of Roger Williams*, vol. 2, 654.

18. John Garrett, *Roger Williams* (New York: Macmillan, 1970), 214.

19. Perry Miller, *Roger Williams: His Contribution to the American Tradition* (Indianapolis: Bobbs-Merrill, 1953), 29.

20. Caroline Robbins, "The Efforts of William Penn to Lay a Foundation for Future Ages," *Aspects of American Liberty* (Philadelphia: The American Philosophical Society, 1977), 72.

21. *Poulson's American Daily Advertiser* (Philadelphia), October 26, 1826.

22. William Penn, *The Great Case of Liberty of Conscience*, in *The Select Works of William Penn* (New York: Kraus Reprint Company, 1971), vol. 2, 136; hereinafter cited as *SWWP*.

23. William Penn, *An Address to Protestants of all Persuasions*, *SWWP*, vol. 3, 155.

24. William Penn to the Prince of Orange, February 26, 1680, *PWP*, vol. 2, 27.

25. William Penn, *A Persuasive to Moderation to Church Dissenters*, *SWWP*, vol. 2, 534.

26. *The Complete Writings of Roger Williams* (New York: Russell & Russell, 1963), vol. 3, 36, 94, 147.

27. William Penn, *The Great Case of Liberty of Conscience*, *SWWP*, vol. 2, 146.

28. *SWWP*, 2, 130.

29. Henry Cadbury, "Persecution and Religious Liberty, Then and Now," *Pennsylvania Magazine of History and Biography* 68, no. 4 (October 1944): 371.

30. *SWWP*, vol. 2, 150.

31. William Penn, *England's Present Interest Considered*, *SWWP*, vol. 2, 307.

32. Mary M. Dunn, *William Penn, Politics and Conscience* (Princeton, N.J.: Princeton University Press, 1967), 64.

33. *SWWP*, vol. 2, 307.

34. *SWWP*, vol. 2, 150.

35. William Penn, *A Persuasive to Moderation to Church Dissenters, SWWP*, vol. 2, 510.

36. *WWP*, vol. 2, 52.

37. William Penn, *An Address to Protestants of all Persuasions*, *SWWP*, vol. 3, 133.

38. William Penn, *A Letter to the Council and Senate of the City of Emden; England's Present Interest Considered; SWWP, vol.* 2, 201, 307.

39. William Penn, *The Great Case of Liberty of Conscience, SWWP*, vol. 2, 135.

40. *SWWP*, vol. 2, 135, 156.

41. William Penn, *England's Present Interest Considered, SWWP*, vol. 2, 299.

42. *SWWP*, vol. 2, 273.

43. *SWWP*, vol.2, 272.

44. Cadbury, "Persecution and Religious Liberty," 359.

45. Cadbury, "Persecution and Religious Liberty," 364.

46. William Penn, *England's Present Interest Considered, SWWP*, vol. 2, 299.

47. Locke, *Letter*, 18.

48. Edmund S. Morgan, "The American Revolution Considered as an Intellectual Movement," in *Paths of American Thought*, ed. Arthur M. Schlesinger, Jr., and Morton White (Boston: Houghton Mifflin, 1963), 14.

49. Jerome Huyler, *Locke in America: The Moral Philosophy of the Founding Era* (Lawrence: University Press of Kansas, 1995), 199.

50. Perry Miller, *The New England Mind from Colony to Province* (Cambridge, Mass.: Harvard University Press, 1953), 165, 167.

51. Huyler, *Locke in America,* 194.

52. Elisha Williams, *The Essential Rights and Liberties of Protestants* in *Political Sermons of the American Founding Era 1730-1805,* ed. Elliot Sandoz (Indianapolis: Liberty Fund, 1991), 59, 61, 65, 85, 87, 96-97.

53. William McLoughlin, ed., *Isaac Backus on Church, State and Calvinism* (Cambridge, Mass.: Harvard University Press, 1968), 376, 382.

54. Boyd, *Jefferson Papers,* vol. 1, 548.

55. Robert A. Rutland and William Rachal, eds., *The Papers of James Madison* (Chicago: University of Chicago Press, 1973), vol. 8, 299.

56. Westmoreland County Petition to the Virginia General Assembly, November 2, 1785, Virginia Religious Petitions, Library of Virginia.

57. Madison to William Bradford, April 1, 1774, *Madison Papers*, vol. 1, 112.

58. Thomas Jefferson, *Notes on the State of Virginia,* ed. William Peden (Chapel Hill: University of North Carolina Press, 1955), 160.

59. Virginia Religious Petitions, Library of Virginia.

60. Westmoreland County Petition, November 2, 1785, Virginia Religious Petitions, Library of Virginia.

61. Notes for Debates on the General Assessment Bill, December 23-24, 1784, *Madison Papers,* vol. 8, 302.

62. Memorial and Remonstrance, [June 20], 1785, *Madison Papers,* vol. 8, 302.

63. "The Writings of the Reverend William Tennent, 1740-1777," *South Carolina Historical Magazine* 61, nos. 3-4 (July-October 1960), 204.

64. *Hyde v. United States,* 225 U.S. 347, 391 (1912).

65. John Stuart Mill, *On Liberty,* ed. Charles W. Eliot (New York: P. F. Collier & Son, 1909), 224.

66. For a complete text of the Declaration, see Gregory Baum, ed., *The Teachings of the Second Vatican Council* (Westminster, Md.: Newman Press, 1966), 366-83.

67. John T. Noonan, Jr., *The Lustre of Our Country: The American Experience of Religious Freedom* (Berkeley: University of California Press, 1998), 331-53.

68. Baum, *The Teachings,* 367, 375 ff.

69. For an excellent account of these difficulties, see Mary Ann Glendon, *A World Made New: Eleanor Roosevelt and the Universal Declaration of Human Rights* (New York: Random House, 2001).

70. Ronald Dworkin, *Taking Rights Seriously* (Cambridge, Mass.: Harvard University Press, 1977), 188.

71. James H. Hutson, "The Emergence of the Modern Concept of a Right in America: The Contribution of Michel Villey," *American Journal of Jurisprudence* 39 (1994): 215.

72. William Penn, "Fundamentall Constitutions," *WWP,* vol. 2, 143.

73. William Penn, Petition to Charles II, *WWP,* vol. 2, 55.

74. William Penn, *The Sandy Foundation Shaken, SWWP,* vol.1, 129.

Chapter 6

James Madison and Religion: Radicalism Unbound

Thomas Jefferson overshadowed his close friend and coadjutor, James Madison, in many ways but in one, at least, Madison was demonstrably superior to his Monticello neighbor—in his ability to keep his religious views private.[1] Despite a desire to be "most scrupulously reserved on the subject" of religion,[2] Jefferson by the end of his life revealed more about his faith than any other Founding Father. He divulged so much about so sensitive a subject for one reason only: to defend himself against Federalist charges, broadcast in the election of 1800, that he was an atheist. Jefferson spent the last twenty-five years of his life refuting these aspersions, although at no time did he conceal his deviations from orthodox Christianity; the Trinity, for example, he dismissed as the "abracadabra of the mountebanks calling themselves the priests of Jesus";[3] the vicarious atonement was a compound of "follies, falsehoods, and charlatanisms";[4] predestination and original sin were "heresies of bigotry and fanaticism."[5] With breathtaking intellectual audacity Jefferson compiled an edition of the New Testament containing what he judged to be the authentic sayings of Jesus, an exercise he

155

considered as easy as finding "diamonds in a dunghill." As a result, it is possible to ascertain precisely what aspects of Christianity Jefferson accepted and what he rejected. The abundance of evidence allows us to fix him, as his grandson did, on the Unitarian band of the religious spectrum of his day.[6]

Madison, on the other hand, defies definition or description. Seeking evidence of his faith quickly leads to the conclusion that there is, in the words of the poet, no there there, that in the mature Madison's writings there is no trace, no clue as to his personal religious convictions. Educated by Presbyterian clergymen, Madison, as a student at Princeton (1769-1772), seems to have developed a "transient inclination" to enter the ministry.[7] In a 1773 letter to a college friend he made the zealous proposal that the rising stars of his generation renounce their secular prospects and "publicly . . . declare their unsatisfactoriness by becoming fervent advocates in the cause of Christ."[8] Two months later Madison renounced his spiritual prospects and began the study of law. The next year he entered the political arena, serving as a member of the Orange County Committee of Safety. Public service seems to have crowded out of his consciousness the previous imprints of faith. For the rest of his life there is scarcely any mention in his writings of Jesus Christ[9] nor of any of the issues that might concern a practicing Christian. Late in retirement there are a few enigmatic references to religion, but nothing else.[10] With Madison, unlike Jefferson or any of the other principal Founding Fathers with the possible exception of Washington, one peers into a void when trying to discern evidence of personal religious belief.

Scholars, nevertheless, have tried to construct from this unyielding evidence a religious identity for Madison. He is such a commanding figure in the Founding Period's controversies over religion's relation to government that a knowledge of his personal religious convictions is sought as a key to his public posture on church-state issues. The very paucity of evidence has permitted a latitude of interpretation in which some writers have created Madison in the image of their own religious convictions. To Christian scholars Madison is a paragon of piety; to those of a more secular bent he is a deist. His major nineteenth-century biographer, William C. Rives, a pillar of the church in Virginia, argued that on Christianity's "doctrinal points" Madison was a model of "orthodoxy and penetration."[11] Madison's major twentieth-century biographer, Irving Brant, bluntly pronounced him a deist.[12] Reacting to this ascription, a Presbyterian minister-scholar, James Smylie, asserted in 1966 that Madison was nothing less than "a lay theologian."[13] Another twentieth-century biographer, Ralph Ketcham, seems, initially, to have subscribed to Rives's view, asserting in 1960 that Madison was a man of "humble faith," who had a "deep personal attachment to some general aspects of Christian belief."[14] By 1971, however, Ketcham appears to have veered toward Brant's view, asserting that even in his college days Madison was no "more than conventionally religious" and that he later became a deist.[15] A third twentieth-century biographer implies that Brant may not have been bold enough in assessing Madison's convictions. Writing in 1995, Lance Banning noted, as others had, that Madison's "more mature opinions are a matter for conjecture, for religious topics simply disappear from his surviving writings after 1776." Then Banning added an arresting suggestion: "there is reason to believe that he [Madison] continued to accept a rational Christianity at least into the middle 1780s."[16] And after the middle 1780s, what? A plausible inference, which Banning may have wanted to invite, is that after that date Madison abandoned even his "rational" brand of Christianity. Within the past few years, John Noonan, a Catholic intellectual and jurist (now joined by the Baptist scholar Garrett Sheldon) has pushed the pendulum back toward Rives by insisting that Madison was "a pious Christian," a "true follower" of Jesus and that he was guided by a "faith . . . palpably alive, a faith stupendous in modern eyes, a faith that God in us speaks to us." He spoke, Noonan concluded, "as a believer in Christianity's special light," as one who "looks to the evangelization of the world."[17]

These differences can, perhaps, be bridged by arguing that an eighteenth-century deist could be a "true follower" of Jesus' moral teachings and have a strong faith in God but it is not clear that Noonan or those sharing Brant's view would accept this attempt at reconciliation. The strongest evidence produced by Noonan for Madison's exemplary faith are calculated compliments to Christianity, included in a document written to appeal to evangelical forces during a petition campaign in 1785,[18] and a statement in 1833 in which the aged ex-president lauded Christianity as the "best & purest religion."[19] This endorsement, however, sounds very much like the deistical maxim, frequently indulged by Jefferson, that the religion of Jesus was, indeed, "pure" but that it had been unconscionably corrupted by the apostle Paul and the early church fathers whose legacy continued to disfigure the orthodox Christianity of his own day.[20]

To make his case, Brant relied on the testimony of Madison's contemporaries, one of whom knew the fourth president well, the Reverend Alexander Balmaine, the husband of one of Madison's favorite cousins and the Episcopal priest who officiated at his marriage to Dolly Paine Todd. Brant also used the testimony of the Episcopal bishop of Virginia, William Meade, who claimed, on at least one occasion, to have talked religion with the former president. Balmaine's account, as recorded by Meade, asserted that after returning to Montpelier from college Madison

> Offered for the Legislature, and it was objected to him, by his opponents, that he
> was better suited to the pulpit than to the legislative hall. His religious feeling,
> however, seems to have been short-lived. His political associations were those
> of infidel principles, of whom there were many in his day, if they did not actually
> change his creed, yet subjected him to a general suspicion of it[21]

According to Bishop Meade:

> I was never at Mr. Madison's but once, and then our conversation took such a
> turn though not designed on my part as to call forth some expressions and
> arguments which left the impression on my mind that his creed was not strictly
> regulated by the Bible.

Brant also cites a Bostonian's account of an 1815 dinner table conversation with Madison:

> He talked of religious sects and parties and was curious to know how the cause
> of liberal Christianity stood with us, and if the Athanasian creed was well
> received by our Episcopalians. He pretty distinctly intimated to me his own
> regard for the Unitarian doctrines.[22]

Two bits of evidence, heretofore overlooked, seem to corroborate the claims of those who assume that the mature Madison either lost interest in religion or migrated spiritually into one of the many mansions of deism. First, there is the curious episode of the publication in 1802 of the sermons of the Reverend John Witherspoon, Madison's mentor at Princeton and, subsequently, his friend and political comrade.[23] As was customary in Madison's day, Witherspoon's writings were published by public subscription. The list of subscribers was so extensive that the promoters of the publication must have scoured the nation to obtain support. The subscribers were a veritable who's who of the nation's political elite: Jefferson, John Adams, John Jay, John Dickinson and many other luminaries. Also included were many of Madison's friends and classmates at Princeton. But Madison's own name was absent. Was the omission accidental? Or had Madison refused to sponsor a theological opus because of disenchantment with its orthodox pieties?

Perhaps a better clue to Madison's outlook is a letter to Jefferson, December 31, 1824, in which he complained about Presbyterian "Sectarian Seminaries," armed with charters of incorporation, disseminating obsolete religious doctrines, by which he clearly meant Calvinism.[24] Unassailable charters allowed a "creed however absurd or contrary to that of a more enlightened Age" to be fobbed off on the faithful in perpetuity. The Reformation itself, Madison continued, must be considered the "greatest of abuses," if legal impediments could prevent its doctrines from being brought up to date. The idea that Madison was espousing, that religious truth must evolve to incorporate the discoveries of science and other branches of modern learning, was anathema to most nineteenth-century American churches. It can be inferred that his own religious views had evolved from the verities he had learned at Princeton, but how far and in what direction is a puzzle that continues to frustrate scholarly inquiry.

Madison's religious practice is better documented than his religious principles. According to Bishop Meade

> Whatever may have been the private sentiments of Mr. Madison on the subject
> of religion, he was never known to declare any hostility to it. He always treated
> it with respect, attended public worship in his neighborhood, invited ministers
> of religion to his house, had family prayers on such occasions though he did not
> kneel himself at prayers.[25]

Note that Meade only attests that Madison attended church when he was at home in Orange County. He was evidently far less conscientious when he was away at Congress for long stretches of time in the 1780s and 1790s. In Jefferson's company in 1791 he allegedly told the governor of Vermont that he had not been in a church for "several years."[26] As president, Madison followed Jefferson's practice of worshiping at both a local congregation and in the hall of the House of Representatives. Madison is said to have been a pewholder at the First Presbyterian Church, located on the site of the present-day Rayburn House Office Building, and to have contributed to its building fund. He attended services in the House of Representatives in style, once arriving, according to the British minister, in a coach and four. On another occasion a Massachusetts congressman reported Madison's presence in the House when a local Masonic lodge attended in a body. Madison's attendance at services in the House indicates that, like Jefferson, he had no objection to religious activities on public property.[27]

Evaluating Madison's motives for attending church services depends on estimating his personal religious convictions. His reasons may have ranged from a genuine devotion to bald political calculations. No office holder in the early republic wanted to be branded an infidel, as Jefferson had been, and Madison certainly knew that public expressions of piety would please the Baptist voters in his political base in Orange County. Jefferson attended church when he was at Monticello, sometimes at a local Episcopal chapel and after his presidency at the Albemarle County Court House, where services rotated weekly between Episcopalians, Baptists, Methodists and Presbyterians.[28] He endured these last services, despite his virulent contempt for the Calvinism that infused them. In partaking of the Court House's often indigestible religious fare, Jefferson was evidently practicing what his friend, the British Unitarian preacher Joseph Priestley called "thinking with the wise, and acting with the vulgar."[29] There is a temptation to apply this epigram to Madison, but given the obscurity of his religious views, it can be done with considerably less confidence than with Jefferson.

The gnawing uncertainty about Madison's personal religious convictions lessens the confidence with which judgments can be made about the motivation of some aspects of his public policy initiatives concerning the relationship of religion to government, an area in which his impact on American law and politics was extraordinary in his own lifetime and continues to be so in modern America. Scholars consider Madison, along with Jefferson, to be the chief advocate and apologist for what is today called the "strict separationist" view of church-state relations, that is, the view that there must be "a complete and permanent separation of the spheres of religious activity and civil authority by comprehensively forbidding every form of public aid or support for religion."[30] Madison has been called an absolutist in his opposition to government assistance to religion.[31] This term fits his career in Virginia politics but distorts, as will presently be shown, his actions at the national level, where he was willing to adjust his church-state convictions, as he was his convictions on other crucial issues, to political realities. Late in life Madison further modified his strict separationist convictions in one particular area, the incorporation of religious societies, by endorsing government intervention in the ecclesiastical sphere to limit the entrenched influence of certain religious institutions.

Madison's passion for the separation of church and state was kindled by exposure as a young man to the sufferings of neighbors enduring religious persecution; like Moses witnessing the beating of the Hebrew slave by the Egyptian taskmaster, Madison was galvanized by this experience toward a lifelong commitment to relieve his countrymen from spiritual oppression. The events that aroused what Madison later called his "very early and strong impressions" in favor of religious liberty were a series of imprisonments of Baptist ministers in 1773-

1774 in Culpeper County for preaching without licenses in violation of the British Toleration Act then in force in Virginia.[32] By this time Baptists were thickly settled in Orange County, so much so that in 1771 5,000 attended an open-air meeting at Blue Run Church near Montpelier. Young Madison informed himself of his neighbors' beliefs and, looking beyond their emotional forms of worship, satisfied himself that they were "in the main very orthodox." He was, therefore, indignant when they suffered from the "diabolical Hell conceived principle of persecution" in adjacent Culpeper County.[33] The plight of the Baptists prompted Madison, characteristically, to reflect on their situation and derive general principles from their misfortunes. The source of all the trouble, it was obvious to him, was the laws establishing the Church of England as the official religion of the commonwealth of Virginia. Establishments of religion, Madison concluded, had broad, deleterious effects on society at large that extended well beyond the violation of individual rights. They had a tendency to produce a mentality susceptible to political "slavery and Subjection" and were unfriendly to "genius," enterprise and economic growth.[34]

Madison actively tried to help the Baptists. On January 24, 1774, he wrote a friend that he had "squabbled and scolded abused and ridiculed" their adversaries. The recipients of his invective are unknown. He may have confronted them as a character witness in judicial proceedings, for there is a tradition that he "repeatedly appeared in the court of his own county to defend the Baptist nonconformists."[35] If so, he was unsuccessful. But the next time Madison appeared in a public forum, he achieved a historic victory for religious liberty.

The occasion of Madison's triumph was the Virginia Revolutionary Convention, May 6-July 5, 1776, which instructed its delegates at the Continental Congress to declare independence, drafted a constitution for the commonwealth, and adopted George Mason's famous Declaration of Rights. The story has been told often and well of how the modest young Madison amended Mason's Declaration, transforming its grant of the "fullest Toleration in the Exercise of Religion" to a guarantee that "all men are equally entitled to the free exercise of religion, according to the dictates of conscience." Brant's estimate of the importance of Madison's amendment is certainly correct: it "asserted, for the first time in any body of fundamental law, a natural right which had not previously been recognized as such by political bodies in the Christian world."[36] Madison offered a corollary to his amendment which would have effectively disestablished the Anglican Church by depriving its ministers of all "peculiar emoluments or privileges."[37] Challenged by the Church's supporters, this initiative failed, sustaining the Anglican Church's power to tax everyone in the state for its support. Virginia's dissenting denominations had now gained equal religious rights but remained tributaries to the old established church, an anomaly that was addressed when the first legislative session under the new constitution convened on October 7, 1776.

Thomas Jefferson, fresh from his own triumphs in Philadelphia, appeared at this session as a representative from Albermarle County and led a campaign, which he later described as inciting the "severest contests in which I have ever been engaged," to bring religious liberty to Virginia in its fullest measure. Jefferson did not achieve everything he sought, which included "totally and eternally restraining the civil magistrate from all pretensions of interposing his authority . . . in matters of religion," but he and his allies obtained their principal goal of liberating dissenters from paying taxes to support the ministers of the Church of England.[38] This exemption weighed so heavily on the Anglicans, who were left as sole supporters of the parish ministry, that they were also relieved of the burden of paying church taxes. The result was that, when the assembly adjourned on December 21, 1776, it had established a sweeping system of voluntary support for religion. Many delegates believed that the assembly had stumbled into the wrong kind of religious equality and that Virginia's public and spiritual interest would be better served by requiring all citizens equally to pay taxes to the churches of their choice, an expedient called a "general assessment." Before adjourning the delegates resolved that because "great Varieties of Opinions have arisen touching the propriety of a general assessment . . . it is thought most prudent to defer this matter to the Discussion and final Determination of a future assembly when the Opinions of the Country in general may be better known."[39] It would take a decade for the assembly to get a definitive reading on public opinion; in the meantime the utility of a general assessment became *the* principal religious issue in Virginia.

Where was Madison during the "desperate contests" in the fall of 1776? He was a passive member, whose youth and modesty, Jefferson later recalled, "prevented his venturing himself in the debate."[40] Nevertheless, he had a ringside seat at the struggle and absorbed the flood of arguments, pro and contra, that inundated the assembly in the form of petitions and declamations on the floor of the house. Many of these he would put to good use later.

In 1777 there was inconclusive skirmishing in the assembly about a general assessment bill. Sentiment, however, began to build for public assistance to religion and in 1779 an assessment bill passed a second reading in the Assembly which compromised the religious freedom guaranteed by the Declaration of Rights by prescribing an official religious creed that entitled subscribers to receive government tax dollars. Once again, Madison, now a member of the Governor's Council, absorbed the arguments without taking a public position and once again the Assembly deferred the vexing issue for further consideration.[41] The conclusion of the war with Britain in 1783 allowed the Assembly to give its undivided attention to domestic issues, one of which was general assessment. In the fall of 1784 its supporters came within a whisker of enacting their favorite measure in the form of Patrick Henry's "Bill Establishing a Provision for the Teachers of the Christian Religion."[42] Henry's bill was more generous in spirit than the 1779 assessment bill, for it required no creedal affirmations and simply allowed each citizen to pay a modest tax to the church of his choice and permitted non-church members to designate their tax for education, a provision intended, apparently, as bait for Jefferson's supporters who had been vainly trying to establish a state system of public education. Henry's bill progressed to the point of being enrolled in anticipation of passage when Madison, fresh from a tour in the Confederation Congress, and his allies persuaded the House of Delegates on Christmas Eve 1784 to defer it until the fall 1785 meeting of the Assembly so that public opinion could be canvassed.

The story of how Madison and a diverse band of evangelicals and civil libertarians mounted, in 1785, a successful public relations campaign against Henry's bill, highlighted by Madison's celebrated religious liberty manifesto, the Declaration and Remonstrance, is a familiar one in American church-state literature, especially since it resulted in 1786 in the passage by the Virginia Assembly of Jefferson's landmark Statute for Religious Freedom. The downfall of the general assessment bill is usually depicted as a kind of graduated Armageddon, in which Madison and his followers, representing the forces of light and progress, vanquish by degrees the legions of reaction who would have dragged America back into the dark ages of religious persecution and bigotry.

There are several things wrong with this interpretation, one being that it can not explain why, if the general assessment bill was so wrongheaded and regressive, it was supported by "most Protestants in Virginia,"[43] not to mention several of the state's most eminent patriots and champions of human liberties, including Henry himself, Richard Henry Lee, John Marshall, Edmund Pendleton and George Washington. Nor can it explain why similar general assessment bills were supported, after 1776, by the legislatures of five other states[44] and by a galaxy of revolutionary heroes, including John Adams, Samuel Adams, John Hancock, Roger Sherman, Oliver Ellsworth, and in neighboring Maryland, Samuel Chase, William Paca and Charles Carroll.

This explanatory failure is the result of a form of scholarly malpractice that Herbert Butterfield denounced early in the last century as the Whig interpretation of history. According to Butterfield, "Whig" historians regularly succumb to the temptation of concentrating on "progress," of focusing on "certain people who appear as the special agencies of . . . progress." Conversely, they routinely ignore the opponents of the enlightened ones, denying them, in Butterfield's words, the benefit of "historical understanding."[45] In Whig eyes Madison and his supporters deserve to be explained and extolled because they are the pioneers of what is currently regarded as the "progressive" doctrine of strict separation of church and state. No time need be wasted on their opponents, as an offhand remark by Irving Brant, a prime example of Butterfield's Whig historian, indicates. Brant noted that Henry's 1784 speech, advocating "religious assessments," had not survived but that this was not a matter of regret, since it would have contained nothing worth reading; "a plea to unite church and state is not," wrote Brant, "of the sort on which libertarian fame is built."[46] Ignoring the case for general religious assessments does not alter the reality that in post-1776 large numbers of Americans, great and small, approved them. We need to know why they did, if we would fully understand Madison's opposition to the state support of religion.

Advocates for assessment endorsed the distinction Virginia's Presbyterian leadership made in 1784 between supporting religion as a "Spiritual system" and "in a civil way."[47] No one wanted to turn the clock back to an era in which the state supported a system of religious beliefs because it purported to offer the one, true path to salvation. What many Virginians wanted, in common with citizens in other states, was to avail themselves of what petitioners to the General Assembly repeatedly called the "Public utility" of religion, by which they meant its capacity to promote the general welfare of society.[48] Not only in Virginia but in Congress and throughout the nation religion was repeatedly acclaimed in the 1780s for its ability to promote happiness, prosperity, peace, order, security and safety.[49] Summarizing the case for the public utility of religion, a Presbyterian minister observed that "if we consider the end of civil society and the evils it was designed to remedy, we will be convinced that from its very nature, that it [government] cannot reach that end, nor guard against those evils, without the aid of religion. Let it suffice to observe that the security of life, liberty and property" is impossible without religion.[50] It is no exaggeration to assert that many, troubled by the unsettled social conditions of the 1780s, and the apparent disintegration of popular morality, regarded religion as the only hope for society's secular salvation.

Religion was expected to come to the rescue by creating a population of law abiding, good neighbors. It would, the citizens of Amherst County confidently predicted, "dispose Men to mutual acts of benevolence and render them dutiful subjects to the state."[51] Why was this so? Because religion was considered to be a uniquely effective incubator of virtue and morality. "The Doctrines of Christianity," asserted Virginia's Episcopal clergy in 1776, " have a greater Tendency to produce Virtue amongst Men than any human Laws or Institutions."[52] "Good morals," added Madison's cousin, Bishop James Madison, "can spring only from the bosom of religion."[53] Religious faith, a "Social Christian" declared in the *Virginia Gazette*, September 18, 1779, "made men more quiet, better members of society." "More than any single thing," it created, "good order, good morals, and happiness public and private. It makes good men and good men must be good citizens."[54] According to Bishop Madison, religion did more; it produced "the perfection of citizens."[55] Religion had an ace in the hole that the secularists lacked: the doctrine of a future state of rewards and punishments, derided as bribes and terror by opponents, but effective nonetheless in guaranteeing virtuous behavior among the people at large. It was a truism of the age that virtue was a prerequisite for republican government. In producing virtue religion enabled the state to achieve its preeminent revolutionary goal: the perpetuation of republicanism.

That the state should concern itself with the character of its citizens was an old idea, stretching back to classical antiquity. That it could use religion to shape civic consciousness was an equally venerable strategy of statecraft which persisted, Madison noted, in the Europe of his own day.[56] No less an authority than David Hume, described by scholars as Madison's mentor in political philosophy, advocated an established church as a way to create a sound citizenry needed to endow government with "security and stability."[57] Hume, as Madison well knew, was but one of many political luminaries who took this position.[58] Other Virginians reminded their fellow citizens that the wisdom of this policy had been acknowledged "at every Period of time and in every Corner of the Globe." "The wisest Legislators of Antiquity," they claimed, were "expressive of their veneration for religion, at least as an assistant to civil Government."[59] Plutarch, for example, had asserted that "a City might be as well built in the air, without any earth to stand upon, as a Commonwealth can be either constituted or preserved without the support of religion."[60]

The contest between the supporters of the general assessment and Madison was not, however, another skirmish in the battle between ancients and moderns, for Henry and his counterparts in the other states were innovators. Heretofore states had promoted religion by "exclusive establishments, " i.e., by supporting one particular denomination. By proposing to give the individual citizen the option of designating his taxes to any one of a number of denominations, the advocates for general assessment had devised a new mechanism which was, in the view of the legal historian, Leonard Levy, unique,[61] a judgment with which Madison agreed. "Experience gives no model of Ge[nera]l Ass[essmen]t," he observed in December 1784.[62] Henry's forces supported their scheme with innovative arguments, the most striking being that it did not violate the freedom of religion clause of the Declaration of Rights of 1776. According to Richard Henry Lee, the Declaration "rather contends against forcing modes of faith and forms of worship than against compelling contributions to support religion in general."[63] How, indeed, could requiring the citizens of Virginia to give financial support to the church of their choice be construed as violating freedom of conscience. People could believe anything they wanted and support any church they wanted. "Men are left as free as Air in the choice of their own religion," claimed petitioners from Surry County on November 14, 1785.[64] The distinguished Virginia jurist and eminent commentator on Blackstone, St. George Tucker saw in the general assessment nothing "incompatible with the most perfect liberty of conscience in matters of religion."[65]

The supporters of general assessment packaged the measure as a panacea for the social instability of the postwar period, promising that it offered a safe, equitable means of empowering the government of Virginia to obtain the highest ends for which it had been constituted in 1776: happiness, prosperity, security, order and perpetuation of republicanism. Why did Madison reject a strategy, endorsed by so many of his fellow Founders, of employing "religion as an engine of Civil Policy"?[66] There seem to have been two reasons; first, his apprehensions, to be described presently, that permitting politicians to promote religion posed a clear and present danger to the existence of a free society; second, his view that the "civil engine" strategy would not work as advertised.

Consider in this respect three statements made by Madison in 1787, all of which were expressed privately, or anonymously, and, therefore, may be presumed to represent his true opinion. In a memorandum, called "Vices of the Political System," which Madison composed in the spring of 1787 to guide his thinking about the forthcoming federal constitutional convention, he speculated about ways to prevent the injustices that seemed to disfigure republican governments. Could religion, Madison asked himself, "be a sufficient restraint? It is not pretended to be such on men individually considered. Will its effects be greater on them considered in an aggregate view? quite the reverse."[67] Madison repeated these views in a speech in the Federal Convention on June 6, 1787, adding that not only was "little to be expected" from religion in a positive way but that it might become "a motive to persecution and oppression."[68] He aired them for a third time in

Federalist 10, published November 22, 1787. In that famous essay Madison inquired how "the public good, and private rights" might be secured against tyrannical majorities. "We well know," he answered, "that neither moral nor religious motives can be relied on as an adequate control. They are not found to be such on the injustice and violence of individuals and lose their efficiency in proportion to the number combined together."[69] If religion could not control violence and injustice, the melioration of which were, after all, its principal professed social goals, it was, in Madison's view, a failure, if not a fraud. His extraordinary trio of 1787 statements betray a pessimism about the social value of religion, as it related to both individuals and groups, so extreme that they separate him from all other Founders, Jefferson included. Arguably, they separate him from any Anglo-American statesman before John Stuart Mill, whose essay, "Utility of Religion" (1858?),[70] was similarly dismissive of the social efficacy of religious faith.

Do any of Madison's subsequent statements mitigate this harsh skepticism about the usefulness of religion? In 1825 he recommended to Jefferson that Washington's Farewell Address, which contained in its middle section an encomium on religion and morality as the "great pillars" of "human happiness" and "political prosperity," be included in the curriculum at the University of Virginia but there is no evidence that these particular passages commended Washington's valedictory to him.[71] There is little else to offset the impression that by the mid-1780s Madison had reached the singular conclusion that religion, as a source of individual social virtue, was so impotent that it was, indeed, no better than the "tinkling cymbal" that the Apostle Paul so famously denounced.[72]

Here, then, was the *practical* reason for Madison's opposition in the crucial years, 1784-1785, to tax support for religion. Government support for religion would not, he was convinced, give taxpayers any of the broad social benefits they were promised. The citizens of Amelia County, who believed that religion would produce "Strength and Stability of Government," the people of Caroline County, who expected that it would bring "peace, order, and decency," and all other Virginians who shared these sentiments were, in Madison's opinion, deceiving themselves.[73]

The *principles* on which Madison founded his opposition to tax-supported religion have had great resonance in American history. These principles were the gravamen of Madison's celebrated Memorial and Remonstrance, written in June 1785. This document has been extolled by Madison's admirers as "the most powerful defense of religious liberty ever written in America," as a manifesto worthy of "Milton, Jefferson, or Mill."[74] The Memorial did, in fact, resemble two of Jefferson's most important state papers. Like the Danbury Baptist letter, "raw political motives" (Thomas Buckley's description)[75] were at work in writing the Memorial, for it was a petition composed with the calculated objective of obtaining signatures sufficient to turn the political tide against the supporters of general assessment. Like the Declaration of Independence, the Memorial was not intended to contain anything "new." Both documents were meant to "assert not to discover truths."[76] In fact, every point in the Memorial had been repeatedly made from 1776 onward by opponents of general assessment. Madison's contribution was to express his fellow citizens' objections with an elegance and lucidity that elevated them from the din of the political controversy to a lofty place in the literature on religious liberty.

The first principle Madison enunciated was that any government embrace of religion violated the fundamental natural right to freedom of conscience which had been reserved by individual citizens when they left the state of nature to enter civil society. This was pure John Locke and, accordingly, scholars have interpreted the Memorial as an expression of Lockean liberalism.[77] In doing so, they have failed to perceive that Madison employed an argument of another school of British political thinkers, equally familiar to the readers of the Memorial, which undoubtedly had a greater impact on them by enabling them to appreciate his contention that the general assessment bill posed a clear and present danger to the people of Virginia.

The nature of the threat was conveyed by a question Madison posed in article three of the Memorial: "Who does not see that the same authority which can establish Christianity, in exclusion of all other Religions, may establish with the same ease any particular sect of Christians, in exclusion of all other sects."[78] Here Madison was warning his audience that the general assessment bill, as innocuous as its supporters made it appear, could lead to an abuse of power—a particularly egregious abuse, he added, for it might lead to nothing less than the establishment in Virginia of the Inquisition or to an effort to establish religious uniformity in the commonwealth on the model of, say, James I, which might drench the land in "Torrents of blood."[79] These were familiar charges— Baptists had warned that the general assessment might lead to the Inquisition[80]— and an anonymous writer in the *Virginia Gazette,* November 8, 1783, anticipated the argument in Madison's Memorial by warning that the general assessment would "certainly open a door for the great red dragon, that horrible monster persecution, to enter into our Western world. For if the Legislature have a power to enforce a maintenance for the Clergy, they must also have a right to impose creeds, and forms of worship, and demand a universal conformity to them, on pain of suffering and punishment for the neglect, as they shall judge proper, both in kind and degree." Other opponents of the tax did not scruple to see that "the severest persecutions in England were ransacked for colors in which to paint the burdens and scourges of religious freedom," not neglecting to cite the possibility of the rekindling in Virginia of the "Smithfield fires" in which Protestant martyrs had been burned alive in the 1550s.[81]

Even to intimate, as Madison did in his Memorial, that Henry, Lee, Marshall, Washington and other supporters of the general assessment favored a policy that could conceivably end in autos-da-fé in Albemarle County appears to be the grossest form of demagoguery, an effort to frighten the citizenry into opposing the general assessment by circulating the crudest kinds of chimeras. Yet Madison was never called to account by either friends or enemies of the religious tax because they recognized that he was employing a thoroughly respectable form of analysis, clothed in impeccable revolutionary credentials..

This mode of analysis derived from what has been called opposition or country ideology, a set of assumptions about political behavior rooted in the English Commonwealth period of the mid-seventeenth century which blossomed in early eighteenth-century Britain among the opponents of Sir Robert Walpole. The central feature of this ideology, which was received in colonial America with an enthusiasm that it never enjoyed in the mother country, was its paranoid-like fear of power, its conviction that the principal feature of power was its "aggressiveness: its endlessly propulsive tendency to expand itself beyond legitimate boundaries" to destroy liberty.[82] One of the principal antidotes prescribed for the menace of the power was jealously, which in the eighteenth century meant suspicion, a hyper-active, deliberately cultivated suspicion which viewed political power with a "watchful, hawk-eyed" vigilance, capable of detecting the first symptoms of aggression.[83] In his famous *Letters from a Farmer in Pennsylvania* John Dickinson had, in 1768, declared that " a perpetual jealousy respecting liberty is absolutely requisite in all free states."[84] In the 1760s and 1770s American leaders worked to cultivate "an extreme spirit of jealousy" in their fellow citizens with such conspicuous success that Charles Carroll of Maryland concluded in 1773 that "jealousy and suspicion had become the vary basis of American politics." Most Americans believed that only by indulging their jealousy had they detected in the British colonial policies prior to 1776 the seeds of slavery meditated for them by George III and his henchmen.

Americans did not simply switch off their jealously after 1776. They now insisted that it was a republican virtue "Republican jealousy," they claimed, "was the guardian angel of these States" and "directed it against themselves."[85]

Explained Senator William Plumer, "the prejudices which the revolution had engendered against the arbitrary government of Great Britain made the people jealous of giving to their own officers so much power as was necessary." "Jealousy," said Silas Deane in 1777, is now "the ruling feature in the American character." The reservoir of jealousy in Virginia in the postwar years was as deep, possibly deeper, than anywhere else in America ; it was Jefferson's credo, for example, that "free government is founded in jealousy." Madison played on this sentiment in his Memorial. "It is proper," he wrote, "to take alarm at the first experiment on our liberties. We hold this prudent jealousy to be the first duty of citizens and one of the noblest characteristics of the late Revolution."[86] Madison then quoted the notorious words of the British Declaratory Act of 1766, "in all cases whatsoever," to alert his readers that the general assessment act was potentially as dangerous as the Stamp Act which preceded it or the Tea Act which followed, to which, in fact, he alluded by mentioning a "three pence" duty, the levy imposed on tea in 1773. Just as Americans had mobilized to defeat these oppressive British statutes, they must do the same to nip the general assessment in the bud. "Let warning be taken at the first fruits of the threatened innovation," Madison enjoined his fellow citizens. And let them arouse themselves to defeat it.

There was, Madison later admitted, a downside to the suspicion he and his supporters were trying to fan in the summer of 1785, which became painfully evident in the effort to ratify the Federal Constitution two years later. In that contest Madison and his fellow Federalists confronted a surfeit of "green eyed hell-born" jealousy in the arguments of the Antifederalists whose credo was that "fear, or jealousy or watchfulness " was "indispensably necessary for the preservation of liberty."[87] The Antifederalists were pure exponents of opposition ideology, for they believed that any grant of power by the people to their elected representatives would be fatally abused. Strengthen the national government, they warned, and it would obliterate the states; give the executive the power to make appointments and he would corrupt the legislators and make them tools of his tyranny. Confronting such arguments as Publius in the *Federalist*, Madison commended the "sober apprehensions of genuine patriotism" but assailed the Antifederalists for surrendering themselves to the "incoherent dreams of a delirious jealousy." They had, he claimed, renounced "every rule by which events ought to be calculated" and substituted "an indiscriminate and unbounded jealousy, with which all reasoning must be vain." "The sincere friends of liberty," he added, "who give themselves up to the extravagancies of this passion are not aware of the injury they do to their own cause."[88] This admonition Madison would not apply to himself when contemplating the prospects of government assistance to religion. Religion, in his view, was a special case, a force against whose aggrandizing impulses and pernicious possibilities no degree of jealousy could be considered excessive.

Madison's Memorial circulated as a petition during the summer and fall of 1785 and was eventually signed by over 1,500 Virginians, an impressive figure but less than one-fifth of all the signatories of anti-assessment petitions.[89] The most popular petitions came from the pens of Baptists, who agreed with Madison's position on the total separation of church and state but argued for it from different premises, from their traditional scriptural view that Christ's kingdom was not of this world rather than from a Lockean theory of the social compact. The Baptists did not scruple to arouse anxiety and jealousy of the general assessment bill, suggesting as Madison had done, that it might set the commonwealth on the path to the Inquisition and conjuring up visions of bonfires for heretics. According to a recent authority, the joint efforts of Madison and the Baptists would have been in vain had the commonwealth's Presbyterians, who had appeared to be gravitating toward support of the general assessment bill in 1784, not returned to the opposition's fold in 1785.[90] The joint efforts of these denominations and Madison's civil libertarian allies led to the decisive defeat of the general assessment bill in the October 1785 session of the General Assembly, thus ending the decade-long battle over the issue of whether the state would be permitted to offer financial support, on an impartial basis, to its Christian religious denominations. In place of the general assessment bill, the Virginia Assembly in January 1786 passed a famous measure strictly separating church and state, Jefferson's Statute for Religious Freedom, which had been languishing in the House for seven years.

Historians have described the passage of Jefferson's Statute at the expense of the general assessment bill as an "anomaly,"[91] because, in the 1780s, the tide on church-state relations was running in the opposite direction in many states. Leonard Levy has argued that "multiple establishments" of religion existed in six states during this period in three of which general assessment measures were written into law.[92] In a campaign that simultaneously tracked events in Virginia in an uncanny way, the Maryland Assembly submitted a general assessment measure, which it hoped to pass, to the people of the state in January 1785, which generated the same deluge of public commentary as its sister measure had done in Virginia.[93] Had Virginia at any time during the first half of 1785 passed the general assessment bill, Maryland might well have followed its example; together the two states would have produced fresh momentum throughout the new nation for state assistance to religion with significant long range consequences for the

American state-church relations. The importance of the contest in Virginia in 1785 transcended the borders of the state, as Madison knew. Virginia, he wrote late in life, had brought "the great and interesting subject" of tax support for religion " to "a decisive test" and set the American nation on its future course.[94]

After 1786 Madison's involvement with church-state issues shifted to the national level. He was a principal architect of the Federal Constitution, written in Philadelphia in the summer of 1787. Although the drafters of the Constitution were far from irreverent, some pious citizens criticized them for paying too little attention to religion. The Constitution dealt with it in Article 6 by proscribing religious tests as a qualification for federal office but it granted the new government no role in promoting religion. With good reason, Madison and most of his colleagues believed, for by denying the government power in matters of religion, they deprived it of the authority to interfere with the peoples' faith and thus protected the freedom of religion. This reasoning failed to satisfy many in Virginia, including Madison's Baptist supporters, who demanded an explicit, written declaration, protecting the free exercise of religion. Both the Baptists and the members of the Virginia Ratifying Convention of 1788 were apprehensive that the new federal government might try to establish religion in the traditional, exclusive sense and, therefore, the latter recommended that its representatives in Congress guarantee that "no particular religious sect or society ought to be favored or established by Law in preference to others."[95] Although Madison was skeptical of the power of "parchment barriers," he agreed to introduce a bill of rights, protecting religious freedom, in the first session of the new federal Congress.

On June 8, 1789, Madison redeemed his pledge by introducing a bill of rights which stipulated that "no national religion be established,"[96] i.e., no single religion legally superior to all others. Although the issue with which Madison was concerned in 1789 was a federal one, far different from the state religious tax at issue in 1785, jurists (those, for example, dissenting in the *Everson* case in 1947) have consulted his opinions in 1785 to discover what he meant in 1789 when he used the term "established" as in the First Amendment expression "establishment of religion."[97] The attempt has been made, in other words, to discover Madison's "original intention" regarding establishment as a means of discovering the "true" meaning of the First Amendment. Madison would have scorned this judicial project, as those writing at the height of the "original intent" controversy in the 1980s pointed out. He believed, as he repeatedly affirmed, that the meaning of a statute must be sought in the intentions of those who ratified it, not of those who drafted it[98]in the case of the First Amendment in the minds of the members of the state legislatures, not of the members of the First Federal Congress.

Madison continued to play a major role in the House of Representatives until he retired from that body in 1797. He returned to public service in 1801 as Jefferson's secretary of state and in 1809 he was elected to the first of two terms as president. In discharging these high offices Madison had an opportunity to correct practices which violated his convictions about the necessity of a strict separation between church and state. That he did not do so has exposed him to charges of political opportunism and hypocrisy. After retiring from public life, Madison composed what has been called his "detached memorandum," well-known to scholars, in which he denounced Congress's appointment of and payment of chaplains, both civilian and military, as inconsistent "with the pure principles of religious freedom."[99] The principle here was precisely the one that made the general assessment bills of the 1780s so controversial: the use of tax dollars to pay ministers of the gospel. Madison moved heaven and earth against the latter, but, as chief executive, suffered the former in silence. He may have felt himself constrained by separation of power considerations from moving against congressional chaplains but military chaplains were executive branch officials whose services he could have terminated in several ways, among others by eliminating their salaries from the executive branch budget. Why did he not do so? The answer, which he himself never ventured to express, seems to be a principle of constitutional construction that permitted him to sign into law a bill establishing the Second Bank of the United States in 1816, even though he had opposed the First Bank as unconstitutional twenty-five years earlier: the conviction that long settled use established a precedent that legitimized a practice. In signing the Second Bank Bill Madison "declared, in accordance with his 'early and unchanged opinion' that such a construction by usage and precedent should override the intellectual scruples of the individual."[100] When Madison became president in 1809, the federal government had been employing and paying chaplains for more than thirty year, ample time, he evidently thought, to give the sanction of precedent to a practice he personally deplored.[101]

The same considerations undoubtedly informed Madison's attitude toward what he assailed in his "detached memorandum" as "Religious proclamations by the Executive recommending thanksgivings & fasts."[102] Madison opposed these on principle, as involving the state in religious exercises. Jefferson, as president, had refused to issue them, even though his predecessors, Adams and Washington, had done so. When requested by Congress at the beginning of the War of 1812 to proclaim a day of "public humiliation and prayer," Madison complied and issued additional proclamations during the course of the war,[103] apparently because he believed these pronouncements had been sanctioned as war measures by the actions of the Continental and Confederation Congresses which issued twenty of them between 1774 and 1784, in the writing of one of which he himself had participated.[104]

If Madison believed that, in these cases, precedent overrode his private, "abstract opinion,"[105] he took a different line when confronted with what he regarded as "innovations" in church-state relations. The general assessment bill had been just such an innovation and so, too, in Madison's opinion were the various proposals that began emerging in the 1780s that the state, or in some cases the federal government, incorporate religious denominations, i.e., make them corporate bodies at law, enabling them to perform such functions as receiving bequests. Madison had supported a bill in the Virginia Assembly in 1784 to incorporate the Episcopal Church, solely because he believed that its passage would alienate the Presbyterians and turn them against the general assessment bill. The legislature's power to issue charters of incorporation he regarded as dangerous, as he explained in the debate in Congress in 1791 over the chartering of a national bank. "He dilated," according House records, "on the great and extensive influence that incorporated societies had on public affairs in Europe. They are a powerful machine, which have always been found competent to effect objects on principles, in a great measure independent of the people." Madison, his jealousy aroused, worried that if Congress were given the power to incorporate a bank, it "might even establish religious teachers in every parish and pay them out of the treasury of the United States."[106]

Madison was proud of the fact that in 1811 he had vetoed a bill to incorporate an Episcopal church in Alexandria. By then the issue of incorporation of religious societies was percolating in Virginia. Representatives of most denominations considered it unfair that the Assembly resolutely refused to give them the benefit of incorporation, even as it issued charters to every conceivable enterprise including railroads, copper mining companies and proprietors of mineral springs.[107] What the churches wanted was an incorporation law, similar to those in other states, which would treat them equally with other organizations and treat each denomination equally with its sister confession, allowing all to obtain routinely charters which would permit a more efficient administration of their affairs and permit them to serve the community more robustly in their role as "religious charities."

The efforts of Virginia's churches to obtain charters of incorporation filled Madison with foreboding. "The dangers of silent accumulations & encroachments, by Ecclesiastical Bodies," he warned in his "detached memorandum," "have not engaged sufficient attention in the U.S." Religious institutions supplicating the assembly must, in his opinion, be watched with extraordinary vigilance, for charters of incorporation might be the "crevices . . . thro which bigotry may introduce persecution; a monster, that feeding & thriving on its own venom, gradually swells to a size and strength overwhelming all laws divine & human." "Are the United States," wrote Madison, now thoroughly worked up, "duly awake to the tendency of the precedents they are establishing, in the multiplied incorporations of Religious Congregations with the facility of acquiring & holding property real and as well as personal."[108] The churches of Virginia could become as bloated with wealth as the English monasteries before their dissolution in the sixteenth century; "how enormous were the treasures of [those] religious societies, and how gross the corruptions engendered by them." Reverting to the lessons of the Revolution, as he had in 1785, Madison suggested that the incorporation of religious societies was potentially as dangerous as the passage of the Tea Act and should be opposed on the same principle. The jealousy of Americans should never sleep; "let them exert the same wisdom [as in 1773], in watching against every evil lurking under plausible disguises and growing up from small beginnings."[109] By 1824 Madison had become so exercised about the dangers of religious corporations that he proposed to Jefferson that the state of Virginia should consider moving against certain theologically retrograde "sectarian seminaries," shielded by the "perpetual inviolability of charters."[110] In 1833, three years before his death, he repeated this proposal, complaining about the "omission of the public authorities, to limit the duration of the charters of religious corporations, & the amount of property acquirable by them [which] may lead to an injurious accumulation of wealth."[111] The sacred principle of separation of church and state could, apparently, be comprised, if the wrong kind of religion or a rich kind of religion was being protected by objectionable legal vehicles.

Despite the emphasis of recent historians on what they variously call the anomalous, the "eccentric," and the "radical," nature of Madison's views on strict separation of church and state,[112] he is regularly appealed to as an oracle on the subject. Why should we listen to him? To this question, Professor Jack Rakove has addressed himself with his customary penetration. We should not, Rakove argues, defer to Madison or any other Founder merely because they were "patriarchs." Neither should we be impressed by "their iconic stature and prestige or the rhetorical advantage we gain by selective quotation" from their writings. Rather, Rakove argues, Madison's ideas are relevant for our times because he was "right" about the "religion question"; he thought "deeply and powerfully" about it and implemented a solution to it that worked as he predicted it would and produced results that have been in the best interests of both religious and secular elements in American society.[113] By championing the "radical" program of "bright line-high wall" separation, Madison compelled religious organizations to rely solely on the voluntary support of their own adherents, a policy which stimulated the explosive growth of American religion after 1800. Madison, Rakove concludes, discovered a formula for religious prosperity that worked as well in its own sphere as the prescriptions for economic growth dispensed by certain modern disciples of Adam Smith.

According to Rakove, Madison foresaw that "religion would never fare better than when it was completely privatized, deregulated, and left open to the market place competition . . . Madison was a veritable Milton Friedman, skeptical of the rationale for public regulation and subsidies, confident in the capacity of consumers to choose, and justified in thinking that competition in the spiritual market place would reduce the transactions costs that would otherwise arise if dissatisfied truth seekers had to struggle against official monopolies to find more efficacious paths to salvation. And to judge by the results, that market-oriented approach offers the best explanation for the remarkable success of the American experiment in religious pluralism."[114]

The evidence Rakove offers to prove that Madison's policy of strict separation-religious voluntarism sparked a boom in American churches is his own statement in 1823 that "there is much more of religion among us now than there ever was before."[115] Madison, in fact, frequently commented after 1819[116] on the vitality of religion in Virginia but it is indisputably clear that this vitality had nothing to do with his policy of depriving the commonwealth's churches of tax support and everything to do with that titanic eruption of religion, called the Second Great Awakening, that poured over the United States at the beginning of the nineteenth century and that ushered in a half century of virtually nonstop revivalism on whose evangelical capitalism the nation is still in some sense drawing. The Second Great Awakening, which was the catalyst for what has been called the "Golden Day of Democratic Evangelicalism"[117] in the United States, seemed to many contemporary observers to be an unfathomable force of nature. The most widely accepted explanation of it and of previous revivals in American history was a theological one, proposed by Jonathan Edwards and adopted by later commentators, that revivals were the "remarkable pourings out of the Spirit of God" at intervals determined by divine and inscrutable wisdom.[118]

The Second Great Awakening is generally considered to have begun in Connecticut in 1798. There it was initiated and nurtured by ministers of the

Congregational Church and there it percolated year after year, decade after decade.[119] Connecticut, of course, was a state in which the Congregational Church was firmly and legally established until 1818, so it would appear that in the new American republic a strong case can be made that Madison, as interpreted by Rakove, was wrong and that a state-subsidized religious establishment was at least as good an incubator of religious energy as a free market in faith. Recall that the only comparable ebullition of religion passion in the country was the Great Awakening of the 1730s and 40s which occurred in areas in which religion was even more firmly established by government than it was at the end of the eighteenth century.

The Second Great Awakening washed over Virginia in the first years of the nineteenth century, producing the religious fervor that Madison described in the letters he wrote late in life. No contemporary Virginian suggested that there was any connection between the revivals and church disestablishment. Madison himself *explicitly denied* that separating church and state had created a bull market in religion. Commenting, in 1833, on the robust condition of religion in Virginia, he conceded that "causes other than the abolition of the legal establishment of religion are to be taken into view" in accounting for its vigor[120] by which he meant that credit must be given to the revivals that were continuing in the commonwealth with barely diminished force thirty years after they burst onto the scene.

In advocating a Friedmanesque free market in religion, Madison may, in fact, have intended to sap its potency. A distinguished line of historians, as noted above, has described him as a disciple of David Hume in both statecraft and church-state policy. A scholar has recently asserted that Hume expressed his argument for religious liberty "in terms that were to stick in Madison's mind" and has called attention to the Humean language in Madison's Memorial and Remonstrance.[121] It would not be unreasonable to assume, therefore, that Madison subscribed to Hume's thesis that religious liberty had the capacity to enfeeble religion. "Open the door to toleration," Hume contended, and the populace's "attachment to particular modes of religion decays." "Unlimited toleration," Hume continued, "is the only expedient, which can allay [religion's] fervour"and transform religious zealots into timeservers and opportunists.[122] If Madison did not imbibe these ideas from Hume, he may have acquired them from the father of laissez-faire himself, Adam Smith, who, like Hume, contended that freedom of religion could enervate religious zeal by reducing it to "pure and rational religion, free from every mixture of absurdity, imposture, or fanaticism, such as wise men in all ages of the world have wished to see established."[123] Hume and

Smith were not singular in supposing that freedom of religion could vitiate its vitality. On this point many of the major thinkers of the 18th century Enlightenment concurred.

Madison did not expect to see religion become politically irrelevant, as Hume and Smith may have privately wished. He believed that, since man was a religious animal, there would always be some sort of religion in society and he further believed that, given the opacity of the spiritual realm, there would always be multiple religious viewpoints and sects promoting them. For Madison the primary advantage of freedom of religion was that it would permit the various sects to emerge and operate in sufficient numbers to prevent the formation of a single religious faction, at once overweening and oppressive. There is no evidence whatsoever that in the 1770s and 1780s Madison assumed that a free market in religion would be a catalyst for the subsequent, pulsating growth of evangelical religion in Virginia or for the growth of any kind of dynamic religious group. What he expected to result from a laissez-faire religious environment was a variety of religious groups, distinguished by moderation and complacency and, conceivably, by the beneficial atrophy that Hume would have welcomed.

Madison cannot, therefore, be credited with inventing a "magic bullet" of religious growth that would validate for modern Americans the correctness of his views on efficacy of the absolute separation of church and state. Nor was he right in his other principal assumption about relations between religion and government, his "country" ideological conviction that Americans must perpetually indulge their "argus-eyed jealously"[124] lest any grant of power to government expand exponentially into temporal or spiritual tyranny. Madison's apprehensions about the dangers of power entrusted to government officials were grossly excessive, for during this century we have experienced what his generation would have regarded as inconceivable amounts of power invested in the federal government with none of the dire results for individual liberties that he and his colleagues predicted. The American people have not been "enslaved" by government, as revolutionary leaders feared, nor have they been devoured by the "red dragon of religious persecution" or incinerated by homegrown inquisitors.

If Madison's views about the church-state issues were anxiety ridden and radically idiosyncratic—especially his denial that religion could be a source of individual social virtue—why does he have a substantial following on the "religion question" in our own day? The answer is simple. For a variety of reasons many present-day Americans agree with the separationist results he sought and, like their fellow citizens at all points on the ideological compass, believe that sailing under the flag of a distinguished Founding Father is a good way to reach their political destination.

NOTES

1. An earlier version of this chapter was delivered at a symposium, March 16, 2001, at the Library of Congress, celebrating the 250th anniversary of James Madison's birth. The symposium, "James Madison: Philosopher and Practitioner of Liberal Democracy," was co-sponsored by the Library of Congress and the Henry Salvatori Center, Claremont McKenna College. I wish to thank the Director of the Salvatori Center, Professor Charles Kesler, for encouraging me to publish a revised version of the original paper here.

2. Charles B. Sanford, *The Religious Life of Thomas Jefferson* (Charlottesville: University Press of Virginia, 1984), 13.

3. Jefferson to Francis A..Van Der Kemp, July 30, 1816. Jefferson Papers, Library of Congress.

4. *Religious Life of Jefferson,* 120.

5. *Religious Life of Jefferson,* 120.

6. *Religious Life of Jefferson,* 5.

7. William Hutchinson, Robert Rutland, J. C. A. Stagg, et. al., eds., *The Papers of James Madison* (Chicago and Charlottesville: University of Chicago Press and University Press of Virginia, 26 vols. to date, 1962—), vol. 1, 52; hereinafter cited as *PJM.*

8. To William Bradford, September 25, 1773, *PJM,* vol. 1, 96.

9. For a reference to the "Saviour," see Elizabeth Fleet, ed., "Madison's 'Detached Memorandum,'" *William and Mary Quarterly* 3, no. 4 (October 1946): 556.

10. See, for example, Madison's letter to Frederick Beasley, November 20, 1825, in which he observed that, beyond presuming the existence of God, human reason could know nothing about the spiritual realm, a statement not inconsistent with pronouncements of the most orthodox Christian thinkers. There is no evidence, however, that Madison took the next step and asserted that faith could supply the deficiencies of reason. Gaillard Hunt, ed., *The Writings of James Madison* (New York: Putnam's Sons, 9 vols., 1900-1910), vol. 9, 229-31; hereinafter cited as *WJM.*

11. *PJM.*, vol. 1, 58.

12. Irving Brant, *James Madison: The Virginia Revolutionist* (Indianapolis: Bobbs-Merrill, 1941), 118.

13. James H. Smylie, "Madison and Witherspoon. Theological Roots of American Political Thought," *Princeton University Library Chronicle* (Spring 1966): 125.

14. Ralph Ketcham, "James Madison and Religion– New Hypothesis," *Journal of the Presbyterian Historical Society* 38 (June 1960): 76, 86.

15. Ralph Ketcham, *James Madison: A Biography* (New York: Macmillan, 1971), 56, 324.

16. Lance Banning, *The Sacred Fire of Liberty: James Madison and the Founding of the Federal Republic* (Ithaca, N.Y.: Cornell University Press, 1995), 80, 430n. Two recent scholars follow the modern biographers by stressing the mature Madison's indifference to issues of religions faith. See Edwin S. Gaustad, *Sworn on the Altar of God: A Religious Biography of Thomas Jefferson* (Grand Rapids, Mich: W. D. Eerdmans Publishers, 1996), 196; William L. Miller, *The First Liberty: Religion and the American Republic* (New York: Knopf, 1986), 90.

17. John T. Noonan, Jr., *The Lustre of our Country: The American Experience of Religious Freedom* (Berkeley: University of California Press, 1998), 87-89; Sheldon asserts that Madison acquired a "Biblical faith" at Princeton which he never relinquished. *The Political Philosophy of James Madison* (Baltimore: Johns Hopkins University Press, 2001), 27.

18. Noonan cites section 12 of Madison's Memorial and Remonstrance of June 1785 in which he refers to the "light of Christianity," describes it as a "precious gift," and speaks of the "victorious progress of the Truth." The Memorial and Remonstrance was a petition, written to obtain signatures in a political contest over tax support for Virginia's churches. Madison evidently saluted Christianity as a means of appealing to evangelical voters, following a carefully calculated strategy that he had employed in composing a speech on religious taxation in December 1784; deliver "a panegyric on it [Christianity] on our side," he reminded himself in notes prepared on that occasion. *PJM*, vol. 8, 199.

19. Madison to Jasper Adams, September 1833, in Daniel L. Dreisbach, ed., *Religion and Politics in the Early Republic: Jasper Adams and the Church-State Debate* (Lexington: University Press of Kentucky, 1996), 117.

20. See, for example, Jefferson to Margaret Harrison Smith, August 6, 1816, in which he attacks the "priesthood" for disseminating "interested absurdities" and for the "artificial structures they have built on the purest of all moral systems." Jefferson Papers, Manuscript Division, Library of Congress. The corruption of Christianity was a constant deistical and Jeffersonian theme. In 1801, for example, Jefferson wrote that, "divested of the rags" in which the priesthood had clothed it and "brought to its original purity and simplicity," Christianity was of incomparable value. Gaustad, *Sworn on the Altar*, 120.

21. For this and the following quotation, see Brant, *The Virginia Revolutionist*, 113.

22. Irving Brant, *James Madison Commander in Chief 1812-1836* (Indianapolis: Bobbs-Merrill, 1961), 364.

23. *The Works of the Rev. John Witherspoon . . . To which is prefixed an account of the author's life* (2nd ed., Philadelphia: William W. Woodward, 1802). Rare Book and Special Collections Division, Library of Congress.

24. Madison to Jefferson, December 31, 1824; January 23, 1825. In the first letter Madison discusses "Sectarian Seminaries" which he identifies in the second letter as being "for the most part Presbyterian." James M. Smith, ed., *The Republic of Letters: The*

Correspondence between Thomas Jefferson and James Madison 1776-1826 (New York: W. W. Norton, 1995), vol. 3, 1913, 1922

25. Brant, *Virginia Revolutionist,* 113.

26. Ketcham, *Madison,* 324.

27. For Madison's activities at the First Presbyterian Church, see *The National Presbyterian Church: The First Two Hundred Years* (Washington, D.C., 1995), 6-7. For his attendance at church services in the House of Representatives, see James H. Hutson, *Religion and the Founding of the American Republic* (Hanover, N.H.: University Press of New England, 6th ed., 2002), 96. See also Abijah Bigelow to Hannah Bigelow, December 28, 1812, Abijah Bigelow Papers, American Antiquarian Society.

28. These rotating services were called "union"services; for Jefferson's attendance at them, see James H. Hutson, "Thomas Jefferson's Letter to the Danbury Baptists: A Controversy Rejoined," *William and Mary Quarterly* 56, no.4 (October 1999): 788.

29. Paul Rahe, *Republics Ancient and Modern* (Chapel Hill: University of North Carolina Press, 1992), 233.

30. *Everson v. Board of Education,* 330 U.S., 31-2, 1947.

31. According to Ralph Ketcham, "religious liberty stands out as the one subject upon which Madison took an extreme, absolute, undeviating position throughout his life." Ketcham, *Madison,* 165

32. *PJM,* vol. 1, 107 n.

33. Madison to William Bradford, January 24, 1774, *PJM,* vol. 1, 106.

34. Madison to Bradford, January 24, April 1, 1774, *PJM,* vol. 1, 105, 112-3.

35. Madison to Bradford, January 24, 1774, *PJM,* vol. 1, 106; Mark A. Beliles, "The Christian Communities, Religious Revivals, and Political Culture of the Central Virginia Piedmont," unpublished paper in the author's possession; Beliles derives his information from Lewis Peyton Little, *Imprisoned Preachers and Religious Liberty in Virginia* (Lynchburg, Va.: J. P. Bell Company, 1938), 130-31.

36. Brant, *Virginia Revolutionist,* 11, 249.

37. *PJM,* vol. 1, 174.

38. Julian P. Boyd, ed., *The Papers of Thomas Jefferson* (Princeton, N .J.: Princeton University Press, 33 vols. to date, 1950—), vol. 1, 527, 531.

39. Thomas E. Buckley, S.J., *Church and State in Revolutionary Virginia, 1776-1787* (Charlottesville: University Press of Virginia, 1977), 35.

40. Brant, *Virginia Revolutionist,* 274.

41. Buckley, *Church and State,* 38, 41-62.

42. Henry's bill is printed in Buckley, *Church and State,* 188-9.

43. Daniel L. Dreisbach, "George Mason's Pursuit of Religious Liberty in Revolutionary Virginia," *Virginia Magazine of History and Biography* 108, no .1 (January 2000): 31.

44. New Hampshire, Massachusetts, Connecticut, Maryland and Georgia. See Thomas J. Curry, *The First Freedoms: Church and State in America to the Passage of the First Amendment* (Oxford University Press, 1986), chapters 6 and 7.

45. Herbert Butterfield, *The Whig Interpretation of History* (London: G. Bell and Sons, 1968), 4, 46.

46. Irving Brant, *James Madison The Nationalist 1780-1787* (Indianapolis: Bobbs-Merrill, 1948), 344.

47. Buckley, *Church and State,* 95.

48. See, for example, the petitions of Lunenburg County, November 3, 1779, and of Amelia County November 8, 1784, in Virginia Religious Petitions, Library of Virginia.

49. For examples of these kinds of testimonials to religion's "public utility," see Hutson, *Religion and the Founding,* 61-9, 80-2.

50. Thomas Reese, *An Essay on the Influence of Religion in Civil Society* (Charleston: Markland and M'Iver, 1788), 5.

51. Amherst County to the Virginia General Assembly, November 10, 1779, Virginia Religious Petitions, Library of Virginia.

52. The memorial of a considerable number of the clergy of the established church in Virginia, November 8, 1776, Virginia Religious Petitions.

53. Bishop James Madison, *An Address to the Members of the Protestant Episcopal Church in Virginia* (Richmond: T. Nicholson, 1799), 4.

54. Hutson, *Religion and the Founding,* 62.

55. Bishop Madison, *An Address,* 23.

56. Madison to Jasper Adams, September 1833, Dreisbach, *Religion and Politics,* 118.

57. Douglass Adair, "'That Politics May Be Reduced to a Science', David Hume, James Madison, and the Tenth Federalist," in Trevor Colbourn, ed., *Fame and the Founding Fathers Essays by Douglass Adair* (New York: W. W. Norton, 1974), 93-106. For Hume's support of an established church, see his "Idea of a Perfect Commonwealth," in T.H. Green and T. H. Grose, eds., *David Hume Essays Moral, Political, and Literary* (London: Longmans, 1898), 485, 490.

58. Madison to Robert Walsh, March 2, 1819, *WJM,* vol. 8, 431.

59. Surry County to Virginia General Assembly, November 14, 1785, Virginia Religious Petitions.

60. The Plutarch quote is from an Anglican minister, Joseph Brett. *A Sermon preach'd in the Cathedral-Church of Norwich* . . . (Norwich: Widow Oliver, 1704). The British Library.

61. Leonard Levy, *The Establishment Clause Religion and the First Amendment* (New York: Macmillan, 1986), 62

62. Madison, "Notes for Debates on the General Assessment," [December 23-4], 1784, *PJM,* vol. 8, 198

63. Richard Henry Lee to Madison, November 26, 1784, *PJM,* 8, 149

64. Surry County to Virginia General Assembly, November 14, 1785, Virginia Religious Petitions.

65. Thomas E. Buckley, "After Disestablishment: Thomas Jefferson's Wall of Separation in Antebellum Virginia," *Journal of Southern History* 61, no.3 (August 1995): 452

66. Madison, Memorial and Remonstrance, June 20, 1785, *PJM*, vol. 8, 301. In this same document Madison asserted that using religion to obtain social and political benefits was "an unhallowed perversion of the means of salvation," a statement that must be weighed cautiously since it was intended to enlist evangelical support in the form of signatures to a petition and may not, therefore, reflect Madison's personal views.

67. *PJM*, vol. 9, 356.

68. Max Farrand, ed., *The Records of the Federal Convention of 1787* (New Haven, Conn.: Yale University Press, 1966), vol. 1, 135.

69. Jacob E. Cooke, ed., *The Federalist* (Middletown, Conn.: Wesleyan University Press, 1961), 61. Madison's statements must be distinguished from a routine Calvinistic-style reflection on the sinfulness of man, which some scholars impute to him; see Sheldon, *Political Philosophy of Madison*, 24-25. All authentic Calvinists of whom I am aware, including such stalwarts as the "Pope" of Connecticut, Timothy Dwight, claimed during this period that religion could neutralize human sinfulness sufficiently to create good, law abiding citizens. Madison appears to have written off religion's meliorative capacities entirely.

70. J. S. Mill, "Utility of Religion," in *The Collected Works of John Stuart Mill Essays on Ethics, Religion and Society*, ed. J. M. Robson et. al. (Toronto, 1969), 10, 403-28.

71. Madison to Jefferson, February 8, 1825, Smith, *Republic of Letters*, vol. 3, 1925.

72. 1 Corinthians 13. Various authors claim that Madison regarded religion as a source of source of civic virtue—"as a useful support for republican government," "as a positive political and social force"—but evidence for these assertions is never produced. See, for example, Ketcham, *Madison*, 57; Joseph P. Viteritti, *Choosing Equality School Choice, the Constitution, and Civil Society* (Washington, D.C.: Brookings Institution Press, 1999), 124. The only positive value that Madison appears to have seen in religion was in its manifestation as multiple sects, whose profusion would prevent the emergence of an oppressive and socially disruptive, dominant sect. On this point, see Jack Rakove, "Once More into the Breach: Reflections on Jefferson, Madison, and the Religion Problem," Diane Ravitch and Joseph Viteritti, eds., *Making Good Citizens Education and Civil Society* (New Haven, Conn: Yale University Press, 2001), 250, 261.

73. Amelia County to the Virginia General Assembly, November 8, 1784; Caroline County to the Virginia General Assembly, December 5, 1777; Virginia Religious Petitions.

74. Irving Brant, *James Madison The Nationalist* (Indianapolis: Bobbs-Merrill, 1948), 352; Ketcham, *Madison,* 163

75. Buckley, *Church and State,* 134.

76. Brant, *Virginia Revolutionist*, 232.

77. Buckley, *Church and State*, 131-33; *PJM*, vol. 8, 297.

78. *PJM*, vol. 8, 300.

79. See sections 9 and 11; *PJM*, vol. 8, 302.

80. For an expression of this charge in 1785, see Baptist General Committee to Virginia General Assembly, August 5, 1785, Virginia Religious Petitions.

81. Buckley, *Church and State*, 31-32.

82. Bernard Bailyn, *The Ideological Origins of the American Revolution* (Cambridge, Mass.: Harvard Univerity Press, 1967), 56.

83. See James H. Hutson, "The Origins of 'The Paranoid Style in American Politics': Public Jealousy from the Age of Walpole to the Age of Jackson," in David D. Hall, John M. Murrin, and Thad W. Tate, eds., *Saints and Revolutionaries* (New York: W.W. Norton, 1984), 332-72.

84. For this and the two following quotations, see *Saints and Revolutionaries*, 343, 346, 347.

85. For this and the three following quotations, see *Saints and Revolutionaries*, 350, 352, 359

86. Section 3,11; *PJM*, vol. 8, 300, 303.

87. Hutson, *Saints and Revolutionaries*, 356-57.

88. *The Federalist*, nos. 46 and 55; Cooke, *Federalist*, 321, 377-78.

89. *PJM*, vol. 8, 297-98.

90. Buckley, *Church and State*, 176.

91. Gordon Wood, *The Creation of the American Republic* (Chapel Hill: University of North Carolina Press, 1968), 427.

92. Levy, *Establishment Clause*, 61.

93. For the campaign for a general assessment in Maryland, see Curry, *First Freedoms*, 153-58.

94. Dreisbach, *Religion and Politics*, 117.

95. Virginia Convention, proposed amendments, no. 20, June 27, 1788, in John Kominski and Gaspare Saladino, eds., *The Documentary History of the Ratification of the Constitution*, (Madison: State Historical Society of Wisconsin, 1993), vol. 10, 1553.

96. *PJM*, vol. 12, 201.

97. See, for example, Justice Rutledge's dissent in *Everson* to which he appended Madison's Memorial and Remonstrance. *Everson v. Board of Education*, 330 U.S., 33-4, 63-72, 1947.

98. H Jefferson Powell, "the Original Understanding of Original Intent," in Jack N. Rakove, ed., *Interpreting the Constitution: The Debate over Original Intent* (Boston: Northeastern University Press, 1990), 83; see also, in the same volume, Charles A. Lofgren, "The Original Understanding of Original Intent?" 135-36,139-141.

99. Fleet, "Detached Memorandum," 558-60.

100. Powell, Lofgren, *Interpreting the Constitution*, 83-4, 139.

101. In this connection the conclusion seems inescapable that Madison would have opposed the Supreme Court's post-World War II interventions against long settled practices such as school prayer

102. Fleet, "Detached Memorandum," 560.

103. For Madison's proclamations of July 9, 1812, July 23, 1813, August 16, 1814, see James D. Richardson, ed., *A Compilation of the Messages and Papers of the Presidents* (New York: Bureau of National Literature, Inc., 1897-1924), vol. 2, 498, 517-18, 543.

104. Hutson, *Religion and the Founding,* 76.

105. Powell, *Interpreting the Constitution,* 84.

106. *PJM,* vol. 13, 375-6, 384.

107. Buckley, "After Disestablishment," 454.

108. Fleet, "Detached Memorandum," 554-55.

109. Fleet, "Detached Memorandum," 557-58.

110. Madison to Jefferson, December 31, 1824, in Smith, *Republic of Letters,* vol.3, 1913.

111. Dreisbach, *Religion and Politics,* 120.

112. Wood, *Creation of the American Republic,* 427; William McLoughlin, "The Role of Religion in the Revolution," in Stephen G. Kurtz and James H. Hutson. eds., *Essays on the American Revolution* (Chapel Hill: University of North Carolina Press, 1973), 222; Rakove, "Once More into the Breach," 235, 245.

113. Rakove, "Once More," 235, 236, 244, 254.

114. Rakove, "Once More," 254.

115. Rakove, "Once More," 254.

116. See, for example, Madison to Robert Walsh, March 2, 1819, *WJM,* vol. 8, 432; Madison to Jasper Adams, September 1833, Dreisbach, *Religion and Politics,* 120.

117. The term is used by Sydney Ahlstrom, *A Religious History of the American People* (New Haven, Conn.: Yale University Press, 1972), 385 ff.

118. Michael J. Crawford, *Seasons of Grace: Colonial New England's Revival Tradition in Its British Context* (New York: Oxford University Press, 1991), 248.

119. Charles Keller, *The Second Great Awakening in Connecticut* (Hamden, Conn.: Archon Books, 1968).

120. Dreisbach, *Religion and Politics,* 120.

121. Mark G. Spenser, "Hume and Madison on Faction," *William and Mary Quarterly* 59, no. 4 (October 2002):, 893-95.

122. Spencer, "Hume and Madison," 894-95.

123. Samuel Fleishacker, "Adam Smith's Reception among the American Founders, 1776-1790," *William and Mary Quarterly* 59, no. 4 (October 2002): 909.

124. Hutson, *Saints and Revolutionaries,* 359.

Bibliography

Bonomi, Patricia, and Peter Eisenstadt, "Church Adherence in the Eighteenth–Century British American Colonies." *William and Mary Quarterly* 39, no. 2 (April 1982): 245-86.

Brant, Irving. *James Madison.* Indianapolis: Bobbs-Merrill, 6 vols., 1941-1961.

Buckley, Thomas E., S. J. *Church and State in Revolutionary Virginia, 1776-1787.* Charlottesville: University Press of Virginia, 1977.

Butler, Jon. *Awash in a Sea of Faith: Christianizing the American People.* Cambridge, Mass.: Harvard University Press, 1990.

Curry, Thomas J. *The First Freedoms: Church and State in America to the Passage of the First Amendment.* New York: Oxford University Press, 1986.

Davies, Paul C. "The Debate on Eternal Punishment in Late Seventeenth and Eighteenth Century England." *Eighteenth Century Studies* 4, no. 3 (Spring 1971): 257-76.

Dreisbach, Daniel L. *Religion and Politics in the Early Republic: Jasper Adams and the Church-State Debate.* Lexington: University Press of Kentucky, 1996.

Dunn, Mary M., and Richard S. Dunn eds. *The Papers of William Penn.* Philadelphia: University of Pennsylvania Press, 4 vols., 1981-1987.

Gaustad, Edwin S. *Sworn on the Altar of God: A Religious Biography of Thomas Jefferson.* Grand Rapids, Mich.: W. D. Eerdmans Publisher, 1996.

Hutson, James H. *Religion and the Founding of the American Republic.* Hanover, N.H.: University Press of New England, 6th printing, 2002.

———. *Religion and the New Republic.* Lanham, Md.: Rowman & Littlefield, 2000.

Ketcham, Ralph. *James Madison A Biography.* New York: Macmillan, 1971

Kramnick, Isaac, and Laurence R. Moore, *The Godless Constitution: The Case against Religious Correctness.* New York: W. W. Norton Publishers, 1996.

McLoughlin, William. *Isaac Backus on Church, State, and Calvinism.* Cambridge, Mass.: Harvard University Press, 1968.

Noonan, John T. *The Lustre of Our Country: The American Experience of Religious Freedom.* Berkeley: University of California Press, 1998.

Penn, William. *The Select Works of William Penn*. New York: Kraus Reprint Company, 3 vols., 1971.

Reese, Thomas. *An Essay on the Influence of Religion in Civil Society*. Charleston: Markland and M'Iver, 1788.

Sandoz, Elliot, ed. *Political Sermons of the American Founding Era 1730-1805*. Indianapolis: Liberty Press, 1991.

Stark, Rodney, and Roger Finke, "American Religion in 1776: A Statistical Portrait." *Sociological Analysis* 49, no. 1 (1988): 39-51.

Thornton, John W. *The Pulpit of the American Revolution*. New York: Burt Franklin, 1970.

Tully, James. "Governing Conduct." Pp. 289-348 in *Locke Volume II*, edited by John Dunn and Ian Harris. Cheltenham, U.K.: Edward Elgar Publishing Limited, 1997.

Villey, Michel. *Lecons d'Histoire de la Philosophe du Droit*. Paris: Dalloz, 1957.

———. *La Formation de la Pensée Juridique Moderne*. Paris: Montchrestien, 1968.

———. *Seize Essais de Philosophie du Droit*. Paris: Dalloz, 1969.

———. *Philosophie du Droit*. Paris: Dalloz, 1978.

Viner, Jacob. *The Role of Providence in the Social Order*. Philadelphia: American Philosophical Society, 1972.

Walker, Daniel P. *The Decline of Hell: Seventeenth-Century Discussions of Eternal Torment*. Chicago: University of Chicago Press, 1964.

Williams, Roger. *The Complete Works of Roger Williams*. New York: Russell and Russell, 7 vols., 1963.

Index

About the Author

James H. Hutson received his Ph.D. in History from Yale University and has been a member of the History Departments at Yale and William and Mary. He is currently the Chief of the Manuscript Division, Library of Congress.

He is the author of the following monographs: *Pennsylvania Politics, 1745-1770* (Princeton, N.J.: Princeton University Press, 1972); *John Adams and the Diplomacy of the American Revolution* (Lexington: University Press of Kentucky, 1981); winner of the Gilbert Chinard Prize, 1981; *To Make All Laws: The Congress of the United States, 1789-1989* (Boston, Mass.: Houghton Mifflin, 2nd ed., 1990); *The Sister Republics: Switzerland and the United States from 1776 to the Present* (Washington, D.C.: Government Printing Office, 4th ed., 1998; French and German editions published by Staempfli Verlag, Bern, 1992); *Religion and the Founding of the American Republic* (Hanover, N.H.: University Press of New England, 6th ed., 2002).

He is the editor of the following volumes: Stephen G. Kurtz and James H. Hutson, ed., *Essays on the American Revolution* (Chapel Hill: University of North Carolina Press, 1973); *A Decent Respect to the Opinions of Mankind: Congressional State Papers, 1774-1776* (Washington, D.C.: Government Printing Office, 1976): *Letters from a Distinguished American: Twelve Essays by John Adams on American Foreign Policy, 1780* (Washington, D.C.: Government Printing Office, 1978); *Supplement to Max Farrand's Records of the Federal Convention of 1787* (New Haven, Conn.: Yale University Press, 1987); *Religion and the New Republic: Faith in the Founding of America* (Lanham, Md.: Rowman & Littlefield), 2000).

DATE DUE

GAYLORD			PRINTED IN U.S.A.